The Rise of Architectural History

The Rise of Architectural History

DAVID WATKIN

The University of Chicago Press

The University of Chicago Press, Chicago 60637

The Architectural Press Ltd, London

© 1980 by David Watkin

All rights reserved. Published 1980

University of Chicago Press edition published 1983

90 89 88 87 86 85 84 83 54321

Library of Congress Cataloging in Publication Data

Watkin, David, 1941–
    The rise of architectural history.
    Reprint. Originally published: London: Architectural
Press, 1980.
    1. Architecture—Historiography. I. Title.
NA190.W37   1983   720'.9   83-10430
ISBN 0-226-87486-9 (pbk.)

Set in 11 on 12 point Baskerville and printed in Great
Britain by Biddles Ltd, Guildford, Surrey from
composition by Alacrity Phototypesetters, Banwell
Castle, Weston-super-Mare, Avon

Contents

Contents

Preface

This book is a first attempt to sketch the outline of the study of architectural history from the seventeenth century to the present day, primarily in England, though also taking into account German, French, Italian and American historiography. It is strange that so important a topic should have been so widely ignored,[1] because our knowledge of cultural history can be extended in fascinating and unexpected directions by investigation of the ways in which people have thought about and studied architecture, the kinds of values and meanings they think it embodies, and the extent to which these ideas have changed with the varying intellectual climate of successive generations.

It is important at the outset to state the aims of architectural history. These may be summarised under three headings — the practical, the historical, and the aesthetic — which ideally should all cross-fertilise each other. The first, or practical, task is to establish what was built, when it was built, and the names of the patron and designer. In this process the historian will rely on the evidence of any surviving remains, and on architectural drawings, engravings, photographs and the almost endless range of documentary sources which can include anything from letters and journals to parish rate books and records of banking accounts. Where necessary, this information will be accompanied by the preparation of measured drawings, plans and sections. The second task, the historical, is to discover why the building was built. This may well call for considerable religious,

---

[1] Important exceptions include P. Frankl, *The Gothic, Literary Sources and Interpretations through Eight Centuries*, Princeton 1960, and N. Pevsner, *Some Architectural Writers of the Nineteenth Century*, Oxford 1972.

cultural and sociological knowledge, for the precise function of a building may not be as obvious as might at first be imagined. Some buildings may be the product of a building mania which has little functional justification; some will have been erected to serve as displays of wealth or power which may or may not correspond with reality. The final task, the aesthetic, is to describe and perhaps account for the visual or stylistic differences between one building and another; to explain how and why styles change and why one style is adopted rather than another. Here, again, there may be many complications, because forms and styles may become charged with different meanings at different times — and may sometimes have no meaning. We shall see in the present book the fascinating variety of explanations which have been introduced to explain style: religious, political, Hegelian, Darwinian, economic, racial, nationalist. These are often stimulating and contain valuable truths or hints, but are rarely satisfactory in the end, and tend to shed more light on the time and place in which they were made than on the work of art itself. It may in the last analysis be humbling and salutary for the architectural historian to realise that, though he can work around his subject, lifting veils here and there, he can hardly hope to penetrate the mysterious heart of style. It should be nonetheless valuable to analyse these attempts to explain the pattern of style and stylistic change, because they show clearly how art history is inevitably shaped by a philosphy of history, even though the individual historian may conceivably be unaware of it.

As we shall see, architectural historians have not always applied themselves simultaneously to all three of the tasks which we have just identified as underlying their work: the practical, the historical, and the aesthetic. Thus some writers might give the impression that the establishment of documented facts is the principal task of the architectural historian; for others it might be to demonstrate the history of construction or of materials; another approach might be to postulate a sociological determinism; while others, again, might interpret architecture as an art of pure form, or of space creation, or of inevitable progress towards a stylistic ideal.

We shall also observe the variety of motives which have prompted the writing of architectural history: thus, in the seventeenth and nineteenth centuries the study of mediaeval architecture was often closely bound up with the promotion of specific religious ideas, as it was in the early nineteenth century with the rise of nationalism; the exceptional dominance in England of the country house as a building type and as a social focus from at least the mid-sixteenth to the early twentieth centuries, has understandably been reflected in the scope of modern architectural writing in this country. It will also become increasingly clear that two of the most important and persistent motives which lie behind the production of architectural history are the practice and the preservation of architecture.

The account of the rise of architectural history presented in this book does not claim to be definitive but rather to indicate the range of questions which serious reflection on the changing pattern of historical writings on architecture inevitably raises, such as whether the methods of architectural history can be dated as readily as the buildings themselves. If they can be, then it is important to bear in mind the celebrated advice given by E.H. Carr in *What is History?* (1962): 'Before you study the history, study the historian ... Before you study the historian, study his historical and social environment. The historian, being an individual, is also a product of history and of society; and it is in this twofold light that the student of history must learn to regard him'.[1] Such an approach is especially necessary in the case of architectural history because so much of it has been written by practising architects: a parallel would be if most history books were written by professional politicians. Thus, whereas historians frequently have a concealed axe to grind, generally political or religious, architectural historians have often had an openly displayed axe: the furtherance of a particular type of present-day architecture. This tradition was interrupted in the 1930s by the arrival of distinguished refugee scholars from Germany and Austria who introduced to this country the concept of art history taught in a university as an intellectual discipline with a conceptual framework of its own. Though this tradition has richly fertilised a more amateurish, native English tradition, it had a greater long-term influence in this country on the history of painting than of architecture.

[1] p.38.

What has risen to the fore is the renewal of a relationship between architectural history and conservation. Thus, though architectural historians are no longer practising architects, many of them have close and active links with the preservationist world, and if this book strikes a topical note it is because the fate of buildings in a conservation-conscious age seems often to be determined by architectural historians. The successive and chronological rehabilitation, in works of architectural scholarship, of the Georgian, Victorian, Edwardian and post-Edwardian periods has gone hand in hand with the rise of societies dedicated to the preservation of the actual buildings of these periods. A perfect example of the fusion between architectural history and architectural preservation is that in December 1978 Mark Girouard used the prize money he had just received for his new book *Life in the English Country House, a Social and Architectural History* to charter an aeroplane to take him to Edinburgh to confront the Chairman of the Standard Life Assurance Company which was supporting the controversial redevelopment of the late eighteenth-century warehouses of the East India Company in Cutler Street in the City of London.

The present book naturally reflects the tastes and interests of its author, and was commissioned by its publishers as a *short* study: these circumstances help explain some of the inevitable omissions, including important topics like the architecture of industry, transport, engineering and town-planning. An attempt has also been made to avoid reference to works of architectural theory and to the study of archaeology, although the dividing line between these fields and architectural history is often very fine. Another area which has been excluded is the history of the changing representation of buildings through the medium of drawings, engravings and photographs. This fascinating and important subject, which is in some ways more closely related to developments in architectural practice than in architectural history, deserves a separate book to itself. There is a different explanation for the absence of a separate section on what has been written by architectural historians in this country about the history of the Modern Movement. The reason here is that very little serious historical writing has so far appeared on this subject, apart from Reyner Banham's *Theory and Design in the First Machine Age* (1960), though there has been a good deal of

journalism by Banham, Charles Jencks and others. The absence
of historical writing is scarcely surprising since it is hard to be
objective about contemporary events and impossible to write
with any perspective about a movement which is not yet ended.
Now that the Modern Movement is over, the historians can get
to work and we shall doubtless see the emergence of some lively
new perspectives during the next few years.

I should like to express my gratitude to Professor Edward
Shils, Dr Robin Middleton and Dr Gavin Stamp for their
comments on the first draft of this book, and to Mr H.M.
Colvin, Mr John Cornforth and Dr Roger Scruton for their help
with specific points.

Bibliographical note

In the text, footnotes and bibliography, the place of publication
is London unless otherwise stated, and the following abbrevia-
tions have been used:

Arch. Hist.	*Architectural History*
Arch. Rev.	*Architectural Review*
Burl. Mag.	*Burlington Magazine*
JSAH	*Journal of the Society of Architectural Historians*
JWCI	*Journal of the Warburg and Courtauld Institutes*

I
The Continental
Background 1700-1914

1 Germany

It was in Germany that history of art was first elevated to the
status of an academic discipline, long before any other country
in Europe. It is therefore inevitable that we should give far more
space to developments in Germany than to those in contemporary France or Italy. From the ancient world up to the time
of Vasari in the sixteenth century, critics wrote about *contemporary* artists, but in the eighteenth century both the German
Neo-Classicists like Winckelmann and English Gothicists like
Essex and Walpole, looked to the *past* for standards. Thus it is
that Johann Joachim Winckelmann (1717-68) is sometimes
regarded as the father of modern art history. However, we
should not overlook the Viennese Baroque architect, Johann
Bernard Fischer von Erlach (1656-1723), who published his
Entwurff einer historischen Architektur (Vienna 1721) with a text in
German and French. A second edition of 1725 was reprinted in
1730 with an English translation by Thomas Lediard under the
title, *A Plan of Civil and Historical Architecture, in the representation of
the most noted buildings of foreign nations, both ancient and modern.* This
book, which has some claim to be the first comparative history
of world architecture — certainly the first to illustrate Egyptian,
Chinese and Islamic buildings — consists basically of eighty-six
double folio plates with a combination of imaginative grandeur
and creative eclecticism which was a potent influence on
eighteenth century taste. Although the overall mood of his
reconstructions of ancient buildings is Baroque, they were based
on serious, scholarly investigations in which he drew on ancient
authors, coins, the writings of modern archaeologists and travellers, as well as the evidence of the surviving buildings or ruins
themselves. He explains engagingly how 'he undertook this

1

Work only as a Kind of Amusement, at a Time, when the Wars, with which His Imperial Majesty was taken up, left little Time or Employment for *Civil Architecture*'. He claimed that 'Artists will here see, that Nations dissent no less in their Taste for Architecture, than in Food and Raiment, and, by comparing one with the other they themselves make a judicious Choice'. What is remarkable is the apparent detachment with which he surveys the broad world scene, and his lack of interest in tracing a pattern or progress. Thus, although he does claim that 'not withstanding all these Varieties there are certain general Principles in Architecture, which can by no Means be laid aside, without offending the Eye: Such are the Rules of Symmetry; that the Weaker must be supported by the Stronger, and the like', it does not seem to be his primary aim to elevate the classical tradition above all others. However, it should be remembered that one entire book of the five of which the whole work is composed, is devoted to illustrations of his own buildings in the Baroque style.

Fischer von Erlach was something of a maverick without immediate progeny. Far more important was Winckelmann's *Geschichte der Kunst des Alterthums* (Dresden 1764, translated by G.H. Lodge as *The History of Ancient Art*, Boston 1880). Winckelmann applied Vasari's cyclical interpretation of artistic development to ancient Greek sculpture, the rise and decline of which he charted in four stages. His book was also important for establishing the notion of cultural history in which the art of a period is seen as reflecting the spirit of the age. Winckelmann not only put new emphasis on the concept of 'style' but made it clear that for him the artistic style of the Greeks was closely bound up with social and political conditions, customs, climate and religion.

The impact of this on Georg Wilhelm Friedrich Hegel (1770-1831) is evident, although architecture was peripheral to his interests as it had been to those of Winclelmann himself. Since Hegel's influence on intellectual history has been so profound, it is important to define as clearly as possible his understanding of the role of art and architecture as expressed in his *Aesthetics, Lectures on Fine Art* (2 vols., Oxford 1965, transl. by T. M. Knox) and elsewhere in his writings. This is best considered under the two headings of his view of self-realisation and of the philosophy of history. Hegel emphasises self-consciousness (*'Entäusserung'*) as the end point of a process of self-realisation. Art plays a necessary role in the evolution of spirit towards self-understanding. The various forms of art, since they cannot be considered as rival means to a single end but as unique contributions to the self-image of man, must successively give way to each other as the self-image evolves in response to them. Having realised itself through architecture, the spirit seeks for new forms in which to manifest itself, for example in sculpture. Hegel recognised various stages in this process. While these stages can be understood in terms which are not historical — since they are simply levels of development which might or might not have been reached — they are also given an historical meaning. This is because Hegel believed that history had a peculiar form, the form of evolution.

According to Hegel's philosophy, the development of the spirit from immersion in 'subjectivity' or 'appetite' to its full realisation as a self-knowing being is mirrored, not only in the development of the individual, but also in the process of history. Hence history moves always forwards, from the less articulate, less definite, less 'formed', to the more articulate, more precise, more 'realised'. Since art is part of this process of self-realisation, its various stages or 'moments' must therefore be mirrored in its own history: for example, Hegel interpreted the history of art in three stages, symbolical art (i.e. Oriental), classical art (Graeco-Roman), and romantic art (Christian-Germanic).

Finally, it is important to remember that Hegel sometimes associated his theory of history with his theory of logic, according to which truth emerges from the interaction of thesis and antithesis, the latter being spontaneously generated by the former. From this interaction a synthesis is formed which, in turn, generates its own antithesis. Once again the idea is of an inner principle, forcing the argument onwards to its conclusion. Again, it seems, the process may have a temporal representation. Hegelians therefore came to see the whole process of history, including art as one part of it, as a 'dialectical' movement through successive stages, each stage being related to the last as synthesis to thesis and antithesis in a logical argument. But, such was the peculiarity of his logic, that Hegel saw thesis and antithesis not as contradicting but as 'opposing' each other, so that each stage was forced towards a kind of 'completion' in the next. Hence the movement, as reflected in history, has a 'forward-looking' character, the character of *'Aufhebung'* or 'transcendence'. The dialectical historical process which Hegel thought of in spiritual terms was translated into material terms by Karl Marx (1818-83), and a combination of their two approaches has had a profound influence on the way many art historians have described the nature of stylistic development.

It is curious that for the Protestant Hegel in the 1820s, as for the Catholic Pugin a decade later, the essence or spirit of Catholicism was seen as permanently enshrined in Gothic architecture. It was, indeed, in the field of Gothic rather than classical studies that architectural history was to be developed in the eighteenth and early nineteenth centuries in Germany, as it was in England and France. In 1772 the young Johann Wolfgang von Goethe (1749-1832) published his celebrated paean of praise in honour of Strasbourg Cathedral, *Von deutscher Baukunst, D. M. Ervini a Steinbach* (Hamburg 1773). For Goethe the importance of Gothic was that it was an organic style consonant with *nature*. Equally influential for the future was his belief that it was a style of German origin and character. Although Goethe's essay was reprinted in the following year by Johann Gottfried Herder (1744-1803) in his *Von deutscher Art und Kunst, einige fliegender Blätter,* the influence of its powerful poetry was, to begin with, comparatively slight. Though Herder was not an enthusiast for Gothic, he did make an appeal for a history of Gothic architecture, and it was his notions of populism and of unfettered creative genius that fired Goethe's youthful imagination. Hegel and the brothers Schlegel were later to adopt some of Goethe's ideas as can be seen, for example, in Friedrich Schlegel's *Briefe auf einer Reise durch die Niederlande, Rheingegenden, die Schweiz, und einen Theil von Frankreich* of 1806 and especially in the revised edition of 1823 in his *Sämmtliche Werke* (Vienna, vol. VI).

August Wilhelm Schlegel delivered an important series of lectures on literature and art at Berlin from 1801, but architecture was not central to his outlook and the lectures were anyway not published until 1884. However, Berlin had become a centre for architectural education with the founding by David Gilly in 1793 of the celebrated Bauschule, known as the Bauakademie from 1799. Here the great neo-classical architect, Karl Friedrich Schinkel (1781-1841), was taught by leading architects such as David and Friedrich Gilly, Heinrich Gentz and Carl Gotthard Langhans. The brilliant and influential Friedrich Gilly (1772-1800) prepared six superb drawings of the mediaeval castle of Marienburg in East Prussia which appeared as aquatint engravings in *Schloss Marienburg in Preussen. Nach seinen vorzüglichsten äussern und innern Ansichten dargestellt* (Berlin 1799), issued by Friedrich Frick in 1799. They had created a sensation when they had been exhibited at the Berlin Academy in 1795, and helped draw the attention of many, including the young Schinkel, to the merits and beauties of Gothic architecture. Schinkel's history professor was the architect Alois Hirt (1759-1839), friend of Goethe and later Director of the Altes Museum in Berlin, who published a treatise on antique and Renaissance architecture in 1809, *Die Baukunst nach den Grundsätzen der Alten* (Berlin 1809). Perhaps the first history of mediaeval German architecture was *Von altdeutscher Baukunst* (2 vols., Leipzig 1820) by Christian Ludwig Stieglitz (1756-1836). Informed by a romantic nationalism descending from Herder, Goethe and the Schlegels, the book claimed that only the Greeks and the Germans had ever created a really original architecture: Greek architecture was 'plastic' and rational; German (i.e. Gothic) architecture was 'romantic' and mysterious. His articles on 'Baukunst' and 'Kirche' in his *Enzyklopädie der bürgerlichen Baukunst* (5 vols., Leipzig 1792-8), had evinced a much more rational and pre-Romantic interpretation of Gothic in which he had emphasised that Gothic was not a style of German origin.

Romantic nationalism as the basis of an interpretation of German mediaeval architecture is given clear expression in the writings of Johann Dominicus Fiorillo and of Johann Gustav Büsching. Fiorillo, a native of Hamburg, taught the history of art at Göttingen University from 1781-1821 where one of the first chairs in the subject was established for him in 1813. Büsching lectured on German mediaeval history and art at the University of Breslau from 1817. The key works of these two scholars are Fiorillo's *Geschichte der zeichnenden Künste in Deutschland und den vereinigten Niederlanden* (4 vols., Hanover 1815-20), and two books by Büsching, *Reise durch einige Münster und Kirchen des nördlichen Deutschlands im Spätjahr 1817* (Leipzig

1819) and *Das Schloss der deutschen Ritter zu Marienburg* (Berlin 1823).

Though Alois Hirt was not a special admirer of Gothic, the way in which he wrote about buildings as 'an organic whole' was quickly adopted to characterise Gothic architecture by those who were its admirers. It was in these idealist and romantic terms that Schinkel spoke of Gothic in the literary commentaries which accompanied his designs of 1810 for an elaborate Gothic mausoleum for Queen Luise of Prussia. Following Friedrich Schlegel, he spoke of Gothic as 'higher in its principles than the architecture of the ancients' because it was based not on practical considerations like Greek architecture but on the expression of an idea and on a notion of the infinite. More important was the poetic interpretation of Gothic as the national German style which coloured a report submitted by Schinkel four years later in connection with his designs for a Gothic memorial cathedral in Berlin. However, instead of realising this project Prussia cooperated with the other German states in the completion of Cologne Cathedral, a building which had always aroused national sentiment. The guiding spirit behind the exceptionally bold and dramatic undertaking at Cologne was Sulpiz Boisserée (1783-1854) who published in 1823 a magnificent set of engravings of the cathedral as well as an explanatory text entitled *Geschichte und Beschreibung des Doms von Köln* (Stuttgart 1823). Boisserée was a serious architectural historian who opened Friedrich Schlegel's eyes to Gothic architecture in Paris and became a close friend of Goethe. He and Georg Moller (1784-1852) discovered lost mediaeval plans for Cologne Cathedral which enabled him to reconstruct the supposed original design. His understanding of the development of the Gothic style in the Middle Ages was, however, severely limited by his determinedly nationalist or racialist interpretation. The fact that he saw it as an essentially Catholic style had a great influence on the Romantic Movement in Germany and, for example, played a part in Friedrich Schlegel's conversion to the Roman Catholic Church. The completion of Cologne Cathedral became a symbol of the new Germany that had been built up from the rebirth of the national spirit under the Napoleonic yoke. Interest in Gothic architecture in England at this time lacked this strongly nationalist and patriotic element.

For Pugin, Gothic was first and foremost Catholic art, whereas his opposite number in Germany, August Reichensperger (1808-95), published his appeal for Gothic architecture under the title, *Die christlich-germanische Baukunst* (Trier 1845). Incidentally, he later published a monograph on Pugin called *Augustus Welby Pugin, der Neubegründer der christlichen Kunst in England* (Freiburg i.B. 1877). It is interesting to note in this connection that when Sir George Gilbert Scott won his celebrated victory over German competitors in the Nikolaikirche competition in 1844, he wrote: 'When my drawings arrived and were exhibited with the rest, the effect upon the public mind in Hamburg was perfectly electrical. They had never seen Gothic architecture carried out in a new design with anything like the old spirit, and as they were labouring under the old error that Gothic was the German ("Alt Deutsch") style, their feelings of patriotism were stirred up in a wonderful manner'.[1]

Georg Moller, who had contributed drawings to Boisserée's great book on Cologne Cathedral, published *Denkmäler der deutschen Baukunst* in three folio volumes (Darmstadt 1815-21) which appeared in an English translation by Priestley and Weale as *An Essay on the Origin and Progress of Gothic Architecture* (1824). It was also translated by W. H. Leeds in 1836 as *Moller's Memorials of German-Gothic Architecture*. Moller's work was important for its accurate measured drawings of mediaeval buildings, but its text, though sensible as far as it goes, was hampered by his lack of knowledge of French and English Gothic. Moller was also the leading architect in the state of Hesse-Darmstadt and was a pupil of the distinguished neo-classicist, Friedrich Weinbrenner (1766-1826), whose *Architektonisches Lehrbuch* (3 vols., Karlsruhe and Stuttgart, 1810-25), echoed the stern functionalism of Carlo Lodoli. Unlike the majority of scholars who studied Gothic architecture at this time, Moller did not consider it suitable as a basis for present-day architecture. He believed that the Gothic style was rooted in the circumstances and way of life of its time, as opposed to the principles of Greek architecture which constituted a language of permanent validity.

In some ways more perceptive than Moller was the less well-

---

[1] G.G. Scott, *Personal and Professional Recollections*, 1879, pp.118-19.

known Johannes Wetter (1806-97) who published a small guide book in 1835, *Geschichte und Beschreibung des Domes zu Mainz* (Mainz 1835). As Frankl has explained, Wetter 'comprehended Gothic as an entity, as *system*, and essentially as a constructive system. In this he goes beyond Rickman, de Laborde, and all the others'.[1] Wetter's matter-of-fact approach contrasts with that of his contemporaries, for example Carl Schnaase (1798-1875) who published an intensely reflective volume of travel letters in 1834, *Niederländische Briefe* (Stuttgart and Tübingen 1835), and also a great eight-volumed *Geschichte der bildenden Künste* (Leipzig 1843). A pupil of Hegel, Schnaase was anxious to interpret architectural style as the result of the *Zeitgeist*, the spirit of the age, and of the *Volksgeist*, the spirit of the nation. On the other hand, he rejected the recently established romantic tradition of interpreting a building as something which had grown as 'an organic whole', because he feared that a belief that a building 'worked' like the human body, might lead to a modern architecture of pure functionalism.

Schnaase's rejection of organic growth was opposed by the leading architectural historian, Franz Theodor Kugler (1808-58), who became Professor of Art History in the Academy of Art in Berlin in 1833. According to Pevsner, 'he is the first man whom we can call an art historian, and who was [also] Professor of the History of Art'.[2] He published a *Handbuch der Kunstgeschichte* (Stuttgart 1841-42) and *Geschichte der Baukunst* (4 vols., Stuttgart 1856-72), and on the whole he has a workmanlike and straightforward approach which contrasts with that of Schnaase. He is important for ending the dominance of mediaeval architecture as the principal subject of study for architectural historians.

This new emphasis on the Renaissance is reflected in the work of Gottfried Semper (1803-79), who was perhaps the most important architect of his day in Germany. His buildings, such as the Opera Houses, Picture Gallery and Oppenheim Palace in Dresden, and his two museums in Vienna, are mainly in a Renaissance or Baroque style. He also taught architecture and

[1] P. Frankl, *op. cit.*, p.527.
[2] 'An Un-English Activity? I. Reflections on Not Teaching Art History', *The Listener*, XLVIII, 1952, p.715.

thought deeply about the nature and history of ornament. His work as an architectural historian is contained in his *Die vier Elemente der Baukunst* (Brunswick 1851) and *Kleine Schriften* (Berlin and Stuttgart 1883), both of which include lectures he had delivered in London in 1851-55. Semper's 'four elements' were the processes of weaving textiles, moulding ceramics, building in timber and building in stone. The making of patterns preceded the development of structural form, so that at the beginning of his *Der Stil* (2 vols., Frankfurt and Munich 1860 and 63), Semper offers not Laugier's primitive hut, but a wreath as man's first consciously ornamental and constructive achievement. He had originally intended completing his greatest work, *Der Stil*, with a third volume 'on the Styles of Architecture', but in the end incorporated much of this material into the first two volumes. The fact that he saw architecture as emerging from the crafts has suggested that his conception of it was utilitarian, and indeed there are passages in his writings which confirm this and for which art historians like Worringer were subsequently to condemn him. However, he firmly believed that religious and political ideals, no less than functional requirements, can shape architecture: 'Monuments of architecture', he wrote, 'are in fact nothing but the aesthetic expression of social, political, and religious institutions'. Semper had read Darwin's *The Origin of Species* as soon as it came out in 1859, and his approach to the history of art can be seen in some sense as Darwinian: it is for him a continuous process of development without abrupt changes of direction, forming a pattern of growth which is built up, like those of nature herself, from a few basic types.

Semper the historian is closely related to Semper the architect. He reacted against the extreme eclecticism of his master, Friedrich von Gärtner (1792-1847), who, with Leo von Klenze (1784-1864), developed Munich in a variety of historical styles for Ludwig I of Bavaria. It was partly Semper's impatience with this purely pictorial approach to style that led him to investigate and establish what he felt to be the first principles of style in his extensive writings. He believed that for present-day architecture the style of the Italian Renaissance should be adopted because its forms enshrined permanent expressions of true or perfect types and, equally importantly, because it had never been taken to its full development in the sixteenth century. He refers in the second volume of *Der Stil* to a forthcoming history of his favoured style by Jacob Burckhardt (1818-97), professor of history at Basel University. This was the *Geschichte der Renaissance in Italien* which Semper had presumably read in manuscript and was published in 1867 as Part I of the 4th volume of Franz Kugler's *Geschichte der Baukunst* (4 vols., Stuttgart 1856-72). Burckhardt's most important book, *The Civilisation of the Renaissance in Italy*, had appeared in 1860. Burckhardt found the modern age in which he lived debased and materialist so that he looked back to the Renaissance as representing not merely an artistic ideal but also a social, political and religious ideal — just as Winckelmann had looked back to ancient Greece, and Pugin to mediaeval England. Like Pugin, Burckhardt was a romantic conservative and saw the revival of an earlier architectural style as a way of improving the quality of modern life. This is partly why Semper, with his professional interest in the Renaissance Revival in architecture, referred to Burckhardt's work with such enthusiasm in *Der Stil*.

Two distinguished followers of Burckhardt were Heinrich von Geymüller (1839-1909) and Heinrich Wölfflin (1864-1945). Geymüller's greatest achievement was his *Die Architektur der Renaissance in Toskana* (11 vols., Munich 1885-1908, abridged transl. 2 vols., New York 1924), produced in collaboration with C. von Stegmann, but he also published *Architektur und Religion* (Basel 1911) which enables one to appreciate the strength of his interpretation of beauty as a conscious reflection of God. Wölfflin developed some hints from Burckhardt so as to form a very different conception of style and of architectural history. Most of his work is concerned with the history of Renaissance painting, but his first book, *Renaissance und Barock* (Munich 1888), described the transition in Italian architecture from Renaissance to what is now often known as Mannerism. He attempted to establish a set of 'laws', applicable to the art of different periods, which would explain the recurring pattern of stylistic transitions. He formed this ambition in the light of an observation of Burckhardt's that 'Art has its own life and history', and possibly also as a kind of parallel to Darwin's 'laws' of Evolution. The tendency of his work is thus to minimise the importance of iconography, the influence of religion, of social and political conditions, and the personality of the individual artist. In its most extreme form this approach can be summed up in Wölfflin's statement that 'What matters is not the individual products of an age, but the fundamental temper which produced them'.[1] However, Wolfflin's great genius lay precisely in his sensitive reaction to the visual appearance of the individual work of art; indeed his constant comparing and contrasting of one object with another has formed the basis of the way in which the history of art and architecture is taught to this day: for example, professional art historians nearly always illustrate their lectures with *pairs* of lantern slides, a comparative technique which seems to go back to Wölfflin's *Renaissance and Baroque*. Wölfflin, who was Professor of Art History at Berlin and, from 1893, at Basel where he succeeded Burckhardt, differed from many of the historians whom we shall investigate in nineteenth-century Germany and France, in not having his roots in archaeology, topography, ecclesiology and religion, or in a romantic, spiritual kinship or identification with a particular culture whose architectural or religious forms he wished to revive. This has tended to enhance his popularity with twentieth-century art historians.

There were naturally reactions against the formalism implicit in Wölfflin's approach. Wölfflin had to some extent ignored and even implicitly condemned full Baroque architecture, but in 1887-9 Cornelius Gurlitt (1850-1938) published a three-volumed history of post-Renaissance architecture in Italy, Belgium, Holland, France, England and Germany, which concentrated on the Baroque and Rococo styles. Gurlitt's remarkable rehabilitation of a period generally regarded as one of decline was followed by August Schmarsow (1853-1936) who interpreted architecture in terms of rhythm and, more importantly, of space in his *Barock und Rokoko, eine kritische Auseinandersetzung über das Malerische in der Architektur* (Leipzig 1897). This emphasis on the creation of space rather than on the forms by which it is surrounded was derived from hints in Hegel and Burckhardt, and was first clearly stated by Schmarsow in his lecture on the nature of architecture, *Das Wesen der architektonische Schöpfung* (Leipzig 1894). It was, of course, an approach especially suited to the new understanding of Baroque and

---

[1] *Renaissance and Baroque*, Fontana Library ed. 1964, p.77.

Rococo architecture with which it went hand in hand. One important pioneer who is sometimes overlooked is the Viennese artist, author and art-educator, Camillo Sitte (1843-1903). His *Der Städtebau nach seinen künstlerischen Grundsätzen* (Vienna 1889) was not only important as one of the first books to describe the city as a work of art but as a positive and original contribution to appreciation of Baroque planning. This enormously popular book had a profound impact on Gurlitt and on the almost equally prolific scholar Albert Brinckmann (1881-1958), who was also influenced by Schmarsow as well as by *Das Problem der Form in der bildenden Kunst* (Strassburg 1893, transl. New York 1907) by Adolf von Hildebrand (1847-1921). Brinckmann's principal works were *Platz und Monument als künstlerisches Formproblem* (Berlin 1908), dedicated significantly to Wölfflin, *Deutsche Stadtbaukunst in der Vergangenheit* (Frankfurt 1911), *Baukunst des 17. und 18. Jahrhunderts in den romanischen Ländern* (Berlin 1915) and *Plastik und Raum als Grundformen künstlerischer Gestaltung* (Munich 1922). Brinckmann extended Hildebrand's concept of space precisely defined in depth, to an unlimited concept of three-dimensional space which could even include town-planning. Brinckmann saw the changing pattern of these space-volume relations as the basis of an explanation of stylistic change. The long-term influence of this tradition of spatial emphasis, coupled with an appreciation of Baroque, first on Frankl, and then on Pevsner (e.g. in his *Outline of European Architecture*, 1943), can hardly be overestimated. The most important early work of the great architectural historian Paul Frankl (1879-1962) was *Die Entwicklungsphasen der neueren Baukunst* (Stuttgart 1914), translated as *Principles of Architectural History, the Four Phases of Architectural Style, 1420-1900* (Cambridge, Mass. 1968, with a foreword by James Ackerman). In this work Frankl drew a distinction between periods like the Renaissance which produced a static architecture based on space addition, and periods like the Baroque with its dynamic architecture based on space division. Like Brinckmann he used these categories to account for stylistic variety.

The immensely industrious Georg Dehio (1850-1932) produced a systematic series of sensitive and scholarly accounts of mainly German architecture, for example *Der kirchliche Baukunst des Abendlandes* (2 vols., Stuttgart 1892-1901), *Geschichte der deutschen Kunst* (8 vols., Berlin and Leipzig 1919-34), and *Handbuch der deutschen Kunstdenkmäler* (5 vols., Berlin 1914-28). In a very different category was the Arts and Crafts architect Hermann Muthesius (1861-1927), who spent the years 1896-1903 as a cultural attaché at the German Embassy in London studying recent English achievement in architecture, especially domestic architecture. His three important works have not been superseded: *Die englische Baukunst der Gegenwart* (Leipzig 1900), *Die neuere kirchliche Baukunst in England* (Berlin 1901) and *Das englische Haus* (3 vols., Berlin 1904-5). Here and in his *Stilcharakter und Baukunst* (Mülheim, Ruhr, 1902), he argued that English Arts and Crafts architecture was the fulfilment of the ideals of functionalism, reason and utility in architecture which had been the basis of the best nineteenth-century German architectural theory, for example in the writings of Schinkel, Bötticher and Semper. To Muthesius this was the perfect expression of what he called *Sachlichkeit*, which was the foundation of the Deutsche Werkbund in 1907, a body intent on improving the quality of design in the German manufacturing industry.

In Muthesius there is thus a close link between the historical period studied and the promotion of a present-day style. In this he was untypical of much German thinking about architecture at the end of the century, and we ought to take up the story of this development at the point where we left it in the work of Wölfflin and Schmarsow. This means turning to what is known as the Vienna School where the great giant was Alois Riegl (1858-1905), keeper of textiles at the Austrian Museum for Applied Arts in Vienna and subsequently a Professor at Vienna University from 1897. Though he was not an architectural historian, his name must be mentioned in any account of the ways in which historians have explained stylistic change. His studies of the then unfashionable Late Antique art, published in *Die spätrömische Kunstindustrie* (Vienna 1901), had led him to dispose of the customary explanation of its forms in terms of Barbarian influence, just as his study of the minor arts had caused him to reject the notion that decorative form was the product of technique and material. He replaced these external determinants with an internal determinant to which he gave the name '*Kunstwollen*'. This verb can be translated in a number of ways of which 'aesthetic urge' may be found most sympathetic by Riegl's admirers, 'will to form' by his opponents. Riegl applied his notion of *'Kunstwollen'* indiscriminately to the individual artist or work of art as well as to an artistic period or a whole nation, and was keen to find it operating equally in different artistic spheres at any one period. His work was also important for ignoring the belief in periods of decline and decay in art which had coloured art-historical writing from Vasari to Winckelmann and beyond. He was, in addition, a pioneer in the investigation of the still unfashionable Baroque, and published posthumously *Die Entstehung der Barockkunst in Rom* (Vienna 1908).

Max Dvořák (1874-1921) and Wilhelm Worringer (1881-1965) were both deeply indebted to the ideas of Riegl. Though not an architectural historian, Dvořák touched on the problems of Gothic architecture in his 'Idealismus und Materialismus in der gotischen Skulptur und Malerei' (Munich and Berlin 1918), reprinted in his posthumously published *Kunstgeschichte als Geistesgechichte; Studien zur abendländischen Kunstentwicklung* (Munich 1924), and translated by R.J. Klawiter as *Idealism and Naturalism in Gothic Art* (Notre Dame, Ind., 1967). Worringer represents even more completely the strengths and dangers which resulted from Riegl because the translation into English as early as 1927 of his most important early work, *Formprobleme der Gotik* (Munich 1912) meant that he was one of the few architectural historians of the new German school whose work was widely known in England at that time. As we shall see later, it was an influence on W.R. Lethaby. Indeed, in the preface to the English edition of 1927, which appeared under the title, *Form in Gothic*, it was acclaimed by Herbert Read. The book was also translated into French, and a new edition of the English translation appeared in 1957.

Worringer had begun his career with the publication of his doctoral dissertation, *Abstraktion und Einfühlung, ein Beitrag zur Stilpsychologie* (Munich 1908, translated into English by Michael Bullock in 1953 as *Abstraction and Empathy, a Contribution to the Psychology of Style*). Worringer's notion of *Einfühlung*, that is to say the spectator's empathy or identification with the particular quality of *life* conveyed in an individual work of art, was borrowed from Theodor Lipps (1851-1914), whose pioneering work in the field of psychological theories of aesthetics was his

Ästhetik (2 vols., Hamburg and Leipzig 1903 and 1906). For Worringer, *Einfühlung* was the basis of classical and Renaissance art in which man is at one with the world around him, while he saw a tendency to abstraction as characteristic of styles such as Egyptian, Indian and Byzantine, produced by men who were in some sense at war with the surrounding material universe. For Worringer the strength of Gothic lay in the fact that it could be seen as in some sense a compromise between *Einfühlung* and *Abstraktion*. However, traditional aesthetics had been based on *Einfühlung* and therefore applied only to classical and representational art, and not to non-European or Gothic art. Since they incorporated an assumption that designers of different periods must ultimately share common ambitions, they placed stress in 'ability' not 'will'. Worringer thus developed Riegl's notion of *'Kunstwollen'* to show that an artist 'can accomplish just as much as he wills, but that he cannot accomplish what is outside the trend of his will'; he argued that 'what we are always taking for the difference between will and ability when we look back in our contemplation of art, is in reality only the difference between our will and the will of past epochs.'[1] The dramatic result of this in terms of an interpretation of Gothic architecture is that 'Gothic has nothing to do with beauty... Let us therefore rid Gothic of any connection with the term aesthetic. Let us strive solely for a psychological interpretation of style in Gothic works of art, which will explain to us the orderly relation between the inner sentiment of Gothic and the outward form of its expression in art; then we shall have done for Gothic what aesthetics has done for classical art'.[2]

The importance of this for defining the nature and potentialities of architectural history is enormous for, as Worringer observes

When we look upon the history of art no longer as a mere history of artistic ability, but as a history of artistic will, it gains a significance in the general history of mankind... For changes in will, whose mere precipitates are the variations of style in the history of art, cannot be purely arbitrary or fortuitous. On the contrary, they must have a consistent relation to those spiritual and mental changes... which are clearly reflected in the historical development of myths, of religions, of philosophical systems, of world conceptions.[3]

[1] p.9.   [2] p.11.   [3] p.12.

The trouble with so grandiose a vision of the role of the architectural historian is that it is hard to conceive that in any one century there could ever be more than one or two at the most who could possibly hope to sustain it. Certainly Worringer himself could not and his book is more interesting as an essay in the history of ideas than useful as a history of Gothic. For one thing, the large vision and the concentration in deeply embedded 'wills' rather than on their 'precipitates' in the form of actual works of art, necessitate a distancing from the individual work of art. The effect of this is brought home most strikingly in *Formprobleme der Gotik* where, amazingly, there is not a single reference to any individual mediaeval building or work of art: a true realisation of Wölfflin's ambition of a 'history of art without names'. Indeed, the whole concept of Gothic style begins to dissolve before our eyes in consequence of Worringer's argument that 'this Gothic will to form dominates, not externally, but internally, Romanesque art, Merovingian art, the art of the Migration period, in short the whole course of Northern and Central European art'.[1] Gothic turns out to be anything Worringer approves of — indeed by the end of the book it seems to include Baroque as well — and the reason that he approves of it is because its 'will' is a reflection of the psychology of northern Germanic man, in other words of Worringer himself. Worringer was conscious that this view could not be very easily reconciled with the birth of Gothic in the Ile de France, and therefore indulged in a kind of word-play which will deceive no one: 'Nevertheless France cannot be called the actual home of Gothic; Gothic itself did not arise in France, only the Gothic system'.[2] His final explanation of Gothic is ultimately racial, as when he claims at the end of the book: 'Wherever Germanic elements are strongly present, a racial connection in the widest sense is observable, which, *in spite of* racial differences in the ordinary sense, is unmistakeably operative, and which is as it were established and recorded for all time in historical phenomena like Gothic. For the Germans, as we have seen, are the *conditio sine qua non* of Gothic'.[3]

Aby Warburg (1866-1929), an older man than either Dvořák or Worringer, had undertaken a study of Renaissance symbols

[1] p.38.   [2] pp.145-6.   [3] pp.180-1.

and allegory which led him away from both Riegl's *Kunstwollen* and from the traditional stylistic approach which tended, from Winckelmann onwards, to isolate monuments and social organisms with a supposedly common theme in order to construct a *Zeitgeist*. Warburg was not, however, an architectural historian and the subject has suffered from the fact that at the moment when German art history had reached in his work one of its highest peaks of subtlety, interest was largely shifted away from architecture. Perhaps Warburg's major impact has been his great library, *die kulturwissenschaftliche Bibliothek Warburg*, and its associated institute devoted to the History of the Classical Tradition, more appropriately considered in the first part of chapter V of the present work.

Before leaving Germany we should consider one more aspect of its remarkable contribution to the development of architectural history at the turn of the century. The establishment of an appreciation of Baroque was immediately followed by pioneering investigations of Neo-Classicism. In his *History of the Modern Styles of Architecture* (1st ed. 1862), Fergusson had not recognised any new approach to architectural design in the course of the eighteenth century and wrote unenthusiastically about nineteenth-century classicism under the heading 'Classical Revival'. In his *Geschichte des Barockstiles, des Rococo, und des Klassicismus in Belgien, Holland, Frankreich, England* (Stuttgart 1888), Gurlitt categorised post-Baroque architecture as 'Klassizismus', which can appropriately be translated as 'Neo-Classicism'. He concentrated largely on Baroque and Rococo, not on Neo-Classical, architecture, but important contributions were soon made by Kurt Cassirer in his *Die ästhetischen Hauptbegriffe der französischen Architekturtheoretiker von 1650 bis 1780* (Berlin 1909), and by Paul Klopfer in an especially useful book, *Von Palladio bis Shinkel, eine Charakteristik der Baukunst des Klassizismus* (Esslingen 1911). Klopfer's richly illustrated study concentrated, despite its title, on the eighteenth and early nineteenth centuries which it surveyed by analysis of building types throughout Europe. It was the penultimate volume in the important series, *Geschichte der neueren Baukunst* (10 vols., Stuttgart 1878-1927), which included works by Lübke, Gurlitt and Schubert, and had begun with a re-issue of Burckhardt's *Geschichte der Renaissance in Italien* of 1867. At the same time there was a revival in architectural circles of interest in Schinkel and in Biedermeier interior design, as can be seen in the work of Peter Behrens (1868-1940) and many other architects. Schinkel was now seen once more, as he had been during his lifetime, as a national hero who first gave German classicism a recognisably German stamp. Books like Paul Mebes's *Um 1800* (2 vols., Munich 1908) and Fritz Stahl's pioneering *Karl Friedrich Schinkel* (Berlin 1911) had their part to play in this movement.

Meanwhile, the Viennese school of art history was having a profound impact on a young Viennese scholar, Emil Kaufmann (1891-1953), who was destined to spend his whole academic career in an attempt to define neo-classicism. Having come under the influence of Max Dvořák, Franz Wickhoff and especially of Riegl with his characteristic interest in periods of transition or of supposed decadence, Kaufmann turned his attention to the dissolution of Baroque and its replacement by neo-classicism. He published the first fruits of his research in an article of 1924, 'Die Architekturtheorie der französischen Klassik und des Klassizismus',[1] in which, like Cassirer, he emphasised the conceptual basis of Neo-Classicism as well as its French origins. The notion that the 'revolutionary' period in French architecture marked the birth of modern architecture began to colour Kaufmann's work more and more as the Modern Movement itself grew in the 1920s and 30s: thus, what is suggested in his article, 'Architektonische Entwürfe aus der Zeit der Französischen Revolution'[2] of 1929, is more clearly stated in his strikingly titled short book, *Von Ledoux bis Le Corbusier. Ursprung und Entwicklung der autonomen Architektur* (Vienna and Leipzig 1933) and in his influential paper, 'Three Revolutionary Architects: Boullée, Ledoux and Lequeu'[3] of 1952. Despite its title, *Von Ledoux bis Le Corbusier* contained no illustrations of twentieth-century buildings, though the work of Le Corbusier, Loos and Berlage is mentioned in the last couple of pages.

In the meantime Kaufmann had been influenced by the writings and career of Sigfried Giedion (1893-1968), the Swiss engineer and architectural historian. Giedion's *Spätbarocker und*

[1] *Repertorium für Kunstwissenschaft*, 64, 1924, pp.197-237.

[2] *Zeitschrift für bildende Kunst*, 63, 1929-30, pp.38-46.

[3] *Trans. of the American Philosophical Soc.*, n.s., vol. 42, part 3, 1952, pp.431-564.

romantischer Klassizismus (Munich 1922) was a Wölfflinian analysis of purely formal artistic values in which he concluded that neo- or romantic-classicism was not a genuine style but purely a fashion. Becoming increasingly concerned with the promotion of Modern Movement design, he was appointed general secretary of CIAM (Congrès Internationaux de l'Architecture Moderne) in 1928 and Professor at Harvard ten years later. His enormously influential *Space, Time and Architecture, the Growth of a New Tradition* (1st ed. Harvard and London 1941) and *Mechanization Takes Command, a Contribution to Anonymous History* (New York 1948) argued that there were 'constituent' and 'transitory' facts in eighteenth- and nineteenth-century architecture and design, the former leading forwards in an inevitable line of shining progress to the glories of the Modern Movement.

Kaufmann's work is thus woven out of a variety of threads, including those originally contributed by Riegl, Wölfflin and Giedion, in which the distinction between the unity of Baroque and the plurality of neo-classicism reflects a distinctly Wölfflinian approach. He thus contrasts tellingly the kind of overall harmony aimed at by both Renaissance and Baroque architects with the attempts of later eighteenth-century architects to achieve 'expression of character, creation of atmosphere and division of the composition into independent units'.[1] Although it is difficult to see how these artistic aims could be the consequence of specific social and political ideals, Kaufmann nonetheless attempts to make the connection, doubtless with the example of Giedion before him. Writing of Boullée and Ledoux, Kaufmann argues that 'Along with the general unrest which was to lead to the political revolution, went a slowly-growing dissatisfaction with the established modes of artistic composition', but that 'In architecture, just as in politics, the reactionaries were to triumph over the inspired, though not sufficiently realistic, modernists'. Both Kaufmann and Giedion were agreed that the style of eighteenth-century French architects should be interpreted and assessed in the light of what had been achieved by modern architects: Kaufmann thus showed, for example, how 'Anticipating the twentieth century, Boullée and Ledoux restored the elementary forms to their rightful place in

[1] *Ibid.*, p.434.

architecture'.[1] He also gave expression to Giedion's determinism in claiming that 'most contemporaries and the following generations were not able to distinguish between those
attempts which were to become fruitful and permanent, and
those which proved to be merely whimsical and transitory'.[2]

In chapter VI of the present work we shall consider briefly
how Kaufmann's deliberately partial interpretation has been
undermined by the researches of recent scholars, including
Herrmann and Pérouse de Montclos, who have paid careful
attention to the origins of Neo-Classicism and to the whole
career, not just to part of it, of Boullée and Ledoux.

Despite the criticisms we have made of German historiography, it should be clear by now that modern architectural
history, in terms of both the description and the explanation
of style, had been established in Germany by 1914 and that
no other European country could show anything like its
intellectual brilliance in this field.[3] It was the fruits of this
tradition which historians like Saxl, Wittkower, Gombrich
and Pevsner, to say nothing of the Warburg Library, brought
in the 1930s to an England that was almost wholly un-
prepared for it.

2 France

It is arguable that some of the earliest architectural historians
are to be found in late seventeenth-century France, particularly
in the circle connected with Colbert's Académie royale d'architecture, founded in 1671. The royal historiographer, Jean-
François Félibien (1658-1733), secretary to the Académie
d'architecture, published a *Recueil historique de la vie et des ouvrages
des plus célèbres architectes* (Paris 1687) which included enthusiastic chapters on the great Gothic architects, Robert de Luzar-
ches, Thomas de Cormont, Renault, Hugues Libergier, Jean de
Chelles, Pierre de Montreuil and Erwin von Steinbach. These

[1] *Ibid.*, p.558. [2] *Ibid.*, p.434.
[3] C. Eisler, in *The Intellectual Migration*, ed. D. Fleming and B. Bailyn,
Cambridge, Mass., 1969, speculates interestingly on the cultural pressures
which may have directed German Jews to the study of art history, emphasising
that the legislation preventing Jews from teaching subjects other than medi-
cine and philology in universities only began to be repealed from the 1840s.

attempted to bring together information from the various published guides to mediaeval buildings. The book is important also as one of the first detached accounts of past architecture with no attempt to justify it as merely a prelude to the superior merits of modern architecture. It is this approach which separates him from a Renaissance writer like Vasari. Félibien later published *Les plans et les descriptions de deux des plus belles maisons de campagne de Pline le Consul avec des remarques sur tous ces bâtiments,* to which was appended a *Dissertation touchant l'architecture antique et l'architecture gothique* (Paris 1699, London 1707). Much of this *Dissertation* consists of a commentary on Colonna's celebrated *Hypnerotomachia Polyphili* (Venice 1499), but Félibien also shows great feeling for the constructional principles of Gothic, remarkable for that date: 'The use of stilted arches and of ribs served to diminish the thrust of the vaults, and also was a cause of substantially reducing their weight and thickness'.[1]

Félibien seems to have been an influence on Florent le Comte (d. 1712) who published *Cabinet des singularitéz d'architecture, peinture, sculpture et gravure* (vol.I, Paris 1699), which contains what may be the first account of the history of French architecture. Another author influenced by Félibien is his younger brother, Dom Michel Félibien (1666-1719), a monk of the Benedictine Abbey of S. Denis, who wrote *Histoire de l'abbaye royale de Saint Denis en France* (Paris 1706). This contains a good biography of Abbot Suger as well as a description and plan of the church itself.

Guides to some of the major Gothic buildings of Paris and the Ile de France were published in the first half of the seventeenth century, and in 1632 it was decided that the newly founded Benedictine congregation of St Maur, centred on the abbey of St Germain-des-Prés, should concentrate its efforts on historical research. One of the greatest of the Maurist historians was Dom Jean Mabillon (1632-1707), who attempted a documented history of the Benedictine order and produced the *De Re Diplomatica* (Paris 1681), a pioneering attempt at establishing the date and authenticity of mediaeval manuscripts and charters. Pommeraye's histories of St Ouen at Rouen and of Rouen Cathedral, published respectively in 1662 and 1686, are

[1] Frankl, *op. cit.*, p.119.

of no great architectural value, but Dom Michel Germain (1645-94) prepared 168 engravings of the monastic buildings of the congregation of St Maur as part of the *Monasticon Gallicanum*. This was intended to parallel Dugdale's *Monasticon Anglicanum* (3 vols., 1655-73), which we shall glance at in the next chapter, but it was not in fact published until 1871.

François Roger de Gaignières, a frequent visitor at the Benedictine community of St Germain-des-Prés, was a colleague of the Benedictines of St Maur in the 1680s, and formed an important and widely known collection of mediaeval antiquities. In 1695 he began a systematic survey of French mediaeval architecture, glass, sculpture and inscriptions which eventually comprised thousands of drawings. These still survive in the Bibliothèque Nationale and the Bodleian Library at Oxford. In 1703 he suggested to Louis XIV's Secretary of State that the state should assume responsibility for preserving the antiquities he had recorded. The time was not yet ripe for this. However, little more than a century later, France became a pioneer in the cause of preservation when Louis Philippe of Orléans appointed an Inspecteur des monuments historiques in 1830.

Together with the Benedictine interest in the mediaeval past there was a growing interest in Gothic as a model of rational structure. This was prompted by architects and theorists who did not want to imitate the appearance of Gothic architecture but believed that its daring constructional principles could be employed to rationalise and improve the design of classical buildings. Perhaps the earliest statement of this can be found in a revolutionary little book by Michel de Frémin, the *Mémoires critiques de l'architecture, contenans l'idée de la vraye et de la fausse architecture* (Paris 1702). Opposing ornament and the classical orders, Frémin argues for a mechanistic type of building produced simply in response to the materialist requirements of function. The Abbé de Cordemoy, who was a canon at the abbey of St Jean-des-Vignes at Soissons, produced his *Nouveau traité de toute l'architecture* (Paris 1706), which took up Frémin's theme but in a less extreme form. Later in the century the Abbé Laugier developed the same arguments further in his celebrated *Essai sur l'architecture* (Paris 1753) and *Observations sur l'architecture* (The Hague 1765).

Frémin, Cordemoy and Laugier were theorists rather than

historians and as such are not of primary concern to us. However, their equation of architectural beauty with structural honesty, rather than with the surface application of the classical orders, led to a serious investigation of Gothic architecture which culminated in the nineteenth century with the work of Viollet-le-Duc.

The architect Jacques-Germain Soufflot (1713-80), a prominent figure in the tradition deriving from Frémin and Cordemoy, began the great Parisian church of Ste Geneviève (today the Panthéon) in the 1750s with the aim of 'combining the lightness of construction found in Gothic buildings with the purity and grandeur of Greek architecture'.[1] In 1741 Soufflot delivered a lecture at the Académie des Beaux-Arts under the title, *Mémoire sur l'architecture gothique*. This paper, which may have been known to Laugier, was remarkable for its sympathetic approach to Gothic as a valid architectural style, as worthy of study as any other. Its argument was developed by Louis Avril, a sometime Jesuit, who published *Temples anciens et modernes, ou observations historiques et critiques sur les plus célèbres monumens d'architecture grecque et gothique* (London and Paris 1774), under the pseudynom M.L.M. It contains some extremely perceptive comments on the structural system of the Gothic church.

Though he was not interested in Gothic, J.-N.-L. Durand (1760-1834) represents the culmination of the drier aspects of this somewhat puritanical rationalism. A pupil of Boullée, he was appointed professor in 1795 at the Ecole centrale des travaux publics which soon after became the Ecole Polytechnique. He held this post until 1830 during which time he published his *Recueil et parallèle des édifices de tout genre anciens et modernes, remarquables par leur beauté, par leur grandeur ou par leur singularité* (2 vols., Paris 1800), *Précis des leçons d'architecture données à l'Ecole Polytechnique* (2 vols., Paris 1802-5) and *Partie graphique des cours d'architecture faits à l'Ecole Royale Polytechnique* (Paris 1821). As a contribution to the development of architectural history, the *Recueil* is noteworthy for its eclectic approach in which Egyptian, Greek, Roman, Gothic and Renaissance buildings are regarded as of equal importance. As an

[1] Letter of Brébion of 1780 quoted in J. Monval, *Soufflot*, Paris 1918, pp.505-6.

eighteenth-century rationalist, however, Durand redraws all
the buildings so as to make them more neat and orderly with
any oddities ignored or eliminated. They are all drawn to the
same scale and arranged for comparison as particular building
types. For Durand architecture was nothing more than the
rational solution of practical problems: its aim was not to please
but to contribute to 'l'utilité publique et particulière'. With the
Recueil was published an *Essai sur l'histoire générale de l'architect-*
ure . . pour servir de texte explicatif au Recueil et parallèle . . par J. N. L.
Durand (Paris 1800, rev. ed. 1809, reprinted Brussels 1842),
which was the work of the architect and architectural writer,
J. -G. Legrand (1743-1807).

The years round 1800 also saw a revival of interest in the more
austere types of Italian Renaissance architecture which were
illustrated in chill outline engravings in a number of books
including Percier and Fontaine's *Palais . . . modernes . . . à Rome*
(Paris 1798) and *Choix des plus belles maisons de plaisance de Rome*
(Paris 1801), Grandjean de Montigny and Famin's *Architecture*
Toscane (Paris 1806), Haudebourt's *Palais Massimi à Rome* (Paris
1818), Schuelt's *Recueil d'Architecture, dessiné et mesuré en Italie, dans*
les années 1791, 92 & 93 (Paris 1821), and most splendid of all,
Letarouilly's *Edifices de Rome moderne* (3 vols., Paris 1840-57). At
the very heart of this tradition was A.-C. Quatremère de Quincy
(1755-1849), Permanent Secretary of the Académie Royale des
Beaux-Arts for over twenty years from 1816. The Académie ran
the Ecole des Beaux-Arts so that Quatremère, as a fierce
opponent of Gothic and upholder of Antiquity as the sole
pattern for modern architecture, exercised a powerful influence
on the education of young architects. Archaeologist, author and
politician, his outlook is characterised in his *Histoire de la vie et des*
ouvrages des plus célèbres architectes du XIᵉ siècle jusqu'à la fin du XVIIIᵉ
(2 vols., Paris 1830). Despite the broad span promised in its title
the book concentrates on the Italian Renaissance and builds up
to a climax in the work of Gabriel, Antoine, Gondoin and
Soufflot. Gondoin's Ecole de Chirurgie of 1769 is praised as
'l'ouvrage le plus classique du dix-huitième siècle'.[1] The book is
illustrated with outline drawings of a quality and finesse typical
of their date.

---

[1] II, p.332.

We should not neglect the romantic interpretation of architecture which in France, as in all European countries at the beginning of the nineteenth century, was inseparable from the rise of interest in Gothic. The nationalism that was so often part of this new historical preoccupation is immediately obvious in the title of the four-volumed *Antiquités nationales ou recueil de monuments pour servir à l'histoire générale et particulière de l'empire français* (Paris 1790-9) by Aubin-Louis Millin (1759-1818). The volumes contain a rather confused assembly of mediaeval buildings, tombs and Baroque sculpture. Of more powerful appeal was the Musée des Monumens Français set up in 1795 by Alexandre Lenoir (1761-1839) in the former Couvent des Petits Augustins, dismantled in 1816 and incorporated into the Ecole des Beaux Arts. This remarkable and poetic assembly of mediaeval fragments saved from buildings ravaged in the Revolution had a formative influence on a generation of Frenchmen including, for example, François-René de Chateaubriand (1768-1848) and the great historian Jules Michelet (1798-1874), whose *Histoire de France* appeared between 1833 and 1860. Chateaubriand's *Génie du Christianisme* (Paris 1802), which contains a celebrated evocation of the poetic mystery of Gothic in the chapter on Gothic churches, owes much to the spirit of Lenoir's Musée. Chateaubriand's interpretation of Gothic as the natural and permanent manifestation of Catholicism was to be a powerful influence in nineteenth-century France and, perhaps almost more, in England.

J.-B.-L. Séroux d'Agincourt (1730-1814) produced a remarkable *Histoire de l'art par les monumens depuis sa décadence au IVᵉ siècle jusqu' à son renouvellement au XVIᵉ* (6 vols., Paris 1811-23) which, in an age of increasing nationalism, was notable for its truly European grasp. Even more serious was the great work of Count Alexandre de Laborde (1773-1842), Directeur des ponts et chaussées de la Seine, *Les Monuments de la France classés chronologiquement et considérés sous le rapport des faits historiques et de l'étude des arts* (2 vols., Paris 1818 and 1836). The title indicates clearly enough the scope of the book as an exercise in both cultural history and stylistic history, arranged systematically on a chronological basis: Roman, Romanesque, Gothic and Renaissance. It is well illustrated with line drawings, elevations and plans. An especially elaborate series, in which some of the numerous illustrations were the work of the young Viollet-le-Duc, was published by le Baron Taylor, C. Nodier and A. de Cailleux as *Voyages pittoresques et romantiques dans l'ancienne France* (20 vols., Paris 1826-64).

A significant historian of the next generation who carried Laborde's work a step further was Arcisse de Caumont (1801-73). His principal work was the *Cours d'antiquités monumentales* (12 vols., Paris 1830-41) which presented a scholarly interpretation of Gothic, combining the rational analysis of structure with the more subjective 'spiritual' interpretation associated with Chateaubriand. In 1823 he founded the Société des Antiquaires de Normandie with C.-A.-D. de Gerville and Auguste Le Prévost (1787-1859). Le Prévost had lived as a refugee in England from 1793-1801 and later translated into French a revolutionary book by a young English clergyman, George Downing Whittington (1781-1807), *An Historical Survey of the ecclesiastical Antiquities of France with a view to illustrating the rise and progress of Gothic architecture in Europe* (1809), in which the French origin of Gothic was established. In 1834 Caumont founded the Société Française pour la Conservation et Description des Monuments de France, later the Société Française d'Archéologie pour la Conservation et Description des Monuments Historiques. This was immensely important for uniting the work of regional scholars throughout France, since under its auspices annual conferences were held in different parts of the country with papers which were subsequently printed in the *Bulletin Monumentale*, founded by Caumont in 1834. Caumont's *Abécédaire, ou rudiment d'archéologie* including *Architecture civile et militaire* (Paris 1850), was an important landmark in the development of appreciation, and therefore preservation, of the secular as opposed to the religious architecture of the Middle Ages.

Just as this sober tradition of archaeological enquiry had already been fertilised by the romantic approach of Chateaubriand, so *Notre-Dame de Paris* (Paris 1831) by Victor Hugo (1802-85) inspired a new generation of which the most important members were Adolphe-Napoléon Didron (1806-67) and the Comte de Montalembert (1810-70). An especially potent aspect of Hugo's work from 1823 onwards was his attacks on the vandalising of ancient buildings that had been prevalent since the Revolution. This encouraged Montalembert to publish his open letter on the subject to Hugo in the *Revue des deux mondes* (Paris 1833). Six years later he published his collected articles under the title, *Du vandalisme et du catholicisme dans l'art; (fragmens)*, a slight book which owed something, especially in its pairs of contrasted illustrations, to Pugin's infinitely more powerful *Contrasts* of 1836. More serious, perhaps, was Didron who became editor of the *Bulletin Monumentale* and, in 1844, of the *Annales Archéologiques*.

Such was the background which made it possible for the great historian F.-P.-G. Guizot (1787-1874), on his appointment as prime minister by Louis-Philippe in 1830, to establish the Commission (later Service) des Monuments Historiques and to provide money for the restoration of historic buildings. Though Guizot was partly inspired by an understandable desire to emphasise the stability and continuity of France and its government after numerous political upheavals, his creation of the Commission established the framework which has ever since linked architectural history with preservation at both the governmental and private level. Instrumental in establishing the Commission were men like Hugo, who was one of its earliest members, and Didron, who became Secretary of the Comité des Monuments in 1835. The initial aim of the Commission was to provide an inventory of all buildings with historical associations, date or style which made them noteworthy to archaeologists, historians or artists. The Commission was to have the task of supervising the conservation of these buildings and of dividing them into classes which would indicate their priority for this purpose. Significantly, this latter task was soon abandoned when it became clear that the growth of historical studies would render virtually impossible any permanent consensus of this kind. What survived was the simple *classement* whereby certain monuments would be protected for all time. In 1833 Prosper Merimée was appointed Inspecteur Général des Monuments Historiques and it was he who introduced into the world of historical restoration one of the most influential of all figures in the history of architecture, Eugène-Emmanuel Viollet-le-Duc (1814-79).

In 1839, aged twenty-five, Viollet-le-Duc began work on the restoration of the celebrated Romanesque church of the Madeleine at Vézelay; in 1840 he joined Lassus on the restoration of the Sainte-Chapelle and four years later began the restoration of Notre Dame, also with Lassus. He became architect to the Commission des Monuments Historiques and, in 1853, one of the three Inspecteurs Générals of the Service des Edifices Diocésains. The knowledge he acquired during his extensive restoration work culminated in his most famous book, the *Dictionnaire raisonné de l'architecture française du XIe au XVIe siècle* (10 vols., Paris 1854-68). Though it is one of the most important monuments of architectural history in the nineteenth century, its presentation in the form of a dictionary is, perhaps deliberately, unengaging, and is presumably the consequence of Viollet's desire to present a materialist and 'scientific' interpretation of Gothic in which every feature of a Gothic building is seen as a functional device. Function for Viollet could embody a wide range of political and social aspirations and it is entertaining to watch him, as a man who became increasingly socialist and atheist in outlook, constructing a secularist and egalitarian picture of the Middle Ages in order to 'fit' his interpretation of Gothic.

The grand successor to Viollet-le-Duc's particular interpretation of architecture, which reached back at least to Frémin, was Auguste Choisy (1841-1909), the engineer of the Ponts et Chaussées. In his *L'Art de bâtir* (3 vols., Paris 1873-1904), *Histoire de l'architecture* (2 vols., Paris 1899), and edition of *Vitruvius* (Paris 1909), he interpreted architecture exclusively in terms of the history of construction, demonstrating what he believed to be its essence in a series of grimly clever diagrams. His work is the logical culmination of two centuries of French rationalism and we shall not see its like again.

The ecclesiological and archaeological approach associated with scholars like Arcisse de Caumont continued to bear fruit at the beginning of the twentieth century. A new scholarly impetus was brought to this tradition by Joseph Quicherat who held the chair of history of architecture at the Ecole de Chartes in Paris, which had been founded in 1847. He put a special emphasis on the training of young architectural historians in the use of documents, and from his school emerged great Gothic scholars like E.-A. Lefèvre-Pontalis (1834-1904) whose enormous bibliography included *L'architecture religieuse dans l'ancienne diocèse de*

Soissons au XIe et au XIIe siècle (2 vols., Paris 1894-6); Louis
Courajod (1841-1906), whose lectures on the history of art at the
Ecole du Louvre in Paris were published in 1899; Robert de
Lasteyrie (1849-1912), who maintained a nationalist interpretation of Gothic; and Camille Enlart (1862-1927), who
published an important paper on the 'Origine anglaise du style
flamboyant' in the *Bulletin Monumentale* in 1906.

In the meantime the spirit of poetry and romance associated
with Chateaubriand's and Hugo's interpretation of Gothic was
revived in the work of Joris Karl Huysmans (1848-1907). In his
novel, *La cathédrale* (Paris 1898), inspired by Chartres, he opposed the dry archaeological technique of Quicherat and his
followers, and in his *Trois églises et trois primitives* (Paris 1908) he
wrote in the same vein of flowery symbolism about Notre Dame.
His books made a profound impression on Henry Adams (1838-
1918), whose *Mont-Saint-Michel and Chartres* (Washington 1912)
was widely influential in North America. The great scholar
Emile Mâle (1862-1954) with his Christian, ecclesiological and
iconographical approach, so different from Viollet-le-Duc's, was
not primarily an architectural historian but an iconographer, as
can be seen in his *L'art religieux du XIIIe siècle en France* (Paris 1898),
L'art religieux de la fin du moyen âge en France (Paris 1908), and *L'art
religieux du XIIe siècle en France* (Paris 1910). Mâle is also important
as an art historian who changed his mind about a major topic.
His studies of mediaeval art were carried out in a Puginian
conviction that Catholicism had found its ideal, natural and
perfect expression in Gothic. Possibly as a result of reading
Werner Weisbach's *Der Barock als Kunst der Gegenreformation*
(Berlin 1921), he radically enlarged his cultural sympathies so as
to produce *L'art religieux après le Concile de Trente* (Paris 1932).

The scholar who first attempted to bring French architectural history out of its nineteenth-century archaeological phase
was Mâle's successor as professor of the history of art at the
Sorbonne, Henri Focillon (1884-1943). He inherited from Riegl
and Wölfflin a belief in the autonomous or biological development of artistic forms to which he gave attractive expression in
his *Vie des formes* (Paris 1934), translated as *The Life of Forms in
Art* by C. B. Hogan and G. Kubler (New York 1942 and 48).

The French enthusiasm for academies and for cataloguing
their national achievement produced an impressive series of

scholarly publications such as the editions by J. Guiffrey of *Les comptes des bâtiments du roi sous le règne de Louis XIV* (5 vols., Paris 1881-1901), by A. de Montaiglon and J. Guiffrey of the *Correspondance des directeurs de l'Académie de France à Rome* (18 vols., Paris 1887-1969), and by Henry Lemonnier of the *Procès-verbaux de l'académie royale d'architecture, 1671-1793* (10 vols., Paris 1911-29), as well as *Les vieux hôtels de Paris* (22 vols., Paris 1908-37) by F. Contet and others. Such studies were important for leading to the fresh appreciation of later eighteenth-century French architecture which flowered in the extensive publications of Louis Hautecoeur (1884-1973). Lemonnier had already published a pioneering article in 1910 on 'La mégalomanie dans l'architecture à la fin du XVIIIe siècle',[1] in which he identified megalomania as a constituent of the architecture of Boullée and Ledoux and also anticipated Giedion's thesis by claiming that 'l'espirit romantique est... une adaption particulière du classicisme'. In 1912 Hautecoeur, who had been a member of the Ecole Française à Rome, published two extremely original books: *Rome et la Renaissance de l'antiquité à la fin du XVIIIe siècle* (Paris), printed under the auspices of the Bibliothèque des Ecoles Françaises d'Athènes et de Rome, and *L'architecture classique à Saint-Pétersbourg à la fin du XVIIIe siècle* (Paris). In these important studies he laid the foundations for the rehabilitation of Neo-Classicism which we shall investigate in chapter VI.

3 Italy

Architectural writing in Italy in the later eighteenth and nineteenth centuries tended to be of local rather than European significance. The same is on the whole true of Italian architecture during this period. However, eighteenth-century Italy — like France, but unlike England and Germany — developed a rationalist tradition of Neo-Classical architectural theory. This is really the achievement of one man, the Carmelite priest

---

[1] *L'Architecture*, December 1910, reprinted in H. Lemonnier, *L'art moderne (1500-1800), essais et esquisses*, Paris 1912, pp.273-89. Perhaps the first reappraisal is the anonymous article, 'Les bizarreries de Ledoux, architecte', *Magasin pittoresque*, 1859, pp.27-9.

Carlo Lodoli (1690-1761), who believed that architecture should derive entirely from the nature of materials and the laws of statics. His implicitly anti-ornamental and anti-classical functionalist theories were recorded with varying degrees of approval by his two pupils, Count Algarotti (1712-64) in *Saggio sopra l'architettura* (1756),[1] and Andrea Memmo in *Elementi dell'architettura Lodoliana; ossia l'arte del fabbricare con solidita scientifica e con eleganze non capricciosa* (Rome 1786). Since they constitute a contribution to architectural theory rather than history, these writings are not our prime concern at the moment. However, the approach which they enshrined coloured early Italian architectural historians, especially Francesco Milizia (1725-98), whose principal writings on the history of architecture are contained in his *Le Vite de'più celebri architetti d'ogni nazione e d'ogni tempo precedute da un saggio sopra l'architettura* (Rome 1768) and his *Dizionario delle Belle Arti del Disegno* (Bassano 1797). The title of the *Vite* was subsequently changed to *Memorie degli Architetti antichi e moderni*. It was translated into English in 1826 by Elizabeth Cresy as *The Lives of Celebrated Architects, Ancient and Modern* (2 vols.).

Despite their functionalist bias, the theories presented by Milizia are confused, compromising and eclectic, so that they are closer to Algarotti's somewhat critical presentation of Lodoli's stern doctrine than to Lodoli himself. Especially striking is the illustration on the title-page to the *Vite* which can be seen as a preparation for that of Pugin's *Contrasts* (Salisbury 1836). Milizia depicts a crowded scene in which, on the left hand side, a Corinthian portico and Laugier's primitive hut, fashioned from trees and branches, represent Antiquity and Nature. Pallas, standing in the centre, points approvingly at these, her judgement being confirmed by a tablet beneath them which bears the injunction, *Hoc Amet*. Behind her to the right appear a small Gothic edifice and a much larger building with an undulating Baroque facade inspired by Borromini: these are condemned by the words, *Hoc Spernat*, inscribed on a tablet beneath them.

Despite Milizia's hostility to Gothic, there were those who

---

[1] Printed in his *Opere*, Livorno 1764, II, pp.51-92.

were prepared to investigate the style even in the mid-eighteenth century. Giovanni Lami (1697-1770) published an essay in 1757 on the painters and sculptors from 1000 to 1300, in which he defined the 'Byzantine manner' in painting and the 'Gothic style' in architecture.[1] More important was the Barnabite priest and mathematician, Paolo Frisi, whose *Saggio sopra l'architettura gotica* (Livorno 1766) was translated into German by Herder and published in his *Von deutscher Art und Kunst* (Hamburg 1773), the book which can be seen as the starting point of German Romanticism. Although Frisi was hostile to Gothic, he was interested in the problems of statics posed by Gothic vaults. The content and tone of his essay could thus be scarcely more different from those of Goethe's lyrical *von deutscher Baukunst*, which was also included in Herder's book.

More sympathetic to the mediaeval period was Leopoldo Cicognara who, following Winckelmann, published *Storia della Scultura dal suo risorgimento in Italia sino al secolo di Napoleone, per servire di continuazione alle opere di Winckelmann e d'Agincourt* (3 vols., Venice 1813-18), and *Le Fabbriche più conspicue di Venezia, misurate, illustrate ed intagliate dai membri della veneta reale Accademia delle belle arti* (2 vols., Venice 1815-20, and 1838-40).

The most important figures in the architectural historiography of nineteenth-century Italy are Pietro (Estense) Selvatico (1803-80) and his follower, Camillo Boito (1836-1914). Both were practising architects as well as historians. Their work must be seen against the background of the political unification of Italy in 1861 and the adoption of Rome as the capital nine years later, for the architecture that accompanied this new national self-consciousness was, not surprisingly, generally neo-Renaissance in character, interpreted in the light of Haussmann's redevelopment of Paris for Napoleon III. However, in Italy as in other European countries, the revival of the indigenous mediaeval architecture was also promoted as an expression of the national genius. Selvatico, who published *Sulla architettura e scultura in Venezia, dal Medio Evo sino ai nostri giorni* (Venice 1847), exercised an influence in some sense akin to that of Ruskin. However, as a restorer of mediaeval churches he was closer in spirit to Viollet-le-Duc than to Ruskin: in 1848-50 he

[1] See L. Venturi, *History of Art Criticism*, 1936 (rev. ed. New York 1964), p.36.

added a papery 'Gothick' facade on to S. Pietro at Trent, and in the 1860s was a prominent member of the jury that eventually selected Emilio de Fabris's designs for the west front of Milan Cathedral.

Camillo Boito briefly succeeded Selvatico as Professor at the Academy of Venice in 1855 and was Professor at the Brera at Milan from 1860-1908. A prolific author, architect and authority on restoration, his most influential book was probably *Architettura del Medio Evo in Italia, con una introduzione 'Sullo stile futuro dell' Architettura italiano'* (Milan 1880). In it he looked forward to the emergence of a kind of practical yet organic architecture rooted in the mediaeval past, yet in keeping with the supposed needs of the new age. This enabled him to be resurrected in the mid-twentieth century as a 'Pioneer of the Modern Movement', and indeed Liliana Grassi published a monograph on him in 1959 in the series *Architetti del movimento moderno*. His own architecture did not relate very closely to his theories, and ranged from an astringent style based on Viollet-le-Duc, to the rich North Italian Romanesque of his Palazzo delle Debite at Padua.

The work of art historians such as Cavalcaselle, Morelli and Croce was more important than that of the architectural historians. The emphasis which they placed on the individual work of art, rather than on abstract theories of the explanation of style, influenced Adolfo Venturi whose monumental *Storia dell'arte italiana* (11 vols., Milan 1901-40) contains a workmanlike history of Italian architecture up to the sixteenth century.

II
America

The position of art-historical studies in America has been from the start totally different from that in England. Whereas in England, France and Germany the rise of architectural history from the eighteenth century was especially associated with antiquarian study of the local Gothic past, frequently undertaken in a nationalist or religious spirit, no such development was, of course, possible in America. The development of American art history has been profoundly influenced by the close ties which existed between Germany and the whole American world of scholarship and art throughout most of the nineteenth and early twentieth centuries. There were also significant architectural links with France, so that many hundreds of Americans studied architecture in Paris either at the Ecole des Beaux-Arts itself or in associated ateliers, the first of these being Richard Morris Hunt (1827 or 28-1895) who was admitted to the Ecole in 1846 and did not return to America until 1855. This meant that the heady impact of Ruskin in America was tempered by a strongly rationalist antidote, a combination which is expressed very clearly in the work of two of the principal writers on architecture in nineteenth-century America, Henry van Brunt (1832-1903) and Montgomery Schuyler (1843-1914).

The writings of van Brunt, who was also a distinguished architect and a pupil of Richard Morris Hunt, have been collected by William Coles as *Architecture and Society: Selected Essays of Henry Van Brunt* (Cambridge, Mass. 1969). Van Brunt translated the first volume of Viollet-le-Duc's *Entretiens sur l'architecture* in 1875, but was also favourable to the turn to Beaux-Arts classicism in America which was already under way in the 1880s and was further stimulated by the World's Fair at

Chicago in 1893. A similar duality is noticeable in the writings of Montgomery Schuyler. He was especially associated with the world of architectural journalism which, having got off to an extremely slow start in America, was not properly established until the 1860s. A member of the editorial staff of the *New York Sketch-Book of Architecture*, which ran only from 1874-6, he was later closely involved with one of the most important of the architectural periodicals, the *Architectural Record*, founded in 1891, in which year he published *American Architecture – Studies*. His work has recently been collected in two volumes by W.H. Jordy and Ralph Coe as *American Architecture and Other Writings* (Cambridge, Mass. 1961). He was an influential admirer of the creative eclecticism of the architecture of H.H. Richardson (1838-86), whose rationalist Romanesque breathed the spirit of Vaudremer and Viollet-le-Duc. Schuyler's key concepts were 'organicism' and 'reality', which might be interpreted as reflecting respectively the influence of Ruskin and Viollet-le-Duc. He would probably have written a book on Richardson but for the publication of Mariana Griswold Van Rennselaer's admirable monograph, *Henry Hobson Richardson and his Works* (Boston and New York 1886). A remarkable young widow who was thirty-seven when her study of Richardson was published, Mrs Van Rensselaer was the author of numerous popular books on the history of art and architecture, including *English Cathedrals* (1892) and, on a straight historical subject, *History of the City of New York in the Seventeenth Century* (2 vols., New York 1909).

A central figure in the cultural and academic world at this time was Charles Eliot Norton (1827-1908), Professor of Fine Arts as Connected with Literature at Harvard, friend and disciple of Ruskin and Carlyle, and an influence on Bernard Berenson and Isabella Stewart Gardner. He lamented the visits to German universities of young Americans and the obsession with Teutonic scholarship, but nonetheless insisted as early as 1874 on a working knowledge of German from those attending his Fine Arts classes. The sons of prosperous German Jewish merchants and bankers studied at American universities, especially Harvard, in increasing numbers, and the great museums at New York, Boston and Philadelphia also looked increasingly to German scholars as curators for their collections.

The importation to North America of the forms and ideals of the later Gothic Revival and the Arts and Crafts movement is especially associated with the architect Ralph Adams Cram (1863-1942), who moved in the same cultured Bostonian world as Charles Eliot Norton. Cram worked in partnership with Goodhue and Ferguson in a Perpendicular style developed from Bodley and Sedding, and his principal buildings include St Thomas's church, New York City, the Military Academy, West Point (1908) and the Graduate College, Princeton (1909-13). An Anglo-Catholic with a Puginian vision of mediaeval society, Cram was also a prolific author of books on Gothic architecture and the spirit of craftsmanship.[1] As a young man in Boston in the 1880s Cram had been a friend of Berenson. It was also Cram who persuaded the historian Henry Adams (1838-1918) to publish his *Mont-Saint-Michel and Chartres* (Washington 1912), that powerful Huysmansesque study which had originally appeared in a privately printed edition of a hundred copies in 1905.

The period from roughly 1910-30 saw an exceptionally attractive flowering of the American art-historical tradition. The astonishing achievement of the methodical Lithuanian-born scholar, Bernard Berenson (1865-1959), is echoed in the work of Marquand, Clapp and Earl Baldwin Smith, and of mediaevalists like Kingsley Porter (1883-1933), Albert M. Friend (1894-1956), and especially Charles Rufus Morey (1877-1955) who founded the Princeton Index of Christian Art in 1917 and helped found the *Art Bulletin* in 1913. The Frick Art Reference Library was founded in 1920. All this activity took place against a background of the connoisseurship of wealthy collectors, many of whom were new to the art world and therefore sought expert guidance. Although architecture was not the primary interest of most of these scholars, a good deal of documentary research was undertaken in the history of medi-aeval architecture. The field was opened up by Charles H.

---

[1] For example *Church Building* (Boston 1901), *The Substance of Gothic* (Boston 1907), *The Gothic Quest* (New York 1907), *The Ministry of Art* (Boston and New York 1914), *Heart of Europe* (New York 1915), *The Catholic Church and Art* (New York 1930), *My Life in Architecture* (Boston 1936), and *Impressions of Japanese Architecture and the Allied Crafts* (New York 1905).

Moore (1840-1930), a friend of Charles Eliot Norton and follower of Ruskin, who published a number of books deeply indebted to the French analytical tradition represented in the work of Viollet-le-Duc: *The Development and Character of Gothic Architecture* (1890), *The Character of Renaissance Architecture* (New York 1905), and *The Mediaeval Church Architecture of England* (New York 1912). These were followed by Kingsley Porter's *Mediaeval Architecture* (2 vols., New York 1909) and *Lombard Architecture* (4 vols., New Haven 1915-17), Clarence Ward's *Mediaeval Church Vaulting* (Princeton 1915), H. C. Butler's *Early Churches in Syria* (1929), and the life-long studies by Kenneth Conant (born 1894) into Romanesque architecture, especially Cluny, which were eventually summarised in his *Carolingian and Romanesque Architecture, 800-1200* (1959). Kingsley Porter, incidentally, was a friend and admirer of Ralph Adams Cram, and wrote in 1926 of his completion of the Cathedral of St John the Divine, New York: 'Your design surpasses what the Gothic builders achieved'.[1]

Fiske Kimball (1882-1955), one of the most influential figures in twentieth-century American architectural history, began to apply detailed scholarship to the history of the American tradition in architecture in his *Thomas Jefferson, Architect, Original Designs in the Collection of Thomas Jefferson Coolidge, junior, with an Essay and Notes* (Boston 1916, new ed. New York 1968). He followed this with his *Domestic Architecture of the American Colonies and of the Early Republic* (New York 1922), and *American Architecture* (Indianapolis 1928). He became Director of the Philadelphia Museum in 1925 and gave practical expression to his interest in architectural history by his involvement in preservation and restoration at Williamsburg, Monticello and elsewhere. In 1943 came a new departure with his brilliant study, *The Creation of the Rococo* (Philadelphia). Conscious of the efforts of German scholars to define Rococo and to separate it from Baroque, he produced a careful and detailed Wölfflinian study in which he deliberately eschewed all attempts at relating the style to a 'spirit of the age'. The only drawbacks are his exclusive concentration on Rococo as a style of decoration in

[1] Quoted in D.S. Tucci, *Ralph Adams Cram, American Medievalist*, Boston Public Library 1975.

which its implications for planning and architecture, to say nothing of painting and sculpture, are overlooked.

The architect and architectural historian Talbot Hamlin (1889-1956), who was a lecturer in the theory of architecture at Columbia University, was influenced by Kimball's veneration of the American tradition. The son of A. D. F. Hamlin, who was the author of *A Text-Book of the History of Architecture* (New York 1896), he published *The American Spirit in Architecture* (New Haven 1926), and followed this with his impressive study, *Greek Revival Architecture in America* (New York 1944), which was dedicated 'to all those architects and planners who today are creating the forms that embody the American dream'. A rather different approach to American culture is provided in the voluminous and apocalyptic writings of Lewis Mumford (born 1895), which include *Sticks and Stones* (New York 1924), *The Brown Decades, a Study of the Architecture of America 1865-1895* (New York 1931), *Technics and Civilization* (New York 1934) and *The Culture of Cities* (New York 1938). Mumford, who became Professor of City Planning at the University of Pennsylvania in 1951, was originally inspired by the work of the Scottish theorist of urban planning, Patrick Geddes (1854-1932), but has developed a highly personal and romantic kind of 'biological' Marxism which he applies to the problems of urban architecture as part of his grandiose vision of forming a new world order through intensive community planning — a process which must end by involving the same kind of barbarisms as the technologically dominated and totalitarian states he condemns.

In the 1930s the principal development, as in England, was the arrival of Jewish refugee art historians from Germany and Austria. Far more, of course, settled in America than in England, especially in New York with its large Jewish population and its proliferation of universities, museums, libraries and research institutes. This pattern of migration was simply an extension of current practice: for example, one of the most distinguished of them, Erwin Panofsky (1892-1968), had been a visiting professor of Fine Arts at New York University since 1931 when, in 1934, he decided to settle permanently in the United States. An early product of his type of Warburgian art history was *Classical Mythology in Mediaeval Art*, published in the Metropolitan Museum Studies (1933), which he had written jointly with Fritz Saxl. The graduate Institute of Fine Arts, housed in the New York home of Paul Warburg, brother of the great Aby Warburg, became a centre of intense academic research 'as far removed from the affluent museum-orientated milieu of Harvard's art history department, ensconced in the Georgian splendors of the Fogg, as from the cloistered masculine fastness of Princeton'.[1] In 1935 Panofsky became a Professor at the Institute for Advanced Studies at Princeton, though he continued to teach at New York University. At Princeton he was joined in 1938 by Paul Frankl (1878-1962), who was trained as an architect but became an architectural historian and professor at Halle. We have already briefly investigated his first book of 1914, translated as *Principles of Architectural History, the Four Phases of Architectural Style, 1420-1900* (Cambridge, Mass. 1968). He now produced his monumental bibliographical study, *The Gothic: Literary Sources and Interpretations through Eight Centuries* (Princeton 1960), and his volume for the Pelican History of Art on *Gothic Architecture* (1962).

A prolific scholar with a wider range than Frankl's is his pupil, Richard Krautheimer (born 1897), who came to Louisville from Marburg in 1935, and has subsequently taught at Vassar College and the Institute of Fine Arts at New York University. One of his major achievements, established from hints in Frankl's work, lies in the field of architectural iconography. This art-historical discipline is concerned with the placing of buildings within their cultural context and with the elucidation of the meaning of various kinds of symbolism, especially religious. Krautheimer demonstrated this approach in two papers in 1942: 'Introduction to an "Iconography of Mediaeval Architecture"',[2] and 'The Carolingian Revival of Early Christian Architecture'.[3] His substantial contributions to scholarship have also included the *Corpus Basilicarum Christianarum Romae* (Vatican City and New York, 4 vols., 1937-1970), a

---

[1] C. Eisler, '*Kunstgeschichte* American Style: A Study in Migration', *The Intellectual Migration, Europe and America, 1930-1960*, D. Fleming and B. Bailyn, ed., Cambridge, Mass. 1969, p.573.

[2] *JWCI*, V, 1942, pp.1-33.

[3] *Art Bulletin*, XXIV, 1942, pp.1-38.

major monograph on *Lorenzo Ghiberti* (Princeton 1956) and the Pelican History of Art volume on *Early Christian and Byzantine Architecture* (1965). A similar approach to the meaning of architecture was explored by Karl Lehmann (1894-1960) who left Germany in 1933 and became Professor of Ancient Art and Archaeology at the Institute of Fine Arts of New York University two years later. From the enormous bibliography of this brilliant scholar there is only space to mention here two of his most characteristic articles: on the meaning of the Arch of Titus (1934)[1] and 'The Dome of Heaven' (1945).[2] Earl Baldwin Smith (1886-1956) also published major works of iconographical scholarship in his *The Dome: a Study in the History of Ideas* (Princeton 1950), and *Architectural Symbolism of Imperial Rome and the Middle Ages* (Princeton 1956).

With Albert Friend as its Director of Studies, the Dumbarton Oaks Research Center for Byzantine Studies in Washington attracted European scholars to America and became one of the most important centres of Byzantine scholarship in the world. Its contributions to architectural history eventually included Robert van Nice's *Santa Sophia in Istanbul: an Architectural Survey* (Washington, D.C. 1966 ff.), Paul A. Underwood's *The Kariye Djami* (New York, 4 vols., 1966 ff.), and Ernst Kitzinger's *The Mosaics of Monreale* (Palermo 1960). More recently, Oleg Grabar, born in France in 1924 and now Professor of Fine Arts at Harvard, has applied himself to an interpretation of Islamic art, publishing *The Formation of Islamic Art* (New Haven, Conn. 1973) and *The Alhambra* (1978).

Adolf Katzenellenbogen (1901-65), who left Germany in 1939, taught at Vassar and at Johns Hopkins and published his great work on *The Sculptural Programs of Chartres Cathedral: Christ, Mary, Ecclesia* (Baltimore 1959). Panofsky also published two books on mediaeval architecture after the war. His *Abbot Suger on the Abbey-Church of St-Denis and its Art Treasures* (Princton 1946) brought brilliantly to life one of the great art-historical documents to survive from the middle ages. In *Gothic Architecture and Scholasticism* (Latrobe 1951) he indulged in a daring if

---

[1] *Bulletino della Commissione Archeologica Communale di Roma*, LXII, 1934, pp.89-122.

[2] *Art Bulletin*, XXVII, 1945, pp.1-27.

idiosyncratic attempt at interpreting Gothic architecture in holistic terms as an expression of the thought-process of the Scholastics. Yet another mediaevalist, Otto von Simson (born 1913), arrived in America in 1939 and became first a Professor at Notre Dame University and then at the University of Chicago. Before resuming his academic career in Germany, he published *The Gothic Cathedral: The Origins of Gothic Architecture and the Medieval Concept of Order* (New York 1956), a distinguished study in the iconography of architecture. It is in this iconographical context that we should mention *Architectural Principles in the Age of Humanism* (1949) by Rudolf Wittkower (1901-71) which demonstrated the religious and symbolical, as opposed to the hedonistic, basis of Italian Renaissance architecture. Since Wittkower lived in England from 1933-56 his career will be more appropriately discussed in the chapter on 'The Establishment of Art History' in England.

Meyer Schapiro is a mediaeval scholar of outstanding quality who is especially well known for his subtle analyses of the forms and meaning of Romanesque sculpture. In the 1930s he was attracted to Marxist interpretations of art and society, though it would be wrong to describe his work as conventionally Marxist in tone or aim. Only a few native Americans have studied Gothic architecture in recent years. Robert Branner (1927-73), of the Department of Art History and Archaeology at Columbia University, made substantial contributions to knowledge of mediaeval architecture in France in the two volumes he published in Zwemmer's Studies in Architecture series: *Burgundian Gothic Architecture* (1960) and *St Louis and the Court Style in Gothic Architecture* (1965). John Fitchen, an architect, published *The Construction of Gothic Cathedrals, a Study of Medieval Vault Erection* (Oxford 1961), and L.R. Selby has produced an interesting edition of mediaeval architectural texts under the title, *Gothic Design Techniques, the Fifteenth-Century Design Booklets of Mathes Roriczen and Hanns Schmuttermayer* (Carbondale, Ill. 1977).

One of the most influential of American-born architectural historians is Henry-Russell Hitchcock (born 1903), who has spent his life in universities as an immensely industrious art historian. He has specialised in nineteenth and twentieth-century architecture, publishing monographs on Frank Lloyd Wright (1928 and 1942) and H. H. Richardson (1936), as well as

Early Victorian Archiiecture in Britain (2 vols., New Haven and London 1954) and the Pelican History of Art volume on *Architecture: 19th and 20th centuries* (1958). Everything he writes is thorough and workmanlike, though lacking in the kind of conceptual or intellectual interest which characterises the work of German-inspired art historians. He early identified himself with a campaign to import the International Modern Movement into North America as is clear from his *Modern Architecture: Romanticism and Reintegration* (New York 1929), and *The International Style: Architecture since 1922* (New York 1932), written with the architect Philip Johnson. He has played a leading role in the Society of Architectural Historians and its journal since its foundation in 1940.

The work of Hitchcock's contemporary, Donald Drew Egbert (born 1902), who has been an influential teacher of art history at Princeton since 1929, is characterised by its conceptual and sociological basis. His insistence on interpreting architecture through social history and the history of ideas can be appreciated in his paper on 'The Idea of Organic Expression and American Architecture' (1950),[1] in 'Religious Expression in American Architecture' (1961),[2] and, though he is not a Marxist, in his studies of *Socialism and American Art in the Light of European Utopianism, Marxism and Anarchism* (Princeton 1967), and *Social Radicalism and the Arts, Western Europe: a Cultural History from the French Revolution to 1968* (New York 1970).

Vincent Scully (born 1920) and Carroll Meeks (1907-66) have made major contributions often in similar areas to those worked by Hitchcock. Meeks produced *The Rail-Road Station, an Architectural History* (New Haven and London 1957) and *Italian Architecture 1750-1914* (New Haven, Conn. 1966). Like Hitchcock, Scully has chosen to identify himself closely with the current American architectural scene, beginning with *The Stick Style, Architectural Theory and Design from Richardson to the Origins of Wright* (New Haven and London 1955), and moving on to *Modern Architecture: the Architecture of Democracy* (New York 1961),

---

[1] Published in *Evolutionary Thought in America*, S. Person, ed., New Haven, Conn. 1950, p.356-96.

[2] Published in *Religious Perspectives in American Culture*, J.W. Smith and A.L. Jamison, ed., vol. II, Princeton 1961.

Frank Lloyd Wright (New York 1960), and *American Architecture and Urbanism* (1969). He has also emphatically associated himself with the architectural work of Robert Venturi to whose book, *Complexity and Contradiction in Architecture* (New York 1966) he wrote an adulatory preface. His *The Earth, the Temple, and the Gods, Greek Sacred Architecture* (New Haven and London 1962) was a valiant and poetically presented attempt to import into the closed world of classical archaeology the techniques pioneered by German art historians, in particular the study of symbolism and of iconography, as well as the feeling for space. He was also, of course, influenced by the brilliant book published posthumously by the South African architect, R. D. Martienssen (1905-42), *The Idea of Space in Greek Architecture, with Special Reference to the Doric Temple and its Setting* (Johannesburg 1956).

The study of Renaissance and Baroque architecture has been associated with an unruffled monumental scholarship, some of which may be due to the impact of Rudolf Wittkower who left England to settle in New York in 1956. John Coolidge, who was the author of the enterprising *Mill and Mansion: a Study of Architecture and Society in Lowell, Massachusetts* (New York 1942), published in 1943 a major article on 'The Villa Giulia: a Study of Central Italian Architecture in the Mid-Sixteenth Century'.[1] Howard Hibberd's principal achievement is his *Carlo Maderno* (1973). James Ackerman (born 1919) has published *The Cortile del Belvedere* (Bibliotheca Apostolica Vaticana 1954), *The Architecture of Michelangelo* (2 vols., 1961), *Palladio* (Harmondsworth 1966), and *Palladio's Villas* (New York 1967), which emphasised the importance of the contemporary economic, social and agricultural background. Frederick Hartt produced a major two-volumed study of *Giulio Romano* (New Haven, Conn. 1958), David Coffin *The Villa d'Este at Tivoli* (Princeton 1960), Richard Pommer *Eighteenth-Century Architecture in Piedmont: the Open Structures of Juvarra, Alfieri and Vittone* (New York 1967), and E. J. Johnson *S. Andrea in Mantua, the Building History* (Pennsylvania 1975). In 1968 Hitchcock published two useful studies of eighteenth-century German architecture, *German Rococo, the Zimmerman Brothers,* and *Rococo Architecture in Southern Germany.* Continuing interest in social and iconographical interpretations

¹ *Art Bulletin,* XXV, 1943, pp.177-25.

of Renaissance architecture has recently been expressed in several distinguished works.[1]

Spanish Renaissance and Baroque art has attracted the attention of Harold E. Wethey who published *Alonso Cano: Painter, Sculptor, Architect* (Princeton 1955), and Earl E. Rosenthal who published *The Cathedral of Granada: a Study in the Spanish Renaissance* (Princeton 1961). George Kubler (born 1912) has made an especially important contribution with his *Mexican Architecture of the Sixteenth Century* (2 vols., New Haven 1948), and his two Pelican History of Art volumes, *Art and Architecture in Spain and Portugal and their American Dominions 1500-1800* (1959), with M. Soria, and *The Art and Architecture of Ancient America* (1962). He has also produced a stimulating work of theory, a rare topic for an American art historian, in *The Shape of Time: Remarks on the History of Things* (New Haven 1962). His complex understanding of change in the visual arts seems to be influenced by Semper, by Focillon, who taught in America from 1939-43, and by modern developments in anthropology, biology and the history of science. In a beautiful and sensitive book, which is free from jargon, Kubler argues for the replacement of the conventional biographical, stylistic or iconographical approach to art history, by 'the idea of a linked succession of prime works with replications, all being distributed in time as recognizably early and late versions of the same kind of action'.[2]

The subject of Neo-Classicism has been much less studied in America than in England, though the Viennese scholar Emil Kaufmann (1891-1953), whom we have already met in chapter I, settled in America where he produced his influential paper, 'Three Revolutionary Architects: Boullée, Ledoux and Lequeu' (1952),[3] and his posthumously published *Architecture in*

---

[1] George Hersey, *The Aragonese Arch at Naples, 1443-1476* (New Haven and London 1973), and *Pythagorean Palaces, Magic and Architecture in the Italian Renaissance* (Ithaca, New York 1976), C. W. Westfall, *In this Most Perfect Paradise: Alberti, Nicholas V, and the Invention of Conscious Urban Planning in Rome, 1447-55* (Pennsylvania 1974), and E. Verheyen, *The Palazzo del Te in Mantua, Images of Love and Politics* (Baltimore and London 1977).

[2] *The Shape of Time*, p.130.

[3] *Trans. of the American Philosophical Soc.*, n.s., vol. 42, part 3, 1952, pp.431-564.

the Age of Reason, Baroque and Post-Baroque in England, Italy and France (Cambridge, Mass. 1955). A very different approach from Kaufmann's to architectural history and theory from the late eighteenth century has been admirably demonstrated by the English-born architect and architectural historian, Peter Collins, Professor of Architecture at McGill University, Montreal. His *Concrete, the Vision of a New Architecture* (1959) was a learned study of nineteenth-century French rationalism and of one of its expressions in the architecture of Auguste Perret (1874-1954). Collins's *Changing Ideals in Modern Architecture 1750-1950* (1956) was an interpretation of the history of architectural development from the Neo-Classical period onwards as part of the history of ideas. It is a book of great quality on a subject which has attracted much false and tendentious writing. One of the best recent interpretations of neo-classicism has been Robert Rosenblum's learned and thoughtful iconographical study, *Transformations in Late Eighteenth Century Art* (Princeton 1967). There is also Hermann G. Pundt's *Schinkel's Berlin, a Study in Environmental Planning* (Cambridge, Mass. 1972), and Dora Wiebenson's *Sources of Greek Revival Architecture* (1969), which is really a publishing-history of Stuart and Revett, and her *The Picturesque Garden in France* (Princeton 1978).

English Victorian and Edwardian architecture has been much less studied in America. Phoebe Stanton is the leading authority in any country on Pugin, but so far her knowledge remains largely unpublished save in her brief monograph on Pugin (1971) and her generous assistance to the work of other scholars. She is the author of an admirable work on *The Gothic Revival and American Church Architecture: an Episode in Taste, 1840-1856* (Baltimore 1968). Other volumes in the Johns Hopkins Studies in Nineteenth-Century Architecture, of which Professor Stanton is herself the General Editor, are George Hersey's somewhat bizarre *High Victorian Gothic, a Study in Associationism* (Baltimore 1972), and James D. Kornwolf's comprehensive *M. H. Baillie Scott and the Arts and Crafts Movement* (Baltimore 1972). Voysey has now found a suitable biographer in David Gebhard: *Charles F. A. Voysey, Architect* (Los Angeles 1975), and, more importantly, there is L. K. Eaton's study entitled *American Architecture Comes of Age, European Reaction to H. H. Richardson and Louis Sullivan* (Cambridge, Mass. 1972). *Camillo Sitte and the Birth*

of Modern City Planning (London and New York 1965) by
G. R. and C. C. Collins was an exceptionally well-documented
study of a Viennese critic of fundamental importance in his
field. A Canadian historian, Robert R. Taylor, has begun to
apply the techniques of iconographical scholarship to the architecture of Nazi Germany. His *The Word in Stone, the Role of
Architecture in the National Socialist Ideology* (Berkeley, Calif. 1974)
continued the pioneering work of Barbara Miller Lane in her
Architecture and Politics in Germany, 1918-1945 (Cambridge, Mass.
1968). Quite closely related is *The German Werkbund, the Politics of
Reform in the Applied Arts* (Princeton 1978) by Jean Campbell.

The field of research which has been most extensively
cultivated is American architecture itself. The work of Kimball
was continued by A. F. Downing and V. Scully in *The Architectural Heritage of Newport Rhode Island 1640-1915* (Cambridge,
Mass. 1952), and by the English émigré Marcus Whiffen (born
1916) in *The Public Buildings of Williamsburg* (Williamsburg
1958, reprinted 1968). Studies of this kind have been succeeded
by an astonishing proliferation of sensitively written and well-
illustrated local inventories and guides which are an impressive
reflection of the increasing interest and pride taken by ordinary
Americans in their architectural environment. These have been
accompanied by a spate of scholarly monographs which include
Harold Kirker on Charles Bulfinch (1969), Donald Hoffmann on
John Wellborn Root (1973), Robert Alexander on Maximilian
Godefroy (1974) and Thomas Hines on Burnham of Chicago
(1974), as well as Esther McCoy's *Five Californian Architects* (New
York 1960) and H. Allen Brooks's *The Prairie School, Frank Lloyd
Wright and his Mid-West Contemporaries.* (Toronto 1972). General
histories have included *American Buildings and their Architects* (4
vols., New York 1970 in progress) by William H. Jordy and
William H. Pierson, and *American Architecture since 1780, a Guide
to the Styles* (Cambridge, Mass. 1969) by Marcus Whiffen.

Books of this kind have generally relied on a conventional
stylistic approach. Urban and technological history have also
played an understandably important part. Carl W. Condit's
two volumes on *American Building Art* in the nineteenth and
twentieth centuries (New York 1960-1) and his *The Chicago
School of Architecture* (Chicago and London 1964) were especially

illuminating on the history of building technology. Equally striking has been the individual contribution of James Marston Fitch, from his *American Building: the Environmental Forces that Shape It* (1st ed. 1947 and 48, rev.ed. Boston 1972), to his *Architecture and the Aesthetics of Plenty* (New York 1961). An especially impressive achievement has been that of E. A. Gutkind, Research Professor at the Institute for Environmental Studies of the University of Pennsylvania until his death in 1968, who has produced an *International History of City Development* (8 vols., New York 1964-72).

Kubler's subtle questioning of the techniques of contemporary art history in *The Shape of Time* (1962) was followed by a cruder attack on conventional architectural history by J. Maass in the *Journal of the Society of Architectural Historians* in March 1969.[1] He calculated that of the 461 contributions, including book reviews, which had been published in the *Journal* from 1958-67, 359 had been written by members of the staff of colleges and universities and virtually none of them by architects, and that only 13 of the 257 articles dealt with vernacular architecture. He decided that modern architectural history exhibited the following eight faults: 'The Bourgeois Standard', 'Racial Bias' (i.e. almost entirely Western or European), 'The Beaten Path' (i.e. Europe of the Grand Tour), 'The Genteel Tradition' (i.e. avoiding industrial architecture), 'The Surface Treatment' (i.e. avoiding technical aspects of structure), 'The Isolated Building' (i.e. avoiding studies of the community and the setting), 'The Isolated Art' (i.e. avoiding discussion of painting, sculpture, drama, music, pageantry), and 'The Isolated Discipline'. He concluded that the architectural historian should be trained in the social sciences, economics, political history, literature and psychology. The tradition which Maass admires is represented by the popular illustrated surveys of world vernacular architecture compiled by Bernard Rudofsky: *Architecture without Architects, an Introduction to Non-Pedigreed Architecture* (New York 1965) and *Streets for People, a Primer for Americans* (New York 1969), and also, presumably, *Learning from Las Vegas, the forgotten Symbolism of Architectural Form* (Cam-

[1] XXVIII, 1969, pp.3-8.

idge, Mass. 1972, rev.ed. 1977) by R. Venturi, D. Scott Brown and S. Izenour, and Reyner Banham's *Los Angeles, The Architecture of Four Ecologies* (1971).

In America, as in England, the Modern Movement has now come to the end of its totalitarian phase in which it was regarded as exercising over-riding moral and social claims over us in every kind of situation as part of the establishment of a new order of society. In terms of architectural history this new mood has been expressed in a renewed interest in the principles and forms of classicism, sometimes promoted by those who had earlier been identified with the Modern Movement. The leading architect Philip Johnson (born 1906) has now abjured his Modernist past by designing a classically-inspired skyscraper with a 'Chippendale' top, and major studies of Sir Edwin Lutyens (1869-1944) by Allan Greenberg and Robert Irving are announced for publication in 1980. In 1967 a society called Classical America was formed with the aim of 'promoting the classical tradition in the arts of our nation'. The editor of the society's journal, *Classical America,* is William Coles who edited Henry van Brunt's architectural writings and also published with Henry Hope Reed *Architecture in America: a Battle of Styles* (New York 1961). Scholarship of outstanding quality has recently been applied to the neglected heritage of nineteenth-century French rationalism and classicism: in 1975 came Neil Levene's three-volumed dissertation for Yale University on 'Architectural Reasoning in the Age of Positivism: the Néo-Grec Idea of Henri Labrouste's Bibliothèque Sainte-Geneviève', which was followed in 1977 by *The Architecture of the Ecole des Beaux-Arts.* Based on the impressive exhibition devoted to the same subject which was held at the Museum of Modern Art in New York in 1975-6, this superbly produced book was edited by Arthur Drexler, Director of the Department of Architecture and Design at the Museum, and contains essays by Neil Levene, Richard Chafee and David yan Zanten. In America, as in England, architectural historians are ready to rewrite the history of modern architecture.

III
English Antiquarians
and the Gothic Revival

1 The Seventeenth and Eighteenth Centuries

We have already seen the first stirrings of architectural history in France in the seventeenth century in the circle of Benedictine historians of the congregation of St Maur. A similar pattern was established in England where between about 1660 and 1730 there took place an extraordinary flowering of mediaeval research and Anglo-Saxon studies. The clergymen, squires, lawyers and doctors of Stuart England became absorbed in a process of historical contemplation in which it is not always easy to separate the strands of religion and patriotism. The key work is the monumental history of the English monasteries and religious houses by Sir William Dugdale (1605-86) and Roger Dodsworth (1585-1654), the *Monasticon Anglicanum* (3 vols., 1655-73). The text was basically the publication of historical documents and charters, which was revolutionary enough for that date, but it contained nothing on the buildings themselves. What is important from our point of view is the presence of the plates, engraved by Daniel King and Wenceslaus Hollar, which make the book the first illustrated history of mediaeval architecture. Dugdale's *The History of St Paul's Cathedral in London from its Foundation until these Times* (1658) marked an advance on the *Monasticon Anglicanum* in that its superb plates by Hollar were accompanied by a serious architectural text. Though Dugdale surveys the world history of religious architecture in the text, it does not seem to occur to him to describe St Paul's itself in any significant detail.

The first attempt to establish the chronology of English mediaeval architecture was the *Chronologia Architectonica* written in the 1670s by the archaeologist and scientist John Aubrey (1626-1697). Aubrey illustrated this manuscript treatise with chronologically arranged drawings of features, especially window tracery, which could be fairly precisely dated by documentary or other means. In dating the buildings of Oxford, to which a good many of the fifty drawings were devoted, Aubrey relied on the *Antiquities of Oxford* (Oxford 1674) by the remarkable Oxford antiquary, Anthony Wood (1631-95). Wood had himself doubtless been inspired by books like Dugdale's *St Paul's* and *Antiquities of Warwickshire illustrated from Records*... (1656).

The growth of architectural history was, on the whole, related to a gradual rehabilitation of Gothic, but the diarist and traveller, John Evelyn (1629-1706), is something of an exception. In 1664 he published a translation of Fréart de Chambray's *Parallèle de l'architecture antique et de la moderne*. This, of course, is a treatise concerned with theory rather than with history, but to it Evelyn appended an essay of his own entitled *Account of Architects and Architecture,* which is simply a statement of the superior claims of the Renaissance over all other styles of architecture.

The tradition established by Dugdale was continued by the pleasingly eccentric antiquarian, Browne Willis (1682-1760), who published *A Survey of the Cathedrals of York, Durham, Carlisle, Chester, Man, Lichfield, Hereford, Worcester, Gloucester, and Bristol* (1727), following this with similar studies of other cathedrals during the next fifteen years. Though there is a ground plan and an exterior elevation for each of the cathedrals described, Willis's interests were in ecclesiastical rather than architectural history, and the text is scarcely more illuminating architecturally than that of the *Monasticon Anglicanum.* Willis is also important as a founder-member of the Society of Antiquaries in 1717. It was through this distinguished and influential group of scholars that what has been called 'the Renaissance sense of the past' became part of the intellectual equipment of the well-educated country gentleman and clergy of eighteenth-century England. It has been calculated, for example, that between 1710 and 1730 about twenty books on British and Roman-British antiquities were published. The aims of the Society can be clearly appreciated from the following statement in the Society's first minute-book, dated 1 January 1718:

whereas our own Country abounds with valuable Relicks of former Ages, especially of the Romans which are at present in the Custody of private Gentlemen, or lying in Obscurity, and more are daily discovered by chance or the diligence of such as tread in the commendable footsteps of those who revived the Spirit of this kind of learning among us in the last Century : to the end that the knowledg of them may become more Universal, be preserved and transmitted to Futurity: several Gentlemen have agreed to form themselves into such a Society here in London with a design at their own charge to collect and print and keep exact Registers under proper heads Titles of all Antient Monuments that come to their hands whether Ecclesiastic or Civil.[1]

This is written in the hand of the secretary to the Society, William Stukeley (1687-1765) who published *Itinerarium Curiosum... an Account of the Antiquities and Remarkable Curiosities in Nature or Art observed in Travels through Great Britain (1725)*. This book was important as one of the first to contain plans of mediaeval buildings, just as Francis Price in *The Cathedral Church of Salisbury* (1753) was perhaps the first to use sectional drawings. Stukeley also helped popularise the notion that Gothic is based on imitation of nature, for example an avenue of trees with touching branches. Certainly his enthusiasm for Gothic, including his recommendation that it be imitated in modern buildings, is remarkable for this date. We know that he put his advice into practice by erecting in his garden at Stamford a Gothic Temple of Flora, fitted out with mediaeval stained-glass windows.

In the meantime, the Society of Dilettanti, founded in 1733, was beginning to play a decisive role in the growth of archaeology. Though it has seemed to the present writer that the story of classical archaeology is on the whole a separate one from that being traced in this book, it is important not to forget that great chain of scholarly publications which links the first volume of Stuart and Revett's *Antiquities of Athens*, published in 1762, with C.R. Cockerell's *The Temples of Jupiter Panhellenius at Aegina, and of Apollo Epicurius at Bassae* of 1860.

A central figure in the Society of Antiquaries and in the foundation of art history in this country was the scholar and engraver, George Vertue (1684-1756). In 1758 Horace Walpole bought from his widow forty volumes of the manuscript notes on the history of English art and artists which he had been compiling since 1713. These formed the basis of the brilliant and

[1] Quoted from J. Evans, *A History of the Society of Antiquaries*, Oxford 1956, p.58.

racy *Anecdotes of Painting in England, with some . . . incidental notes on other arts, collected by the late Mr George Vertue, digested and published from his original MSS. by the Hon. Horace Walpole* (4 vols., 1762-80). On to Vertue's patient scholarly search for documented facts Walpole grafts an interpretation of historical development culminating in what he regarded as the perfections of mid-eighteenth-century taste. He thus believed that James Wyatt's Pantheon in Oxford Street, 'uniting grandeur and lightness, simplicity and ornament, seems to have marked the medium where Taste must stop'.[1] Architectural taste reached its lowest level in the work of Vanbrugh who 'seems to have hollowed quarries rather than to have built houses',[2] but gradually improved thanks to the efforts of Gibbs and Campbell until, in the reign of George II, 'Architecture resumed all her rights'[3] with the designs and the patronage of the Earl of Burlington and Henry Herbert, Earl of Pembroke. An especially attractive and novel feature of the fourth volume is Walpole's chapter 'On Modern Gardening'. He traces the history of garden design, reaching its climax in the modern landscape garden which he equates with Whiggish Liberty and Whiggish opulence: he thus argues, as only one could *before* the creation of Nash's Regent's Park, that 'A landscape and a crown-surveyor are incompatible'.[4]

As one would expect from the creator of Strawberry Hill, the chapter on mediaeval architecture is sympathetic in tone: 'One must have taste', Walpole claimed, 'to be sensible to the beauties of Grecian architecture; one only wants passions to feel Gothic. In St. Peter's one is convinced that it was built by great princes — In Westminster-abbey, one thinks not of the builder; the religion of the place makes the first impressions — and though stripped of its altars and shrines, it is nearer converting one to popery than all the regular pageantry of Roman domes'.[5]

The possibility that mediaeval antiquarianism might arouse deep sympathies for Catholicism was a very real one. Not only was George Vertue himself a devout Roman Catholic but William Cole (1714-82), who was one of the two scholars who gave greatest assistance to Walpole in the compilition of *Anecdotes of Painting*, had often been tempted by the thought of

[1] IV, p.xi.   [2] II, p.297.   [3] IV, p.207.   [4] IV, p.281.   [5] I, p.200.

conversion. Anthony Wood's religious convictions seem to have been the same as Cole's, while we know that the *Monasticon Anglicanum* was as much resented and feared by the Puritans and Protestants as it was welcomed by Catholics.

William Cole, who spent a large part of his life at or near Cambridge, left to the British Museum on his death a hundred manuscript volumes including his extensive notes for a 'History of the Parochial Antiquities of Cambridgeshire.' Some of his diaries have been published, including *A Journal of my Journey to Paris in the Year 1765* (ed. F.G. Stokes, 1931) in which his enthusiasm for Gothic architecture, especially Notre Dame, is evident. He had been at Eton with Horace Walpole, who remained a life-long friend, and with the poet Gray who supplied Walpole with information for his chapter on medi-aeval architecture in *Anecdotes of Painting*. The third in the distinguished triumvirate of Cambridge antiquarians at this time was James Essex (1722-84). It may not generally be realised that in the 1740s Cambridge assumed a dominant position in the study of mediaeval architecture which it sustained for over a century till it reached a climax in the varied but remarkable contributions of the Cambridge Camden Society, William Whewell, Robert Willis and G.G. Scott, junior. The son of a Cambridge carpenter and joiner, James Essex acquired an exceptional understanding of Gothic and skill as a Gothic designer, which commended him to the most distinguished antiquaries of the day from Walpole to Cole. Like Cole, unfortunately, he was more given to planning than to publishing books. In 1740 he proposed a book called 'The Antiquities of Cambridge', and in 1756 issued 'Proposals for publishing Plans, Elevations and Sections of King's College Chapel, in Fifteen Plates with Observations on the Original Contracts'. Though the book on King's Chapel was not published, Essex's measured drawings survive in the British Museum, and in 1769 the first guide book to the chapel was published by Henry Malden[1] in which a serious attempt is made

[1] *An Account of King's College-Chapel in Cambridge*, 1769 (reprinted 1973). Though the name of Malden, the Chapel Clerk, appears on the title-page, it was written by Thomas James with assistance from the Bursar, Edward Betham, who was an accomplished antiquary.

to identify the various building phases by close attention to the fabric and to surviving documents.

Essex was elected to the Society of Antiquaries in 1772 and published a number of articles on mediaeval buildings in *Archaeologia*, the Society's journal which had been founded in 1770. His principal unpublished work was his 'History of Architecture', which eventually became a History of Gothic Architecture in England. A large number of drafts and illustrations survive at the British Museum[1] but form a heterogeneous collection of scholarly information in no way ready for publication. His belief that the thirteenth century was the style of perfection was uncharacteristic of the taste for Gothic in his day which generally favoured the Perpendicular style; he also made a careful illustrated study of Gothic vaults, arches and tracery, and expressed displeasure at the ignorance shown by eighteenth-century imitators and restorers of mediaeval buildings. Essex himself carried out work in the Gothic style at King's College Chapel, Cambridge, and at Strawberry Hill, as well as undertaking extensive and on the whole sensitive restoration and rebuilding at Ely and Lincoln Cathedrals.

Another important member of the Cambridge group including Essex, Gray and Cole, was James Bentham (1708-94), who graduated from Trinity College in 1730, became a minor Canon of Ely in 1737, and published a noble book on *The History and Antiquities of the Conventual Church and Cathedral of Ely, from the Foundation of the Monastery, A.D. 673 to the year 1771* (Cambridge 1771). Other members of the Society of Antiquaries who published works of topographical interest were Francis Grose, Richard Gough and John Carter: for example, Grose's *Antiquities of England and Wales* (4 vols., 1773-87) and *The Ancient Architecture of England* (1795-1814), Gough's *Sepulchral Monuments of Great Britain* (1786-96), and Carter's *Views of Ancient Buildings in England* (6 vols., 1786-93). John Carter (1748-1817) was perhaps more important for his persistent attacks, published anonymously in the *Gentleman's Magazine* from 1798-1817, on the needless destruction and ignorant restoration of mediaeval buildings, in particular those by James Wyatt. A close associate of Carter was the remarkable and pugnacious Catholic bishop,

[1] Add. MSS. 6760-73, 6776.

Dr John Milner (1752-1826), Vicar Apostolic of the Western District of England, who, with Carter's help, built a Catholic chapel at Winchester in 1792 in a simplified Perpendicular style. In 1798 Milner published *The History, Civil and Ecclesiastical, and a Survey of the Antiquities of Winchester* (2 vols., Winchester 1798-1801), of which the most important section was reprinted as an essay 'On the Rise and Progress of the Pointed Arch' in a volume published in 1800 under the title, *Essays on Gothic Architecture by the Rev. T. Warton, Rev. J. Bentham, Captain Grose and the Rev. J. Milner*. Milner's reference to 'that beautiful style of architecture properly called the *pointed*, and abusively the *Gothic*, order',[1] shows how far the term 'Gothic' was from being accepted at the turn of the century, even though Warton had made a serious attempt at promoting and defining it as early as 1762 in the second edition of his *Observations on the Fairy Queen of Spenser*. Milner also demolished the view, which went back to Evelyn and Wren, that Gothic had Saracen or Moorish origins, although he could only offer in its place an accidental origin in the intersecting round arches of the Normans.

The last decade of the eighteenth century was especially rich in historical reflections on Gothic architecture which, like Milner's, exhibit a wide range of interpretations from romantic fantasy to sober factual analysis. This variety and uncertainty of tone and aim is perhaps not surprising when one considers the extent to which these students of Gothic were in advance of other European scholars. Thus, whereas a structural interpretation of Gothic is proposed by Michael Young in 'The Origin and Theory of Gothic Architecture' (1790),[2] and by James Anderson in 'Thoughts on the Origin, Excellencies and Defects of the Grecian and Gothic Styles of Architecture' (1800-1),[3] a far more romantic account was offered by James Cavanagh Murphy (1760-1814) and by Sir James Hall (1761-1832). Murphy's sumptuous publication on Portuguese Flamboyant Gothic, *Plans, Elevations, Sections, and Views of the Church of Batalha in the Province of Estremadura in Portugal* (1795), was at the time the

---

[1] pp.126-7.

[2] *Trans. of the Royal Hibernian Acad.*, III, 1790, p.55ff.

[3] *Recreations in Agriculture, Natural-History, Arts and Miscellaneous Literature*, II-IV, 1800-1.

finest set of engravings of Gothic buildings ever to appear in this country. It was prefaced by an 'Introductory Discourse on the Principles of the Gothic Architecture' in which Murphy drew some fanciful analogies between Egyptian pyramids and the spirit of Gothic design. In 1797 the distinguished geologist Sir James Hall delivered an 'Essay on the Origin and Principles of Gothic Architecture'[1] which he later published in book form, expanded and illustrated, as an *Essay on the Origin, History, and Principles of Gothic Architecture* (London and Edinburgh 1813). This is a colourful but belated attempt to prove that Gothic architecture had developed gradually from wicker huts! What is interesting is that it should have been precisely these two books by Murphy and Hall which attracted attention in Germany at the beginning of the Romantic Movement. Murphy's *Batalha* caused Herder to look sympathetically at Gothic in the last year of his life, 1803; it was also well known to the early architectural historians of Germany like Boisserée, Moller and Stieglitz, and was even translated into German in 1813 by J.D.E.W. Engelhard. Hall's theory of the organic origins of Gothic was discussed and rejected around the year 1820 by Friedrich Schlegel, Johann Gustav Büsching and Georg Moller.

2 1800-1840

Controversy in England at the turn of the century raged over two principal points, one concerning the nomenclature of the style, and the other the origin of the pointed arch. From the great flood of books and pamphlets one in particular should be singled out, *An Historical Survey of the Ecclesiastical Antiquities of France with a view to illustrate the rise and progress of Gothic Architecture in Europe* (1809, 2nd ed. 1811), by the Rev. G.D. Whittington (1781-1807), Fellower Commoner of St John's College, Cambridge. This gifted young Etonian travelled in France and Italy in 1802-3 with the 4th Earl of Aberdeen, better known as an enthusiast for Greek architecture, and on his return began to prepare, but never completed, his study of French Gothic architecture which was published posthumously in 1809 with a preface by Lord Aberdeen. Whittington's original aim, according to Aberdeen, had been to refute 'an hypothesis maintained

[1] *Trans. of the Royal Soc. of Edinburgh*, III, 1798.

by several writers and supported by the Society of Antiquaries, that the style usually called Gothic, really originated in this island, and ought therefore in future to receive the denomination of English architecture'.[1] To this ambition Whittington had added that of outlining the history of the development of Gothic in France, and of describing in detail a few of the major monuments as well as providing 'An Enquiry into the Origin of Gothic Architecture'.

Whittington's lucid, fresh and readable book is remarkable as the first history of French mediaeval architecture — unless we count Florent le Comte's *Cabinet des singularitéz d'architecture, peinture, sculpture et gravure* (3 vols., Paris 1699-1700) and also as the first statement that Gothic was invented in France in the first half of the twelfth century. In fact, little attention was paid to Whittington's convincing proofs of this claim, so that Didron, for example, could falsely argue that it was he who had first made it. Whittington's book is arresting, well-documented and enlivened by close attention to the surviving fabric. He writes boldly that 'the architecture of France underwent a total change in the course of the twelfth century... [so that] before the end the ancient heavy manner was everywhere discontinued, and the new airy unmixed Gothic universally adopted'.[2] His special *forte* is stylistic comparison, of an almost Wölfflinian kind, between French and English Gothic in order to establish the chronological precedence of the former. His detailed comparison of Amiens and Salisbury is especially memorable. Here he is on the west front of Reims:

The diminishing or pyramidal form is in itself more graceful, and it is certainly more congenial to the character of the Gothic style, than the square fronts of our cathedrals. It has the advantage which is possessed too by some of ours, of having no mixture or confusion of design; but here how nobly has the invention and taste of the architect displayed itself! He has surpassed every other front in richness, at the same time that he has excelled them in lightness; he has judiciously placed all his heavy magnificence below, and has gradually lightened and relieved his ornaments as they rise to the summit; the eye is delighted, without being confused; every thing partakes of the pyramidal and spiral form, and the architecture is preserved as delicate and light as possible, as a contrast and relief to the sculpture'.[3]

[1] pp. vi-vii.   [2] pp. 62-4.   [3] pp. 161-2.

An entertaining feature of the book is the account of Lenoir's Musée des Monumens Français. While welcoming Lenoir's general aim of rescuing characteristic monuments from the destruction which occurred during the Revolutionary period, Whittington, as a non-Romantic, could find 'no good reason or excuse... for [Lenoir's] baffling and confusing us by an incongruous mixture of styles in almost every century'.[1]

Whittington is important as perhaps the earliest example of a recognisably 'modern' architectural historian conducting a detached and scholarly investigation into a past style in a country other than his own. He has no special non-architectural axe to grind: he is not a topographer recording the history of his own county or church; he is not a Romantic seeking experiences of the Infinite; he is not a nationalist arguing that his own country must have given birth to the style of his choice; nor is he an ecclesiologist studying Gothic as the basis for a revival of mediaeval design or liturgy in the modern church. Indeed, his brief account of the adoption of Renaissance forms in sixteenth-century France, though written without enthusiasm, has a carefully impartial air.

Whittington was not entirely alone. The Rev. James Dallaway (1763-1834) published *Observations on English Architecture, Military, Ecclesiastical and Civil* (1806) which shares something of his detached tone and contains some account of the lives of mediaeval architects. Like Whittington, with whom he may possibly have been in touch, he recognises the importance of Suger's St Denis in the origins of Gothic. He also brought out a useful edition of Walpole's *Anecdotes of Painting* in 1826-8. Another Cambridge scholar who will certainly have been known to Whittington is Thomas Kerrich (1748-1828), Fellow of Magdalene College from 1771-5 and University Librarian from 1797-1828. He had preserved James Essex's manuscript 'History of Architecture' and had presented it to the British Museum together with 48 volumes of his own antiquarian notes and drawings. He drew on Essex's papers for a lecture which he delivered at the Society of Antiquaries in 1809, published as 'Some Observations on the Gothic Buildings abroad, particularly those of Italy, and on Gothic Architecture in general'.[2]

[1] p.207. [2] *Archaeologia*, XVI, 1809, pp.292-325.

Preoccupied with the problems of nomenclature and classification, he rejected the title 'Pointed architecture', arguing that this limited what should be seen as a total style to one of its constituents. His solution was simply to refer to it by centuries since they roughly corresponded with the principal phases of its stylistic development. This suggestion is often adopted today, although it is combined with the familiar nomenclature of Norman, Early English, Decorated (English) and Perpendicular, proposed by Thomas Rickman (1776-1841) in his celebrated *Attempt to Discriminate the Styles of English Architecture, from the Conquest to the Reformation; Preceded by a Sketch of the Grecian and Roman Orders, with Notices of Nearly Five Hundred Buildings* (1817).[1] Rickman had a sharp eye and was, for example, the first to distinguish authoritatively between Saxon and Norman architecture, a subject about which there had been almost unbelievable confusion throughout the seventeenth and eighteenth centuries. He was a practising architect and wanted his book to be of use to restorers of mediaeval buildings, to designers of new ones in mediaeval styles, and to the layman as a popular practical handbook. It fulfilled all these ambitions and became one of the most widely known architectural books of the nineteenth century, reaching its seventh edition in 1881.

Other architects who made minor but significant contributions were George Saunders and Samuel Ware who published specialised papers on the construction of Gothic vaults in *Archaeologia*. Rickman was quite content to design in the classical style on occasion, and Saunders and Ware virtually designed in nothing else. The researches of Saunders and Ware can thus be seen, like those of Whittington, as an exercise in detached scholarship. We have emphasised how far English scholars were in advance of those on the continent, and French antiquarians now became acutely conscious of the lead which the English had given in architectural history. Auguste Le Prévost, for example, translated Whittington, and Pevsner has assembled a pleasing group of tributes by Frenchmen which it is worth citing here: Caumont, who translated in 1823 Andrew Ducarel's *Anglo-Norman Antiquities* (1767), wrote, 'Je cite les antiquaires anglais

---

[1] First published in James Smith's *The Panorama of Science and Art*, 2 vols., Liverpool 1815, I, pp.125-81.

parce que je n'en connais pas d'autres qui se soient occupés de l'architecture du moyen-âge'; in 1824 Gerville wrote, 'Ni l'architecture romane, ni celle qu'on appelle communement gothique, n'ont attiré l'attention des antiquaires français... C'est en Angleterre que nous devons chercher des auteurs pour nous diriger dans l'étude de notre architecture ecclésiastique'; but perhaps the best tribute comes from Stendhal in 1838: 'Notre archéologie nous est venue de l'Angleterre, comme la diligence, les chemins de fer et les bâteaux à vapeur'.[1]

Amongst those whom these Frenchmen will have had in mind is the prolific entrepreneur, John Britton (1771-1857). His first work was the *Beauties of England and Wales* (10 vols., 1801-14), which was of topographical rather than architectural interest. This was followed by the far more serious *Architectural Antiquities of Great Britain* (5 vols., 1807-26), in which many of the major mediaeval and Tudor monuments of ecclesiastical and domestic architecture were provided with an elevational drawing, measurement, plan, cross-section and brief commentary. To answer those who felt that, though excellent in detail, the overall conception was unsystematic, Britton published in the fifth volume 'A Chronological History and Graphic Illustrations of Christian Architecture in England'. This represents an important attempt to synthesise the information contained in writings on the subject from the seventeenth century onwards. Indeed Britton draws up a useful list of sixty-six items to which he has referred, beginning with Wootton.

In the meantime he had launched another and even more important series of illustrated books, entitled the *Cathedral Antiquities of England* (14 vols., 1814-35). Here for the first time was a thorough and beautiful survey of the mediaeval cathedrals, with accurate measured plans, sections and elevations. The series is a triumph of scholarship and of book production. Britton quickly followed it with *Specimens of Gothic Architecture* (2 vols., 1820-5), produced in association with E.J. Willson and A.C. Pugin, and *Specimens of the Architectural Antiquities of Normandy* (plates 1825-7, text 1833), produced with A.C. and A.W.N. Pugin, and J. and H. Le Keux.

[1] N. Pevsner, *Some Architectural Writers of the Nineteenth Century*, Oxford 1972, p.22.

Britton dedicated the second volume (1809) of his *Architectural Antiquities of Great Britain* to the influential connoisseur, author and designer, Thomas Hope (1769-1831): 'no one', Britton claimed, 'can be better qualified to appreciate the subject than him who has carefully, and critically examined the ancient architecture of Greece, Italy, and Western Europe'. [1] In the 1820s Britton prepared for Hope a book on his Picturesque country-house, the Deepdene, as a parallel to his publication on Sir John Soane's Picturesque town-house in Lincoln's Inn Fields. It was not, however, until 1835 that the extensive knowledge of European architectural history with which Britton had credited Hope a quarter of a century earlier, was publicly exhibited in book form. In that year, four years after Hope's death, his eldest son, Henry Thomas Hope (1808-62), published *An Historical Essay on Architecture by the late Thomas Hope, illustrated from Drawings made by him in Italy and Germany* (2 vols., 1835). It is one of the most impressive and eccentric publications of its time. But what is its time? How far, indeed, does the book as published represent Thomas Hope's intention? It is surely extremely unlikely that the mature understanding of the structural and aesthetic basis of Gothic architecture, which comes over very clearly in the book, could have been acquired as early as 1809. There are few references in the text to the work of other scholars which might help us date the composition: Milner, Warburton, Milizia, D'Agincourt and, the most recently published, C.F. von Wiebeking's works of the 1820s and 30s. [2] In the introduction, Henry Hope quotes from a pamphlet written by his father in 1804 and claims that the present work was 'Written at a later period'. [3] Apologising for its defects due to lack of 'revision or reconstruction by the Author', he nonetheless justifies his decision to publish it in its present form because of his knowledge that 'the drawings were intended for publication, and the following pages destined, in a shape similar to the present one, to accompany them.' [4]

---

[1] II, p.iii.

[2] Hope seems to have owned Wiebeking's *Theoretisch-praktische bürgerliche-Baukunde* (4 vols., Munich 1821-6). See The Hope Heirlooms Sale Catalogue, Christie, Manson & Woods, Library, July 1917, Lot 561.

[3] p.ix.   [4] p.xi.

Without this confirmation from his son it might be difficult to accept that the curious balance of subject matter could have represented anything like Hope's own intention. This Neo-Classical pioneer of the Greek Revival and introducer of the French Empire Style to England produced a history of European architecture in which out of a total of 561 pages less than thirty are devoted to Greek architecture. In fact half the book and virtually all of the ninety-seven illustrations are devoted to Romanesque (which he calls Lombard) and Gothic (which he calls Pointed). It seems, then, that Hope must have been sensitive to the current intellectual climate where the problems surrounding the origins and nomenclature of Gothic were precisely those on which the study of architectural history, a subject then in its infancy, cut its teeth. Indeed Hope devotes chapters 34-39 to the question of who invented Gothic and comes down firmly in favour of Germany. Despite this, and many other quaint ideas and erroneous dating, he has, as we have already asserted, a real understanding of Gothic which makes large tracts of the book a pleasure to read. The weakest section is on the Renaissance (called the 'cinque-Cento'), a style of which he disapproves because he thinks that Revivals are impossible. 'The real antique style', he claims, 'when it first arose, sprung gradually, and connectedly, out of the climate and institutions for which its buildings were required. It resembled a plant'[1] and therefore could not be uprooted and planted in another soil and climate.

Hope's *Historical Essay on Architecture*, which was widely consulted by Freeman, Ruskin and others, is a work of major importance because of its impressively broad European scale — it even takes in Russian and Moorish architecture. The sheer number of buildings mentioned from the well-known to the obscure, is astonishing: indeed an additional index volume was published in 1836. The *Historical Essay* undoubtedly played a part in the *Rundbogenstil*, i.e. revival of round-arched architecture, which was such a feature of the 1830s and 40s, especially in Germany. The principal German architects who worked in varieties of this style were Lassaulx, Hübsch, Schinkel, Klenze, Persius and Gärtner, backed up by the historical researches of Moller, Boisserée, A.F. von Quast, Heideloff, and K.J. Bunsen

[1] p.529.

in his monumental *Die Basiliken des Christlichen Rom* (1823-43). The principal architects in England were John Shaw, James Wild and T.H. Wyatt, and the most important books were Kerrich's pamphlet of 1810 which contained illustrations of Italian Romanesque churches, E. Cresy and G. Ledwell Taylor's *Architecture of the Middle Ages in Italy* (1829), Whewell's *Architectural Notes on German Churches* (1830), Hope's *An Historical Essay on Architecture* (1835), and Gally Knight's *The Normans in Sicily: being a sequel to 'An Architectural Tour in Normandy'* (1838), and, of more importance, his *Ecclesiastical Architecture of Italy from the Time of Constantine to the fifteenth century* (2 vols., 1842-4). We thus see once again a close relationship between architectural history and architectural practice. The *Rundbogenstil* was seen as a compromise between antiquity and the middle ages which appealed to those who had become bored by the aridity of the later Greek Revival but were reluctant to go completely Gothic. Hope himself seems to have preferred Romanesque to Gothic, partly on the grounds that the element of fantasy in Gothic eventually destroyed its credibility as a style. How far he was committed to a Romanesque Revival is unclear, and his book ends with an appeal for unbridled eclecticism combined with modern techniques and materials so as to produce for the first time an architecture which we might justly call '*Our Own*'.[1]

If Hope's book helped to give an impetus to the comparatively minor Romanesque Revival in this country, the numerous publications of John Britton, which formed a great corpus of reliable representations of mediaeval buildings and details, undoubtedly exercised considerable influence on the development of the Gothic Revival. The accompanying, though sometimes separate, tradition of original and scholarly enquiry into Gothic architecture and structure — particularly associated with Cambridge since the days of Essex — came to a climax in the work of two brilliant Cambridge scholars, William Whewell (1794-1866) and Robert Willis (1800-78). Whewell, who was an expert in an astonishingly wide range of subjects from philosophy to mineralogy and was Master of Trinity College from 1841-66, published anonymously *Architectural Notes on German Churches, with Remarks on the Origin of Gothic Architecture* (Cambridge 1830). The subject was even less known in England then

[1] p.561.

than today, and this pioneering book clearly aroused interest for it had gone into three editions by 1842. At Trinity, Whewell was tutor to the brilliant young undergraduate, Kenelm Henry Digby (1796-1880), whom he accompanied on an architectural tour of Picardy and Normandy in 1823. Digby was a key figure in the romantic world of Catholicism, mediaevalism, heraldry and chivalry, of which Pugin was to be the crowning glory. In 1822 Digby produced the first of the three editions of his *The Broad Stone of Honour: or, Rules for the Gentlemen of England*; in 1825 he was received into the Roman Catholic Church; and from 1831-42 he published the eleven volumes of his *Mores Catholici: or, Ages of Faith*. This was one direction in which Whewell could conceivably have moved, as did Digby's friend, Ambrose Phillipps de Lisle (1809-78), who was received into the Catholic Church in 1824, came up to Trinity in the following year, and subsequently became a friend and patron of Pugin. However, Whewell's scientific cast of mind turned him in other, more materialistic directions, and it is significant that when he made a second architectural tour of Normandy and Picardy in 1831, he did so in the company of Thomas Rickman (1776-1841). In the preface to his *Architectural Notes on German Churches* he emphasised his debt as an architectural historian to Rickman's 'fixation of the language of the science . . . [by] a phraseology so exact that . . . the student should be able to draw the design from the description'.[1]

In the course of his penetrating analysis of the aesthetic and structural essence of Gothic, Whewell claimed that it was 'a connected and organic whole', governed by 'general laws',[2] and was characterised by a new sense of '*decorative construction*', which often involved 'The introduction of several planes of decoration'.[3] He concentrates on German Late Romanesque and Transitional architecture which he contrasts illuminatingly with the contemporary yet different Early English style of England. He directed his huge intelligence to an absolutely fundamental problem in architectural history which is the difference between what he called the 'theoretical history of architecture which is derived from the relations of style', and 'the actual history of buildings, which must rest upon docu-

---

[1] 3rd ed., p.xiv.   [2] p.3.   [3] pp.5-7.

ments and dates'.[1] He realised that the latter was 'a far more laborious and difficult process' than the former, but that the two must be combined in the best architectural history. To make up for his own deficiencies in the latter process he thus appended to the second and third editions of his book in 1835 and 1842 a series of notes on Rhineland churches by his friend, Johann Claudius von Lassaulx,[2] a Prussian student of mediaeval architecture and designer of *Rundbogenstil* buildings. In the first and possibly the only book published in England on German mediaeval architecture, it is not surprising to find Whewell paying generous tribute to the work of Moller and Boisserée as well as to that of Lassaulx. In 1833 we find Boisserée in turn praising Whewell's researches in his *Denkmäle der Baukunst vom 7ten bis zum 13ten Jahrhundert am Nieder-Rhein* (Munich 1833).

Robert Willis, who was probably the greatest architectural historian England has ever produced, was the same kind of dazzlingly gifted early-Victorian polymath as Whewell. Appointed Jacksonian Professor of Natural and Experimental Philosophy at Cambridge in 1837, he had published his first book two years earlier: *Remarks on the Architecture of the Middle Ages, especially of Italy* (Cambridge 1835). His scientific love of classification stood him in good stead in dealing with a new subject and his skills in engineering, coupled with his visual sensitivity, made him especially aware of the presence in Gothic architecture of both 'mechanical and decorative construction' existing side by side. Viollet-le-Duc's interpretation of Gothic did not always allow for this kind of subtlety. An admirable example of Willis's skill in this area is his paper 'On the Construction of Vaults in the Middle Ages' (1842)[3] which, in Pevsner's words, 'established a standard of insight and meticulous accuracy which has never since — in England or anywhere else — been surpassed'.[4]

In 1846 the Archaeological Institute of Great Britain and Ireland was founded, a society in which Willis played a con-

[1] pp.xii-xiii.

[2] It is very puzzling that Whewell should refer to him on the title-page as F. de Lassaulx.

[3] *RIBA Trans.*, I, part 2, 1842, pp.1-69. Reprinted 1910.

[4] Pevsner, *op. cit.*, p.54.

siderable part. He published some of his most important papers on English cathedrals in its journal, which was published from 1845 onwards: e.g. on Canterbury (1845), Winchester (1846), York (1848), Lichfield (1861) and Worcester (1863).[1] In the preface to his account of Winchester Cathedral Willis gives an admirable statement of his methods as an architectural historian, which were 'to bring together all the recorded evidence that belongs to the building; to examine the building itself for the purpose of investigating the mode of its construction, and the successive changes and additions that have been made to it; and, lastly, to compare the recorded evidence with the structural evidence as much as possible'. Willis's approach, or at any rate, this statement of it, lacks not only stylistic analysis but also an appreciation of architectural history as cultural history: this last is probably due to the attempt which both he and Whewell made, in a polemical age, to keep religion out of architecture.

In 1844 Willis published *The Architectural Nomenclature of the Middle Ages* (Cambridge and London) which was based on the terms he had found in English mediaeval documents and in French and Italian books. In some ways his greatest memorial is his posthumously published *Architectural History of the University of Cambridge* (4 vols., Cambridge 1886), which was completed by his nephew, John Willis Clark. Once more, one has to say of a work of Willis that it has simply never been superseded. With seemingly superhuman energy and dedication, Willis combed the extensive and uncatalogued archives of the Cambridge colleges from the thirteenth to the nineteenth centuries, 'and related what he found to the evidence of the surviving fabric, so as to produce a work of unparalleled scholarship.

Willis was a friend of C.R. Cockerell (1788-1863), the distinguished classical architect and archaeologist who produced at the end of his life a monumental study of *The Temples of Jupiter Panhellenius at Aegina, and of Apollo Epicurius at Bassae* (1860).[2] Despite his profound attachment to the classical tradition, Cockerell, just as Hope had done before him, nevertheless

---

[1] These have now been collected as *Architectural History of Some English Cathedrals*, 2 vols., Chicheley 1972-3.

[2] For a full discussion of Cockerell as an architectural historian, see my *The Life and Work of C.R. Cockerell, R.A.*, 1974.

allowed himself to be absorbed as an architectural historian into the dominating topic of the day: mediaeval architecture. Thus, though the primary aim of his lectures of 1841-56 as Professor of Architecture at the Royal Academy was to extol the classical language of architecture, they contained much perceptive analysis of Gothic. Moreover, he played with Willis an important role in the early years of the Archaeological Institute: for example, on the same morning in 1845 that Willis delivered his brilliant paper on Winchester Cathedral, Cockerell gave a lecture on the architectural patron, William of Wykeham, which was published in the same year, a model of architectural history; in July 1848, the Institute met at Lincoln where Cockerell read a paper on the sculpture of the Cathedral, F.C. Penrose on the system of proportions in the nave; in 1849 Cockerell spoke on the sculpture of Salisbury, and Willis on the architecture; and similarly in 1851 Cockerell spoke on the sculpture of Wells, and Willis on the architecture.

Cockerell was also central to the world in which architecture became established as a profession with its own professional scholarly journals. Indeed the rise of architectural journalism is one of the most important developments of these years. 1835 saw the founding of the Institute of British Architects and the publication of the first volume of its *Transactions;* Cockerell became its first professional President in 1860. J.C. Loudon founded the *Architectural Magazine* in 1834; the *Civil Engineer and Architect's Journal* was founded in 1837; and, ten years later, came the Architectural Association. *The Builder*, the most influential architectural periodical of the nineteenth century, appeared in 1843 and carried full reports of Cockerell's Royal Academy lectures in its earlier numbers. Cockerell was also significant for his devotion to Sir Christopher Wren. He wanted the architectural profession of his own day to reflect something of the grandeur, dignity and intellectual distinction that he found in Wren's career. In 1838 he prepared his remarkable water-colour, 'A Tribute to the Memory of Sir Christopher Wren', which depicted all of Wren's major works; ten years later John Clayton dedicated to Cockerell his great folio volume on *Wren's City Churches*. In considering the revived interest in Wren, we should not overlook the architect James Elmes (1782-1862), a prolific architectural and literary antiquary, who was the author in 1823 of the first documented life of Wren, *Memoirs of the Life and Works of Sir Christopher Wren, with a View of the Progress of Architecture in England, from the Reign of Charles I to the End of the Seventeenth Century.* Elmes's *Lectures on Architecture* (1821) are less impressive, presenting an interpretation of architecture in which the level of skill once attained by the ancient Greeks was not equalled until the advent of James Wyatt, who 'was richer and more learned in his art than either Jones, Wren, or Vanbrugh'.[1]

Another popular architectural historian was Joseph Gwilt (1784-1863) who, like Elmes, was also a minor architect. In the 1820s he had published a new edition of Chambers's *Treatise* and a translation of Vitruvius, and in 1837 he dedicated to Cockerell his *Elements of Architectural Criticism.* Rather curiously, this is an attack on contemporary German architects and critics, particularly Klenze, for what he regarded as their rigid preference for Graeco-Roman architecture as the exclusive model for present-day design. Gwilt favoured a more eclectic approach, though he seems to have had particular sympathy for the Italianate Revival. He later (1842) published an extremely successful *Encyclopaedia of Architecture.*

Another prolific historian, especially associated with the Italianate Revival, is the architect, W.H. Leeds (1786-1866). We have already come across him briefly as the translator in 1836 of Moller's great work, *Denkmäler der deutschen Baukunst* (1815-21), but his career had begun with the text which he wrote for John Britton's beautifully illustrated account of Sir John Soane's house and museum in Lincoln's Inn Fields, published in 1827 as *The Union of Architecture, Sculpture and Painting.* Perhaps his principal work was the portentously titled *Studies and Examples of the Modern School of English Architecture: The Travellers' Club House by Charles Barry, Architect. Accompanied by an Essay on the Present State of Architectural Study, and the Revival of the Italian Style* (1839). This handsomely illustrated book was not only unusual in itself as a monograph dedicated primarily to a single building, but was also influential as propaganda in favour of the Italianate Revival of Barry as against the Greek, Palladian and Elizabethan Revivals of the day. The book may also have helped give favourable publicity to the fact that Barry's

[1] 2nd ed., 1823, p.385.

designs for the club had been selected in 1828 as the result of a
limited competition. From now on, competitions, often disas-
trously conducted, became the normal method throughout the
nineteenth century of procuring designs for major buildings.

The Elizabethan and Jacobean Revival, especially in domestic architecture, was speeded on its way by a striking series of
illustrated books, mainly dating from the 1830s. The chief of
these are T.F. Hunt's *Exemplars of Tudor Architecture adapted to
Modern Habitations* (1830), T.H. Clarke's *The Domestic Architecture of the Reigns of Queen Elizabeth and James I* (1833), which is
probably the first book devoted exclusively to the subject,
J. Hakewill's *An Attempt to determine the exact Character of Elizabethan Architecture* (1835), C.J. Richardson's *Observations on the
Architecture of England during the Reigns of Queen Elizabeth and King
James I* (1837) and *Studies from Old English Mansions* (4 vols.,
1841), H. Shaw's *Details of Elizabethan Architecture* (1839), Joseph
Nash's celebrated *The Mansions of England in the Olden Time* (3
vols., 1839-49), and E.B. Lamb's *Studies of Ancient Domestic
Architecture* (1846). Nash's attractive lithographs were especially
influential in popularising the style, partly because they featured characters in 'period costume' who brought it entertain-
ingly to life.

3 Pugin to Comper

The 1830s were also, of course, the decade which saw the rise of
A.W.N. Pugin (1812-52), one of the most influential thinkers
about architecture in the nineteenth century. We have delayed
referring to him till now in the hope of emphasising the rich
world of architectural publishing and debate which he entered.
Although he acquired a brilliantly impressive knowledge of
mediaeval architecture, one of his principal aims in so doing was
to construct a theory of contemporary architecture and a
justification for his own design. Pugin the historian was ultimately subservient to Pugin the designer so that his role in the
present book is perhaps less important than might be supposed
at first glance. However, no one in Europe had ever made out so
complete a case for the identification of a desired style with a
desired way of life before the publication of Pugin's series of
polemical books: *Contrasts; or, A Parallel Between the Noble Edifices
of the Fourteenth and Fifteenth Centuries, and Similar Buildings of the*

Present Day; Shewing the Present Decay of Taste (Salisbury 1836), *The True Principles of Pointed or Christian Architecture* (1841), *The Present State of Ecclesiastical Architecture in England* (1843) and *An Apology for the Revival of Christian Architecture* (1843). Pugin saw the beauties of Gothic as coterminous with the truths of the Catholic Church, and in developing this theme in book after book exhibited in high degree the four fallacies that were later so ably defined by Geoffrey Scott: Romantic, Ethical, Mechanical and Biological. He died insane aged only forty, but his ideas lived on after him: in Germany, for example, we have already noted his influence on August Reichensperger, editor of the influential periodical, the *Kölner Domblatt* (1842-92); in France, Montalembert owed much to him, and in 1850 a French translation of *The True Principles of Pointed or Christian Architecture* was published at Bruges (noted in the *Ecclesiologist*, vol. XII, 1851, pp.355-6). It is fitting that he should have been taken so seriously in France and Germany, for his early ideas seem to have been coloured by Schlegel and Chateaubriand as well as by the whole corpus of French rational theory, but it was above all in England that his ideas found overwhelming support. They were enshrined in his lifetime in the Cambridge Camden Society which was founded in 1839 by two undergraduates at Trinity College, Cambridge, John Mason Neale (1818-66) and Benjamin Webb (1819-95). The aims of the Society were to exercise vigilance over the design and fittings of new churches, to preserve and restore existing mediaeval churches, and to introduce the spirit of Catholic worship into the Anglican liturgy. It was the most influential undergraduate society of all time, growing from thirty-eight members in the year of its foundation to seven hundred, including the Archbishop of Canterbury, by 1843. Its rigorous insistence on Gothic as the only Christian style transformed the face of the Church of England with the help of its spirited journal, *The Ecclesiologist* (29 vols., 1841-68), a title which, as Eastlake commented in 1872, 'was at that time a novelty, and to some an enigma'.[1] Countless enthusiasts for the cause lent themselves to a kind of espionage by filling in the Blank Forms for the Description of a Church which the Society issued with the intention of exposing

[1] C.L. Eastlake, *A History of the Gothic Revival*, 1872, p.196.

un-Gothic and un-Catholic deviations. The movement became a popular crusade, a kind of architectural Good Food Guide, in which the world of architectural scholarship of the preceding forty years was opened up to a new audience through the medium of books like *A Few Hints on the Practical Study of Ecclesiastical Antiquities*, published by the Society at Cambridge in 1839. Its intensely polemical character frightened off a few important supporters. Robert Willis resigned amidst some publicity as early as 1841, and C. R. Cockerell, who had been an early Honorary Member, subsequently attacked it in his Royal Academy lectures. In 1844 Montalembert, whose *Du vandalisme et du catholicisme dans l'art* (1839) we have already noted as evidence of Pugin's influence in France, was made an honorary member of the Society, but he rejected the honour and published a pamphlet[1] accusing the members of mortal sin for misusing the term 'Catholic'. Such was the controversy surrounding it that in 1846 it changed its name from the Cambridge Camden Society to the Ecclesiological Society and moved its headquarters from Cambridge to London.

In the meantime, Oxford, which was the centre from which the revival of Catholic doctrine in the Church of England radiated, saw the foundation in 1839 of a parallel society: the Oxford Society for Promoting the Study of Gothic Architecture, which soon changed its name to the Oxford Architectural and Historical Society. Its secretary from 1845 was the remarkably able young scholar, Edward Augustus Freeman (1823-82), who is perhaps best known for his monumental *History of the Norman Conquest* (6 vols., Oxford 1867-76). Architecture was the chief interest of his early years, so that in January 1848, aged only twenty-four, he had completed the manuscript of a book called *A History of Architecture*. The preface to this vigorous work reveals its author as a young man in a hurry with the bold ambitions and the strong prejudices of the young. Regarding architecture as an art, his principal intention was to promote the study of its history as a serious intellectual pursuit. He was convinced that 'Painting and sculpture . . . have never lost the character of arts, they have never been reduced to matters of antiquarian or

---

[1] *A letter addressed to a Rev. Member of the Camden Society* [i.e. Neale] *on the architectural, artistical, and archaeological movement of the Puseyites*, Liverpool 1844.

ecclesiological research. Now architecture has'.[1] He thus
claimed that 'The general design... of the present work is an
attempt at a philosophical history of the science of architecture;
it will be its aim to exhibit its artistic principles, and their
political and religious symbolism — the symbolism I mean of
styles and whole edifices, not that of mere details. Construction,
detail, archaeology, ecclesiology, will only occur as subordinate
and incidental; and technicalities will be avoided as much as
possible'.[2] He believed, however, that there were forces hinder-
ing the advancement of this new and profound science: these
were the archaeological, the ecclesiological and the mechanical
interpretations of architecture. He complained that 'It is not
archaeology in its right place, as something subordinate and
ancillary, but archaeology exclusive, assuming, claiming a rank
which does not belong to it, which is at this present moment the
bane not only of architecture but of a yet nobler study, of history
itself... documents, facts, customs, are continually discovered
and elucidated; but that to which these are but the means, the
enlivening of the dry bones, the connection of the scattered
fragments, is yet wanting'.[3] Of the ecclesiological approach, he
wrote: 'I am persuaded that the Ecclesiological movement,
deeply as I sympathize with its most important bearings, has
been in some respects prejudicial to the view of architecture for
which I am contending'. Because 'architecture is only an
incidental feature in their pursuits', the passionate enthusiasm
of the ecclesiologists for the Gothic style could lead them 'almost
to anathematize even the study of any other'; even within the
field of Gothic, their 'narrowness and prejudice' could lead
them to condemn the Perpendicular style which, to Freeman, is
'on the whole... the best'. He associates a mechanical interpretation with the researches of Whewell and Willis, and 'cannot
consider that line quite such a high one' as that he hopes to take
himself: 'Their writings treat as much of buildings as of architecture; their aim is to exhibit the mechanical rather than the
artistic view'.[4]

The authors to whom Freeman confesses himself most deeply
indebted are, perhaps surprisingly, Thomas Hope and John
Louis Petit (1801-68), from whom 'I have learned far more than

<hr>

[1] pp.xi-xii.   [2] p.11.   [3] p.xv.   [4] pp.xii-xv.

from all other architectural writers put together'.[1] Hope's *Historical Essay on Architecture* appealed to him because of its broad speculative tone, while Petit's *Remarks on Church Architecture* (2 vols., 1841) owed much to Hope, particularly in its enthusiasm for Romanesque. A recent assessment of Petit by Pevsner takes a very different line: 'As a scholar Petit does not count... Finally as a writer Petit cannot count either'.[2]

Nevertheless, Freeman's book is perceptive and intelligent: as a popular text-book it brought an incisive and informed understanding of mediaeval architecture to a wide audience. Especially valuable was his demonstration of the different aesthetic motivations behind the three styles of Romanesque, Early Gothic, and, finally, Decorated and Perpendicular. It was in his analysis of later Gothic architecture which, from its tracery and ornament, he called 'the late or *Continuous* style', that his originality chiefly lay. He regards the history of post-mediaeval architecture, which he dismisses in thirty pages at the end of the book, as an appalling mistake. And no example is more appalling than C.R. Cockerell's Ashmolean Museum and Taylorian Institution at Oxford of 1839-41. His criticism of this great classical masterpiece is worth quoting: he castigates the combination of

the eternal portico with the wildest fantasies that Italianism had previously devised; the said portico attached to a dead wall, with two loftier wings; those wings adorned with columns copied from a solitary example, the least graceful that Grecian art had produced, and these columns having no end but to support vases and images, which vases and images again have no end but to form a finish to the columns; and this composition diversified by windows of the most portentous ugliness that human perversity ever imagined... For the opposite to every principle which Pheidias and Ictinus, no less than Walkelyn and Wykeham, cherished and obeyed, we have only to look to those pursued by the authors and abettors of the Taylor Building, the very Mosynoecians of architecture.[3]

It seems scarcely possible that only twenty-four years later — so fast do fashions change — the architectural historian, James Fergusson (1808-86), could claim of the same building, that 'there is perhaps no building in England on which the refined

---

[1] p.xii.   [2] Pevsner, *op. cit.*, p.100.   [3] pp.450-1.

student of Architecture can dwell with so much pleasure.'[1] Even that austere vernacularist, Philip Webb (1831-1915), smiled on it towards the end of his life when he claimed that it 'expresses what I mean by imagination with graceful simplicity'. [2]

Despite Freeman's grand ambition to construct a general 'philosophical history of the science of architecture', his moralising condemnation of classical architecture reveals him as a true child of Pugin and of the ecclesiological movement in the ancient universities during the 1830s and 40s. Michelangelo and Wren fare no better than Cockerell, so that any qualities possessed by 'St. Peter's at Rome and St. Paul's in London... are lost in the shock sustained by our best ideal of a Christian temple, and in the moral condemnation which a high view of Christian art must of necessity pronounce upon their authors'. [3]

Freeman's other important architectural book was *An Essay on the Origin and Development of Window Tracery in England* (Oxford and London 1851), which was based on lectures he had delivered at the Oxford Architectural Society in 1846-8. In the meantime, the architect Edmund Sharpe (1809-77), a pupil of Rickman, had published *A Treatise on the Rise and Progress of Window Tracery in England* (1849). Freeman pointed out, however, that in contrast with his own approach, 'Mr Sharpe attempts hardly any classification of the minuter varieties of tracery; and his scheme involved but a very slight notice of the Flowing style, and none at all of the Flamboyant and Perpendicular'.[4] Freeman's claims for the superior merits of his own book are undoubtedly justified: with its four hundred clear, if diagrammatic, illustrations, it is a work of reference which has not been superseded to this day.

Perhaps the single most influential individual to feel the force of Pugin's ideas was John Ruskin (1819-1900). His principal contributions to architectural history are contained in *The Seven Lamps of Architecture* (1849), *The Stones of Venice* (2 vols., 1851-3) and the *Lectures on Architecture and Art* delivered at Edinburgh in 1853. *The Seven Lamps* is a work of theory rather than history and is profoundly coloured by Pugin's Ethical Fallacy; more impor-

[1] 2nd ed., II, 1873, p.349.
[2] Quoted from W.R. Lethaby, *Philip Webb and his Work*, 1935, p.138.
[3] p.29.   [4] p.vi.

tant for our purposes is *The Stones of Venice*, which is perhaps the most detailed as well as the most lyrical architectural account of a great city ever written. How can one begin to indicate the broad range, the rich detail and the paradoxes of this monumental work? Paradoxes or contradictions are such a characteristic of Ruskin's vast output that two recent studies of him as an architectural historian have proposed totally different interpretations: K.O. Garrigan, in *Ruskin on Architecture: his Thought and Influence* (Madison, 1973), takes the conventional modern view that Ruskin's understanding of architecture was limited by his concentration on ornament and two-dimensional effects; whereas John Unrau's *Looking at Architecture with Ruskin* (1978), produces much evidence, especially from unpublished manuscript material and drawings, to show that he was keenly sensitive to space, mass and structure. He was undoubtedly especially conscious of the complexities of visual experience and of the optical tricks played by factors such as light, shade, and the scale of ornament. He was also keenly aware of the importance of colour in architecture. Again, this is an area where he has much to teach the modern architectural historian who tends to shy away from this problem, partly because of the difficulties of conveying colour accurately in either words or photography. Perhaps what in the end makes Ruskin uniquely compelling as an architectural historian is his superb poetic command of the English language, his range of speculative enquiry, and the sensational force of his emotional convictions. His belief that architecture *matters*, as well as constituting a passionately beautiful language, has created an intellectual climate that has lasted to the present day.

Ruskin's enthusiasm for Italy was doubtless part of a pattern in which intellectuals in the cold Protestant north, from Winckelmann to Burckhardt and Pater, have sought warmth and colour by absorbing themselves in a southern culture — even if it meant, as in Winckelmann's case, becoming a Roman Catholic as well. However, Ruskin's concentration on *continental* architecture, for whatever reason, was bound to exercise a certain influence. Thus, whereas the beau idéal of Pugin and the Ecclesiological Society had been the English fourteenth century, we find that in the wake of Ruskin a number of architects published accounts of continental Gothic: G.E. Street's *Brick*

and Marble in the Middle Ages: Notes of a Tour in the North of Italy
(1855), R. Norman Shaw's *Architectural Sketches from the Continent*
(1858), W.E. Nesfield's *Specimens of Mediaeval Architecture in
France and Italy* (1862), and William Burges's *Architectural Drawings* (1870). These books need not detain us. Although Street
was an important figure in the Oxford Society for the Propaga-
tion of the Study of Gothic Architecture, his *Brick and Marble* is
not very impressive in tone, with its dates taken from Murray's
Handbook and its Jennifer's Diary language: 'We really enjoyed
Cremona very much indeed',[1] and 'Pavia appeared to me to be
a rather pleasant city, and we had a delightful day there'.[2]
Rather more serious is Street's *Some Account of Gothic Architecture
in Spain* (1865, 4th ed. 1914), a book whose value consisted — as
Street himself was the first to recognise — in being the only
account of its subject in English. The architectural riches of
Spain have, indeed, been persistently ignored by English historians: this is presumably a reflection of English hostility to Spain
from the time of Catherine of Aragon to that of General Franco.

Sir Gilbert Scott (1811-78) was another leading architect of
the Gothic Revival who, even more than Street, saw himself as a
professional historian. If this is so, it is because of his appointment as Professor of Architecture at the Royal Academy in 1868
in succession to Sydney Smirke. Of his eighteen *Lectures on the
Rise and Development of Mediaeval Architecture Delivered at the Royal
Academy* (2 vols., 1879), he had given the first seven in the later
1850s during C.R. Cockerell's tenure of the chair, when Cockerell was prevented from lecturing by illness. They are a workmanlike summary of contemporary knowledge, drawing
heavily on the researches of Willis and on his own painstaking
archaeological investigations carried out as part of his cathedral
restorations, but are intellectually somewhat flaccid. Though
he was conscious of having stormed the citadel of classicism —
he was the first Goth in the distinguished line of Professors at the
Royal Academy — he found on arrival that he had no special
message to deliver the young students. He did not even seem to
mind whether they chose to design in Gothic or classic: 'In these
days of miscellaneous distraction', he told them in his final
lecture, 'it is difficult to give advice as to the choice of a ground-

[1] p.201.   [2] p.209.

work of study. Having no actual style belonging to our age, you must choose between the two Renaissances, — the Classic and the Gothic, — as best you may... Nor is it for me to dictate, were it in my power to do so, what that choice should be'. Once the young architect has made his choice — on grounds which Scott does not begin to explain — all that matters is that he should 'study with diligence, and with the most assiduous attention, the best and purest examples of the style you have chosen'.[1] The notion that both classical and Gothic architecture have a 'best and purest' phase which will be immediately recognisable and universally acknowledged, shows how remote Scott's generation was from the kind of complex stylistic analysis which would shortly be undertaken by architectural historians in Germany. Indeed, Scott has an ambiguous attitude towards the value of architectural history. Noting that it is a new subject which 'has never been viewed as an object of study previous to our own day',[2] he argues that it would be wrong to 'suppose that a knowledge, however intimate or accurate, of architectural history, is of necessity a part of the study of architecture itself. On the contrary, at no period when a genuine, unborrowed style of architecture has prevailed, has *any* knowledge whatever existed of the history of art'.[3]

Another, and far more remarkable, book was published at the very peak of the Gothic Revival, Charles Eastlake's *A History of the Gothic Revival, an attempt to show how the taste for mediaeval architecture which lingered in England during the last two centuries has since been encouraged and developed* (1872). Eastlake's aim in this book, which has some claim to be considered as the first history of modern English architecture, was to describe one of 'the most remarkable revolutions in national art that this country has seen', in order 'to serve as a link between the past and future history of English Architecture'. He saw the result as a work of reference rather than of criticism, stating that 'it was my intention from the first to chronicle facts rather than offer criticisms'.[4] Sir Charles Eastlake (1836-1906) was trained as an architect but became a professional administrator: Secretary to the RIBA from 1866, and Keeper and Secretary to the National Gallery from 1878. Though a passionate supporter of the Gothic

[1] I, p.323.   [2] p.290.   [3] p.293.   [4] p.vi.

Revival, he doubtless saw himself as a broad central figure, and disapproved, for example, of much of the work of the eccentric 'rogue' architects of the Victorian era who are popular today, like Lamb, Bassett Keeling and even Burges. Thus, despite his intention to offer 'facts' not 'criticisms', he does indeed have a particular axe to grind — and one which is closely related to the production of contemporary architectural design, as is made clear in his reference to the 'future' history of architecture. He treats the whole history of the Gothic Revival from the seventeenth century onwards — the work of antiquarians, restorers and architects — as the progressive development of a single theme. His twenty chapters, from which the absence of individual titles serves somehow to emphasise this sense of common aim, move to their appointed climax in Bodley's church of St John, Tue Brook, Liverpool (1868-70), of which, with its wall-paintings by C.E. Kemp, he writes: 'In this truly admirable work the genuine grace of Mediaeval art seems at length to have been reached'.[1]

Only nine years later, George Gilbert Scott, junior (1839-97), a contemporary of Eastlake's, came to a very different conclusion, in *An Essay on the History of English Church Architecture prior to the Separation of England from the Roman Obedience* (1881). Whereas Eastlake's ideal had been the English fourteenth-century style, used as a model by Bodley at St John, Tue Brook, Scott committed himself to the following revolutionary statement: 'I regard the later phase of the perpendicular style as the most original and able thing that the English have achieved in art. It was really the discovery of a new and quite unlooked-for capability in pointed architecture... It is the glory of the English school of architecture that in England alone did the gothic style receive its final and complete development'.[2] In the world of the Ecclesiological Society, Perpendicular had generally been condemned because a late style was seen as inevitably debased, as compared with a style which was in its middle period. Is it a coincidence that the reaction against that view was led by a man who, himself a practising architect, was the son of the architect particularly associated with it? Scott junior's own principal buildings — the tower at Cattistock

[1] p.371.   [2] p.186.

church, Dorset, St Agnes, Kennington, and All Hallows, South-
wark — move decisively away from his father's Anglo-French
Gothic of the thirteenth or early fourteenth centuries, towards a
spare but refined Late Gothic style set off by rich furnishings.
Thus, we see once again a close and fructifying relationship
between architectural history and architectural practice. What
we can also perhaps see in Scott is the impact of his conversion to
the Catholic faith in 1880, the year before the publication of his
Essay on the History of English Church Architecture. It was after a
meeting with Cardinal Newman that Scott finally took the
plunge, and it is perhaps surprising that whereas the Catholic
revival in the Church of England led many Anglican clergy to
follow Newman's example in seceding to Rome, very few
church architects followed Pugin's example.

Scott junior was also a Fellow of Jesus College, Cambridge,
from 1871-2, and his book is infinitely more distinguished
intellectually than anything his father ever wrote. It also has a
European perspective which is closely related to his new-found
Catholicism. His clearly stated aim was 'to exhibit the architectural art of christendom as a part of the great fact of
christianity: to deal with the church architecture of our own
country as but a portion of a great whole, and to display the
essential solidarity of the history of christian art in England with
that of christian art in general, and of christianity itself' .[1] What
this meant in practice was that the first half of this very
substantial, if eccentrically arranged, book contained a good
deal of information on the relationship of early Christian
churches to ancient Roman basilicas, on the orientation of early
churches, and on the early Christian architecture of the Near
East. At every turn in this provocative and stimulating book
Scott forces us to consider how the churches were used and how
liturgy and popular piety were reflected in their design and
decoration. His passionate sense of belonging personally to a
universal Catholic tradition gives an illuminating urgency to his
writings: indeed, his conviction that Europe is the Faith and the
Faith is Europe makes him Bellocian before his time. Moreover,
we know from his unpublished notebooks[2] that his deep hatred
of the Liberal party made him wish to see great landlords

---

[1] p.i.   [2] Preserved in the RIBA Drawings Collection.

replaced by a system of peasant proprietorship — Chesterton's 'distributism' — and that he foresaw the day when Protestants would unite with Liberals in overthrowing Christian society. Of the impact of the Reformation, the first stage in that appalling process, he wrote: 'The divine idea, the electricity of the social order, having been lost, there is no longer any vertical "cleavage", in society. Brute nature asserts itself once again, and the old battle of classes recommences, as if christianity had not been'.[1]

It should not be thought that the whole book is written at that apocalyptic level. Scott shows himself a true disciple of Robert Willis in his brilliant analysis of the vicissitudes in design of King's College Chapel, Cambridge. No one before him had noted that this great church had not been planned for a fan vault but for a complex lierne vault. His keen eye perceived, and made the correct deductions from, the fact that the corbels of the vaulting shafts in the ante-chapel carry seven members (though a fan requires only five), whereas the corresponding corbels in the choir, which were constructed at a later date, carry five.

It should be pointed out that another distinguished late Victorian architect shared Scott's enthusiasm for the Perpendicular style. John Dando Sedding (1838-1901), the Arts and Crafts pioneer, delivered a lecture in 1880 to the St Paul's Ecclesiological Society on 'The Architecture of the Perpendicular Period', in which he hailed the Perpendicular as 'the harvest-time of all our mediaeval endeavour. For in English Gothic, as in Nature, there are three phases of development — first the blade, then the ear, and afterwards the full corn in the ear'.[2]

The ecclesiological movement had a late flowering in the work of the distinguished antiquarian and scholar, Sir William St John Hope (1854-1919). A devout High Churchman and son of an ecclesiologically minded clergyman, he went up to Peterhouse, Cambridge, in 1877 and came under the influence of the great librarian, Henry Bradshaw (1831-86), and of John Willis Clark (1833-1910), who was then completing *The Architectural History of the University of Cambridge* begun by his uncle, Robert

[1] p.iii.   [2] *Trans. of St. Paul's Ecclesiol. Soc., I, 1881-5, p.44.*

Willis. St John Hope was Assistant Secretary of the Society of Antiquaries for a quarter of a century, during which period he acquired considerable standing in the world of English mediaeval studies. The bibliography which was published in 1929 of his publications from 1872-1925 contains over 250 contributions to a wide variety of antiquarian subjects, but his greatest achievement was probably his sumptuously produced *Windsor Castle, an Architectural History* (2 vols., 1913), which almost overwhelms the reader with its elaborate display of documentary scholarship. Sir Lionel Cust later commented wryly, 'King Edward... wished to have a book containing the history of Windsor Castle, such as he could read himself and give away to his friends. This great volume was never at any time the kind of thing which King Edward had in mind... He wanted a book with all the gossip, legendary or historic, connected with the Castle'.[1]

In the late nineteenth century the ecclesiological movement enjoyed a considerable revival and a number of societies were founded with the aim of introducing mediaeval ritual and authentically designed mediaeval furnishings into Anglican churches. This renewed emphasis may have been in part a reaction to the increasing 'triumphalism' of the Roman Catholic church in England, particularly while Cardinal Vaughan was Archbishop of Westminster from 1892-1903, during which period Pope Leo XIII published his dramatic and definitive Bull, *Apostolicae Curae* (1896), declaring Anglican orders as sacramentally invalid. The Henry Bradshaw Society now published scholarly editions for an Anglican audience of mediaeval liturgical manuscripts, while St John Hope edited the first volume of the Alcuin Club Collections, *English Altars from Illuminated Manuscripts* (1899). J. T. Micklethwaite (1843-1906), a pupil of Sir Gilbert Scott and founder member of the Alcuin Society, published *The Ornaments of the Rubric* as the Alcuin Club Collections volume for 1901. The movement was popularised by the Rev. Percy Dearmer (1867-1936) who published *Fifty Pictures of Gothic Altars* for the Alcuin Club in 1910 and the phenomenally successful *Parson's Handbook* (1st ed. 1899). In 1897 the architect Ninian Comper (1864-1960), who kept alive

---

[1] L. Cust, *King Edward VII and his Court*, 1930, p.220.

the traditions of Pugin and Bodley in his own buildings until well into the twentieth century, published in the *Transactions of the St Paul's Ecclesiological Society* a paper on 'The Reasonableness of the Ornaments Rubric, illustrated by a Comparison of the German and English Altars'. In it he wrote:

let us clothe our churches and the ornaments thereof as they were in the Second Year of the reign of King *Edward* the Sixth, that is, in all the beauty of our pure English style. Not the first beginnings of it, however interesting we may feel them to be: for to ignore its latest development by imitating the styles of the thirteenth or fourteenth centuries is purely antiquarian and arbitrary. Nor its debasement by the foreign and pagan renaissance: for that is but broken English. But its full and latest utterance in the architecture which gathers round the fifteenth century... It is not least in ecclesiology, that:

"Nought shall make us rue
If England to itself do rest but true."[1]

Comper's attempt to discover what might be called 'an Anglican style for the Anglican church' should be borne in mind when, in the next chapter, we discuss those architectural historians who believed that there were permanent traits in the English character which were permanently reflected in architectural style.

4 Fergusson to Banister Fletcher

The first serious history in English of world architecture is James Fergusson's *A History of Architecture* (3 vols., 1865-7), a remodelling of his earlier *Illustrated Handbook of Architecture* (2 vols., 1855) and of his *History of the Modern Styles of Architecture* (1862). Both the text and the wood-cut illustrations represent a remarkable achievement in which Fergusson presented the results of the most up-to-date research in an astonishingly wide variety of periods and countries. It was also, as it remains to this day, highly readable. Not surprisingly, it proved instantly popular, a second edition appearing in 1873 and a third in 1891-3.

Born in Scotland in 1808, Fergusson spent his early years as an indigo-merchant in Calcutta where he studied the architecture of India, and also of China, and published two books on Indian architecture in 1854-8. Thus, when he eventually came

[1] IV, 1897, pp.65-97.

to study European architecture he brought to it an especially fresh and independent approach:

My faith in the exclusive pre-eminence of mediaeval art was first shaken when I became familiar with the splendid remains of the Mogul and Pathan emperors of Agra and Delhi, and saw how many beauties of even the pointed style had been missed in Europe and the middle ages... After so extended a survey, it was easy to perceive that beauty in architecture did not reside in pointed or in round arches, in bracket capitals or horizontal architraves, but in thoughtful appropriateness of design and intellectual elegance of detail. I became convinced that no form is in itself better than any other, and that in all instances those are best which are most appropriate to the purposes to which they are applied. [1]

Fergusson, of course, found it impossible to sustain this level of Olympian detachment, so that the book inevitably reflects many of the prejudices of the day, for example the belief that Perpendicular, as a late style, must represent a decline from earlier phases of Gothic: he thus writes of King's College Chapel, after complaining that it 'is too long for its width', that 'It is more sublime than the Saint [*sic*] Chapelle, though, from its late age, wanting the beauty of detail of that building'. [2]

Where Fergusson diverges decisively from the received opinion of his day is in his extraordinarily emphatic rejection of all post-mediaeval architecture as a sham: 'from the building of St Peter's at Rome to that of our own Parliament House, not one building has been produced that is admitted to be entirely satisfactory, or which permanently retains a hold on general admiration'. [3] The reason is clear: 'the fact simply being that no sham was ever permanently successful, either in morals or in art, and no falsehood ever remained long without being found out, or which, when detected, inevitably did not cease to please'. It is fascinating to discover Fergusson deploying the whole Puginian armoury of arguments from human, and ultimately religious, morality, to demolish the very position which Pugin had used them to establish. Fergusson's belief that 'no perfectly truthful architectural building has been erected in Europe since the

---

[1] *A History of Architecture*, I, 1865, pp.xii-xiii.

[2] *History of the Modern Styles of Architecture*, 1893 ed., II, p.397.

[3] *ibid.*, p.7.

Reformation',[1] derives from his unquestioning acceptance that architectural forms are so deeply and irretrievably rooted in particular ways of life that it is impossible to re-use them in a period later than that of their origin:

> It is literally impossible that we should reproduce either the circumstances or the feelings which gave rise to classical art, and made it a reality; and though Gothic art was a thing of our country and of our own race, it belongs to a state of society so totally different from anything that now exists, that any attempt at reproduction now must at best be a masquerade, and can never be a real or an earnest form of art.[2]

Since echoes of this view can still be heard today, it ought to be pointed out that anyone who believes that forms cannot lead new lives in new contexts must, with Fergusson, be prepared to condemn the Renaissance as a fake. The key word for Fergusson is 'real'. Refusing to recognise the fact that architecture is, by its very nature, artificial, he persuades himself that ancient and mediaeval architecture was 'natural' and 'truthful', evolving inevitably in accordance with the great laws of nature, almost without the intervention of the individual man:

> A further consequence of this truthfulness is, that we can reason with regard to buildings of the True Styles with the same certainty, and according to the same rules, which we apply when speaking of the works of Nature. Man's works, though immeasurably inferior in degree, are parts of the same great scheme; and when they are produced by the simple exercise of man's reason, they are as distinctly natural as any of the instinctive functions which can be performed either by man or by any of the lower animals.[3]

In further support of this view, Fergusson argues[4] that no one living in the time of the 'True Styles' ever allowed himself to be inspired by buildings produced in societies or countries other than his own; inevitably, too, mediaeval cathedrals have to be regarded as anonymous emanations of truthfulness, so that 'it would be of the least possible interest to us'[5] to know the names of their architects.

It is perhaps surprising that anyone with so crushingly

---

[1] *ibid.*, p.3.   [2] *A History of Architecture*, I, p.7.
[3] *History of the Modern Styles of Architecture*, I, p.3.
[4] *ibid.*, p.5.   [5] *ibid.*, p.29.

condemnatory a view of all European architecture from the end
of the Middle Ages onwards, should have chosen to write what
eventually became a two-volumed history of it. Fergusson's
book, in which Victorian buildings were roundly condemned
whilst they were being put up, is salutary reading for anyone
who still thinks that the Victorian age was one of complacency.
Indeed, to rescue the book from almost total negativity, the
edition of 1891 was extensively, if eccentrically, interlaced with
comments challenging Fergusson's assumptions, by Robert
Kerr (1823-1904), architect, author and former Professor of the
Arts of Construction at King's College, London. It should,
perhaps, be pointed out finally that so far as contemporary
architectural practice was concerned, Fergusson adopted the
same stance as Semper: that the Italian Renaissance style
should be used because it represented a seam which had not yet
been fully worked out.

Fergusson's great work was intended for an intelligent but
non-specialist audience. In the meantime, Wyatt Papworth
(1822-94) was busy editing an eight-volumed *Dictionary of Architecture* which appeared in instalments between 1853 and 92 and
was intended for a more professional audience. Papworth, who
was a son of the celebrated Regency architect, J. B. Papworth
(1775-1847), was a pupil of his father, worked for a time for Sir
John Rennie, and was Curator of Sir John Soane's Museum in
1893-4. The circular letter which he issued in 1848 proposing
the formation of a 'Society for the Promotion of Architectural
Information', resulted in the founding of the Architectural
Publication Society, under whose auspices the Dictionary was
published. Papworth was the principal contributor to a work
containing over 18,000 articles which, in the words of Colvin,
'laid the foundations of English architectural biography in a
series of scholarly and fully documented articles which have
formed the basis upon which all subsequent research has been
built'.[1]

It seems appropriate to consider after Fergusson the last of the
great nineteenth-century historians of architecture, Banister
Fletcher (1866-1953), who produced, in conjunction with his
father, the celebrated *History of Architecture on the Comparative*

[1] H.M. Colvin, *A Biographical Dictionary of English Architects*, 1954, p.viii.

Method for the Student, Craftsman, and Amateur (1896). The influence of Fergusson on the scale and approach of this book is immediately apparent. Indeed, Fergusson had outlined just such a book as long ago as 1865 when he wrote in the preface to his own *History of Architecture*, 'There is still another work, to the execution of which I have long looked forward, though whether I shall ever see it even attempted seems problematical. It is a New Parallel of Architecture. The only work of the sort which exists... is Durand's... To such a work the present History would form a fitting and appropriate introduction, and such indeed is its proper and intended function'. [1]

The first edition of Banister Fletcher in 1896 is a comparatively modest affair of some 300 pages and 115 plates, but it had already grown by the ninth edition of 1931 to 1000 pages and 4000 illustrations. The characteristic line illustrations, which have the depressing effect of making all buildings look more or less alike (exactly as Durand had already done), made their first appearance in the fourth edition of 1901. Banister Fletcher was an active Freemason and a keen member of the Northwood, Mid-Surrey and Moor Park golf clubs; as a practising architect his output, which may be said to have reached a climax with the Gillette Factory of 1937 on the Great West Road at Osterley, Middlesex, was extensive but commonplace, and one can perhaps begin to make the same kind of criticism of his *History of Architecture*. As Bruce Allsopp has said, 'his book reflects the decline of architectural historical thinking. Climatic, geographical, ethnic and historical causes are cited in tabloid form. There is no challenge to the mind, no weighing of evidence'. [2]

One of the minor curiosities of the book is the description of Indian, Chinese, Japanese, Central American and Saracenic architecture under the heading, 'The Non-Historical Styles', and everything else under the heading, 'The Historical Styles'. The basis for this distinction is ingenuously explained in the following way: 'in the East decorative schemes seem generally to have outweighed all other considerations, and in this would appear to lie the main essential differences between Historical and Non-Historical, Architecture'. [3]

[1] *A History of Architecture*, I, pp.viii-ix.
[2] B. Allsopp, *The Study of Architectural History*, 1970, p.67.
[3] B. Fletcher, *A History of Architecture*, 15th ed. 1950, p.888.

Probably it is in the end unfair to cavil at a book which generations of architectural students have evidently found so helpful. The author of the stately monograph published on him in 1934 wrote, in connection with his work as an educationist and lecturer, of 'his steadily maintained endeavour to secure the recognition of the study of the history of architecture as an essential part of a liberal education'.[1] And that may be the most appropriate note on which to leave the historian who laid the fruits of nineteenth-century architectural scholarship in conveniently potted form at the feet of the twentieth-century architectural student.

5 Lethaby

The architect W. R. Lethaby (1857-1931) was one of the most influential, distinguished and yet eccentric architectural historians of the later nineteenth century. As a key assistant of Norman Shaw from 1879-90, he was an important figure in the formation of the Art Workers' Guild in the circle of Shaw's pupils which included E.S. Prior (1852-1932), Mervyn Macartney (1853-1932), Ernest Newton (1856-1922), and Gerald Horsley (1862-1917). The loose body of opinion and design known as the Arts and Crafts Movement adopted a secular tone in reaction to the doctrinaire intensity of High Victorian Gothic. Although it had historical and literary roots in the writings of Ruskin and Morris, its architectural roots lay in the Domestic Revival of architects like George Devey (1820-86), Norman Shaw (1831-1912) and Philip Webb (1831-1915), which had flourished in various forms, such as the 'Old English' style and the 'Queen Anne' movement. This special emphasis on domestic architecture encouraged sympathetic investigation of the English vernacular tradition in building, which was reflected in a spate of architectural publications well into the twentieth century. What is especially interesting from our point of view is that the reaction by Arts and Crafts architects against what they saw as the tyranny of 'style' and of superficial appearances in favour of the fundamentals of the craft of building, carried with it valuable implications for the architectural historian. Fergusson, as we have seen, reacted against 'styles' and 'shams', but his

---

[1] W. Hanneford-Smith, *The Architectural Works of Sir Banister Fletcher*, 1934, p.viii.

interpretation of architecture did not often penetrate much below the surface. However Lethaby's thoughts on this matter bore fruit in his *Architecture, Mysticism and Myth*, which was published in 1891, though the title-page is dated 1892. This somewhat bizarre little book was based on the view that 'Behind all the minor categories of the "styles" there is a general unity in ancient architecture of the magic type'. He claimed that 'It seems clear at first sight that such a practical art as building developed in the main in response to bodily need, but even this may be doubted. Without the stimulus provided by theories of magic man might have been content with the bare satisfaction of very simple needs; the impetus of magic wonder and the desire to control nature were required to urge him forward to great tasks'.[1] He thus aimed at writing 'a history of architecture in antiquity as thought or idea',[2] on the assumption that 'the development of building practice and ideas of the world structure acted and reacted on one another', and that 'thought of magical properties generally had a very wide and deep influence on the development of ancient building customs'.[3] The thesis may, of course, have been true enough, but, as Lethaby was the first to recognise, the task of presenting a full and coherent picture of the cosmology, religion and magic of the great ancient cultures of the world, called for a man of greater leisure and scholarly attainments than those enjoyed by a thirty-four-year-old practising architect. Lethaby later noted, when the book was out of print, that he was 'pleased that it should be unobtainable', but he nonetheless rewrote it as a series of articles for *The Builder* in 1928 as 'Architecture, Nature and Magic', under which title it was also published in book form in 1956. He had in the meantime been encouraged by reading the discussion on 'arts as human psychology' in the English edition (1927) of Worringer's *Formprobleme der Gotik*.

Though offered as architectural history, Lethaby's book had positive practical hints for the designer. Echoing César Daly's *Des Hautes-Etudes d'architecture* (Paris 1888), he claimed that 'if we would have architecture excite an interest, real and general, we must have a symbolism, immediately comprehensible by the

---

[1] *Architecture, Nature and Magic*, 1956, p.147.
[2] p.40. [3] pp.15-16.

great majority of spectators. But this message cannot be that of the past — terror, mystery, splendour. Planets may not circle nor thunder roll in the temple of the future . . . What, then, will this art of the future be? The message will still be of nature and man, of order and beauty, but all will be sweetness, simplicity, freedom, confidence, and light'.[1] It is thus not surprising that the book was widely read in the 1890s by those interested in mysterious, organic and symbolic design, like Henry Wilson (1864-1934), Harrison Townsend (1851-1928), and Charles Rennie Mackintosh (1868-1928), who quoted from it at length in a lecture of 1893 at the Glasgow Institute of Architecture. Lethaby put his own ideas into practice in 1901 in his idiosyncratic church at Brockhampton, Herefordshire, where stone arches support a concrete vault covered with thatch, so as to create what has been described recently as 'an extraordinary atmosphere of almost primeval sacredness . . . more reminiscent of Glastonbury or Avebury's prehistoric earthworks than a purely Christian place of worship'.[2]

In the meantime, Lethaby's exploration of unfamiliar territories in search of an alliance between symbolism and the building crafts, had led him to study Byzantine architecture. His interest in this subject can be seen as a natural development from Ruskin's *Stones of Venice* which had been dominated by the great Byzantine church of St Mark's. William Morris lectured on Byzantine art in 1879, stressing its importance in the development of mediaeval art. Philip Webb also shared something of this enthusiasm and there are occasional Byzantine mannerisms in his own designs. Lethaby recommended the architect R.W. Schultz to visit Greece in 1887-91 with Sidney Barnsley, which led to their monograph on *The Monastery of St Luke of Stiris in Phocis* (1901) and to Schultz's essay on Byzantine architecture in the *Architectural Review* in 1897.

Lethaby himself now produced a beautifully printed work of scholarship, *The Church of Sancta Sophia, Constantinople, a Study of Byzantine Building* (London and New York 1894). This book was an attractive combination of an English Arts and Crafts approach with a French rationalist tradition which is derived

[1] *Architecture, Mysticism and Myth*, 1892, pp.7-8.
[2] A. Service, *Edwardian Architecture*, 1977, p.118.

from Choisy, whose *L'Art de bâtir chez les Byzantins* is several times cited by Lethaby in his discussion of the construction of vaults and domes. By a happy coincidence, John Francis Bentley (1839-1902) was appointed architect of Westminster Cathedral in the year of publication of Lethaby's book on Santa Sophia. It had already been agreed that the cathedral should be in a non-Gothic style, and in November 1894 Bentley left for Italy to seek inspiration in a four-month tour of Early Christian and Romanesque churches. His ambition of travelling from Venice to Constantinople in February 1895 was thwarted by an outbreak of cholera in Constantinople, but he had Lethaby's book with him and so studied this instead. Thus once again we see the close and fertile link in the nineteenth century between architectural history and practice. In the preface to his book, which begins with the arresting phrase, 'Sancta Sophia is the most interesting building on the world's surface', Lethaby goes out of his way to refer to the problems of contemporary architecture: 'A conviction of the necessity for finding the root of architecture once again in sound common-sense building and pleasurable craftsmanship remains as the final result of our study of S.Sophia... the style cannot be copied by our attempting to imitate Byzantine builders; only by being ourselves and free, can our work be reasonable, and if reasonable, like theirs universal'.[1] Bentley's superb Italo-Byzantine cathedral came to represent for Lethaby and his circle a model of a reasonable modern architecture; Lethaby wrote an article in its praise in *The Architectural Review* in January 1902 and contributed a preface to the biography of Bentley published by his daughter in 1919.

Lethaby continued to think deeply about the relationship between eastern and western art, and in 1904 produced his truly remarkable *Mediaeval Art, from the Peace of the Church to the Eve of the Renaissance, 312-1350*. The book is primarily concerned with architecture and with a discussion of the influences on the formation of Romanesque and Gothic. Professor Talbot Rice, on whom Lethaby had exercised a perhaps undue influence, later explained how, 'In this he attributed a primary role to the East — to the Byzantine world, and beyond it, to Asia Minor

[1] p.vi.

and Armenia. Indeed, he looked upon Romanesque and Gothic as the final expression of a vital trend which was conceived in the Near East in the early days of Christianity'.[1] Lethaby's approach was revolutionary and prophetic, though it brilliantly developed ideas pioneered in the principal books of Josef Strzygowski (1862-1941), the Czech scholar working in Vienna, *Orient oder Rom* (Leipzig 1901) and *Kleinasien, ein Neuland der Kunstgeschichte* (Leipzig 1903). His book is rich, stimulating, and written from the heart about the things he loved best.

What Lethaby was interested in writing came close to what Germans would call *Kulturgeschichte*. He claimed in *Mediaeval Art* that 'Art is man's thoughts expressed in his handwork, the course of art has left a great series of documents for the history of civilisation', and quotes an example of what he means by this: 'Westminster Abbey is a great piece of the middle of the thirteenth century still projecting above the later strata of English life and effort'.[2] Lethaby was Surveyor of Westminster Abbey from 1906-28, and in 1906 published what is probably his major contribution to mediaeval architectural scholarship, *Westminster Abbey and the King's Craftsmen: a Study of Mediaeval Building*. It was his considerable achievement as an archival researcher tq organise and bring to life the contemporary records of the masons and artists who worked on the building: a task for which his own close links with the Arts and Crafts movement gave him a special imaginative sympathy. He added to this a patient illuminating analysis of the building's progress through time as revealed in the constant adaptations and restorations it had undergone: this in itself meant ordering and synthesising the work of scholars, antiquarians, architects and topographers from the sixteenth century right up to Lethaby's own day. His romantic historical imagination, architectural scholarship and sense of identification with what he felt to be the realities of mediaeval life, produced what has been described as 'the outstanding study of any one of our mediaeval buildings'.[3]

Unfortunately, perhaps, Lethaby did not stop here. He had

---

[1] W.R. Lethaby, *Mediaeval Art*, rev. ed. 1940, p.xiii.

[2] ibid., p.1.

[3] B. Ferriday, 'W.R. Lethaby', *Concerning Architecture*, J. Summerson, ed., 1968, p.162.

another quarter of a century to live which he filled with lecturing and writing about the history and practice of architecture. His *Philip Webb and his Work* (1935)[1] is an absorbing and sympathetic study, but in his *Architecture, an Introduction to the History and Theory of the Art of Building* (1911) and *Form in Civilization, Collected Papers on Art and Labour* (1922), the bankruptcy of the tired nineteenth-century Arts and Crafts ideals of 'honesty' in building became increasingly apparent. It may have been stimulating in the 1860s for Fergusson to dismiss all post-mediaeval architecture as a sham, but it was no longer very stimulating for Lethaby to follow his example in 1911 by devoting less than eight pages to the Renaissance, and describing it as 'a style of boredom', in his *Architecture;* Ruskin's distinction between the phrase 'within my walls', which he found unwelcoming, and the warmer 'under my roof',[2] was a useful contribution to the language and understanding of the Domestic Revival when it was made in 1853, but was not helpful when repeated by Lethaby in a condemnation of the skyline of Renaissance buildings on the grounds that '"roof" and "chimney", indeed are almost synonymous with home';[3] it was similarly from Viollet-le-Duc's writings of the 1850s that Lethaby derived his increasing conviction that Gothic was basically an engineering solution to mechanical problems, so that he was led to downgrade both English Gothic and late Gothic generally, for their more frankly ornamental character.

Lethaby's populist attacks on 'taste', 'style' and 'connoisseurship', and his elevation of 'truth', engineering and efficiency, had played a useful enough role in tautening an accepted language like that of the Arts and Crafts Movement in its many varieties in the later nineteenth century, but were exposed as simplistic and destructive with the removal of the historical framework within which they could usefully operate. Exactly the same was true of the similarly puritanical and mechanistic doctrines of Lodoli and Laugier in the eighteenth century,

---

[1] First published as 19 articles in *The Builder*, CXXVIII-CXXIX, 1925.

[2] *The Works of John Ruskin*, ed. E.T. Cook and A. Wedderburn, XII, 1904, p.33.

[3] W.R. Lethaby, *Architecture*, 1911 ed., p.234.

which were fruitful only so long as they were contained within a range of classical expectations.

Lethaby does not represent quite the end of the Arts and Crafts approach to architecture: that place is reserved for the Catholic and neo-Primitivist Eric Gill (1882-1940), who was trained as an architect in the office of W.D. Caröe but abandoned the practice of architecture for the craft of stone-carving and letter-cutting. His outlook is summarised in the neo-functionalist title of his book of 1933, *Beauty Looks After Herself*. As in the later writings of Lethaby, Gill here uses the Arts and Crafts ethic to build the foundations of a new technological and truthful architecture. Thus, 'all ideas which derive from a time before Industrialism must be ruthlessly scrapped', [1] and centuries of classical tradition are to be swept aside: 'From St Paul's Cathedral to the new Regent Street Quadrant we have had nothing but stage effects obtained by viewing the job of building entirely from the outside'.[2] Real buildings, on the other hand, ought to express their actual structure immediately and unambiguously, and should be in total harmony with the technological spirit of the age: 'All architecture which receives its inspiration in an industrial civilisation from any other source [than function] is pure play-acting'.[3]

By pursuing the ideas of Lethaby and even more of Gill, we have been led out of architectural history proper and out of the nineteenth century. They are important for representing one development from the Arts and Crafts Movement; in the next chapter we shall see another long-term influence of that powerful but diffuse movement which had its roots in the work of Ruskin and Morris.

[1] p.128.   [2] p.137.   [3] p.147.

IV
The History of the
'English Tradition': 1900-1945

1 Blomfield and the Edwardians

We have already noted that the intensity of the Gothic Revival faded after 1870 when its place was taken in architecture by the 'Old English' style, the 'Queen Anne' Movement and the Arts and Crafts Movement, all of which had a more secular and more compromising tone. The special emphasis on traditional domestic architecture rather than on ecclesiastical architecture, together with the concentration of interest on 'the English scene' and the wave of nostalgia for old country ways and lost crafts, which was heightened by the increasing pace of industrialisation and of technological advance, was given lasting expression in the mid 1890s in the founding of two institutions which have since become part of the English way of life: the National Trust for Places of Historic Interest or Natural Beauty in 1895, and the magazine *Country Life* in 1897. The first house ever illustrated in *Country Life*, in the first number of 8 January 1897, was the moated Baddesley Clinton, Warwickshire, still in Catholic ownership and perhaps the most perfect late mediaeval manor-house in England. The caption to one of the photographs, 'You can easily forget for the time that you are living in the Nineteenth Century',[1] typifies the dreamy nostalgia of these years. Both the National Trust and *Country Life* have since come to be especially associated with the respective roles of preserving and recording the country house, though in the 1890s those particular functions seemed less necessary than they have since become. In its early years the National Trust was concerned primarily with the preservation of the countryside, especially in the Lake District, and as late as 1934 owned

[1] *Country Life Illustrated*, I, 1897, p.20.

only two major houses. The founding of the National Trust can appropriately be seen as an extension of the ideals which had prompted William Morris to found the Society for the Protection of Ancient Buildings in 1877.

By 1900 a new religion had been invented — or, at least, a new version of an old religion: the worship of England. This came to a natural climax at the time of the Great War when it was given characteristic expression in the following passages: first the familiar opening couplet from the poem of Sir Cecil Spring Rice:

> I vowe to thee my country — all earthly things above —
> Entire and whole and perfect, the service of my love;

and also in the closing couplet, with its near blasphemous echo of the Lord's Prayer, from a less familiar poem by Sir Robert (later lst and last Baron) Vansittart on the death of his brother:

> God of the love that makes two lives as one
> Give also strength to see that England's will be done.[1]

The popular and prolific author, William Le Queux (1864-1927), also conveys the chauvinistic mood of these years in a chance remark in one of his romantic tales of espionage: 'An English country house, with its old oak, old silver and air of solidity, is always delightful to me after the flimsy gimcracks of Continental life'.[2]

W.R. Lethaby, whom we left towards the end of the last chapter, forms a very good introduction to the present chapter because his outlook characterises both the rural vernacular obsession and the obsession with England. In paying tribute to Lethaby in 1932, William Morris's daughter particularly stressed his 'love of the country, and his delight in country crafts',[3] while his 'Englishry' is well conveyed in the following words from a lecture which he delivered at the Arts and Crafts Society in 1916: 'Simple, well-off house-keeping in the country, with tea in the garden; Boy-scouting, and tennis in flannels. These four seem to me our best form of modern civilization, and

[1] R. Vansittart, 'Long Leave', *Collected Poems*, 1934, p.18.
[2] *Secrets of the Foreign Office*, 1903, p.229.
[3] *RIBA Jnl.*, XXXIX, 1932, p.304.

must serve as examples of the sort of spirit in which town improvement must be undertaken'.[1]

Central to this new climate of opinion was the architect Sir Reginald Blomfield (1856-1942), grandson of a Bishop of London and nephew of Sir Arthur Blomfield (1829-99), a coarse and prolific Gothic Revival architect. Reginald Blomfield's Arts and Crafts sympathies are well conveyed in his study entitled 'The English Tradition' which he contributed to *Arts and Crafts Essays by Members of the Arts and Crafts Exhibition Society* (1893), a popular little book with a preface by William Morris, which was twice reprinted in 1903. When Blomfield writes: 'Three great qualities stamped the English tradition in furniture so long as it was a living force — steadfastness of purpose, reserve in design, and thorough workmanship',[2] it seems that he is not so much describing furniture as defining what he regards as the characteristic qualities of the English gentleman.

Blomfield's first book, published when he was thirty-six at a time when his architectural practice had hardly begun, was *The Formal Garden in England* (1892). Attractively illustrated with reproductions of seventeenth and eighteenth-century engravings as well as with modern line drawings by Inigo Thomas, this little book had been through three editions by 1901 and was successful in attracting many clients to Blomfield. In it we find an early expression of the sustaining ideal which lay behind Blomfield's many subsequent books of architectural history: that the decay of English architecture and the abandonment of its essential 'Englishness' began in the mid-eighteenth century. If not a very profound or self-evidently true observation it was, at any rate, a fairly new one and brought encouragement to architects and country-house owners who had previously been told that good taste ended with Queen Anne if not before. In terms of garden design and garden buildings the book was important for showing that the formal garden need not necessarily be Italianate, as had been thought in the days of Sir Charles Barry, because there was a native English, or at least Anglo-Dutch, tradition which had been wantonly destroyed by Kent, Capability Brown and Repton. Blomfield's romantic

[1] W.R. Lethaby, *Form in Civilization*, 2nd ed. Oxford 1957, p.17.
[2] 3rd ed. 1901, p.296.

chauvinism is well expressed in his declaration that 'It is nothing to us that the French did this or the Italians that: the point is, what has been loved here, by us and by those before us. The best English tradition has always been on the side of refinement and reserve'.

In 1897 Blomfield published a two-volume *History of Renais-sance Architecture in England, 1500-1800* which included a develop-ment of the ideas in *The Formal Garden*. He had been pre-ceded by another architect-historian, J. Alfred Gotch (1852-1942), who had brought out *Architecture of the Renaissance in England* (2 vols., 1891-94) and who later produced *Early Renaissance Architecture in England* (1901), *The Growth of the English House* (1909) and *Inigo Jones* (1928). The architect Thomas Jackson (1835-1924) had done much to stimulate interest in Elizabethan architecture by his Examination Schools of 1876, prominently placed in the High at Oxford, and inspired in its design by the Elizabethan courtyard at Kirby Hall, Northamp-tonshire. Based on his home town of Kettering, Northamp-tonshire, Gotch built up an extensive neo-Tudor architectural practice to which his books formed the natural counterpart. Blomfield, who did not want to restrict the range of sources of either his own buildings or of his historical studies to the sixteenth and seventeenth centuries, extended the term 'Renais-sance' to cover eighteenth-century architecture as well. He also interprets everything he admires about English architecture as the expression of permanent racial characteristics. This racial interpretation of style is extraordinarily close to the long established German tradition from Schnaase to Worringer — which found a late expression in Pevsner's *The Englishness of English Art* (1955) — though it seems unlikely that Blomfield could have known much about this tradition.[2] Blomfield is nonetheless emphatic that 'the individuality of race is stronger than that of genius', and that as a result of 'the psychological standpoint which results from the mental and moral qualities of

---

[1] p.236.

[2] German art history also moved into an increasingly racially conscious phase in these years, as can be seen in Alfred Woltmann's *Germanen und die Renaissance* (1905), Ottmar Rutz's *Menscheitstypen und Kunst* (Jena 1921), Josef Strzygowski's *Die Krisis der Geisteswissenschaften* (Vienna 1923), and Hans Günther's *Rasse und Stil* (Munich 1926).

the race... it is very doubtful if any foreigner can fully understand the art of an alien race'.[1] It is thus possible to 'define
tradition as an inherited psychological standpoint in regard to
art': Blomfield claims, for example, that in English, as opposed
to French or Italian, Romanesque sculpture, we find that
'something of the vigorous open-air energy of the northern
people seems to have stamped itself on their work — the
simplicity of taste and directness of purpose of a race who spent
the best part of their existence in fighting by land and sea. One
finds in it, if one may so put it, a certain sportsmanlike contempt
for anything trivial or irrelevant'.[2] So far from being sportsmanlike was the French Romanesque craftsman that it is clear from
his work that 'In his veins still lingered the blood of the men who
had no instinctive aversion to cruelty'. In England, by contrast,
'The race asserts itself at once', so that our architecture is always
marked by 'sober dignity', 'artistic reticence' and 'sober sanity of
thought'. Comparing Salisbury Cathedral and Notre Dame,
Blomfield is, somewhat surprisingly, struck by the fact that
'Always in the Frenchman one finds a certain expansiveness, an
irresistible impulse to let himself go'.[3] Apparently these racial
characteristics survived both the Protestant Reformation and
the introduction of classicism: 'the essential point is, that after
the forms and methods of mediaeval architecture had died out,
there yet survived this permanent element of English tradition,
an element outside all changes of style'.[4] It survived, at any rate,
until the time of the brothers Adam, whose 'art was essentially a
morbid development, evidence of the slow decay that was surely
overtaking the once magnificent school of English architecture'.[5] Thus, whereas the seventeenth-century Banqueting
House 'is unmistakeably English',[6] the nineteenth-century London club-houses are not.

Most people today would probably concur in regarding this
approach as a farrago of mischievous nonsense. But at the turn
of the century its jingoistic note echoed a popular mood of which
the acceptable face today is, perhaps, the music of Elgar. The
revival of the lost folk-music of England, particularly associated
with the endeavours of Cecil Sharp (1859-1924), is a close
parallel to the Englishry and vernacularism of the Arts and

[1] II, p.398.   [2] p.399.   [3] p.400.   [4] p.401.   [5] p.252.   [6] p.402.

Crafts Movement in architecture. Indeed, Sharp's interest in folk-music is said to have grown out of his earlier enthusiasm for the indigenous English genius as reflected in our mediaeval cathedrals. It certainly seems to be from the Arts and Crafts Movement that Blomfield derived his own version of this historical preoccupation.

In 1913 Blomfield applied his racial interpretation of style to Gothic architecture in a lecture called 'Atavism in Art' which he subsequently published in *The Touchstone of Architecture* (Oxford 1925). In his bold search for the origins of Gothic Blomfield rejected Viollet-le-Duc's explanation of Gothic as a lay reaction against feudalism, and emphasised the role of the Celts who occupied north-west France and England before and during the Roman occupation. Thus the key to the understanding of Gothic is 'the Celtic race, long in abeyance, never wholly extinguished, still vital today': Gothic 'represents the re-emergence of the Celtic temperament... [and] the rise of Gothic architecture is a tremendous example of atavism'.[1] When we ask the question 'what spirit inspired and expressed itself in Gothic on the one hand, Neo-Classic on the other... we must make the attempt to drive back to these root instincts of our race'.[2] Such arguments strike a Germanic note so that it is not surprising to find the great Viennese art-historian, Hans Sedlmayr (born 1896), explaining the Gothic cathedral as the product of Celtic forces in his *Die Entstehung der Kathedrale* (Zurich 1950).

Just as the Gothic Revival had been accompanied by serious restoration of the fabric of mediaeval churches, so the extension of 'Englishry' to the post-mediaeval period, as in Blomfield's books, led to increasing concern for the condition of the characteristic post-mediaeval building-type, the country house. We know from Blomfield himself that both his *Formal Garden* and *Renaissance Architecture* led to many commissions for the reconditioning or careful enlargement of historic country houses: for example, at Apethorpe, Northamptonshire, Brocklesby, Lincolnshire, Chequers, Buckinghamshire, Drakelowe Hall, Derbyshire, Garnons, Herefordshire, Godinton Park, Kent, Heathfield Park, Sussex, Knowlton Court, Kent, Mellerstain,

[1] pp.84-5.   [2] p.93.

Berwickshire, Stanstead Park, Sussex, and Waldershare Park, Kent. What Blomfield enjoyed at these houses as much as the exercise of his architectural talents was the excellent shooting which so many of their proprietors were kind enough to offer him. Indeed in his prosperous and crowded career one thing always seemed to lead to another: thus he discovered in the great Adam library at Mellerstain, a fine collection of seventeenth-century French topographical engravings by Pérelle, Marot and Silvestre which, with Lord Binning's permission, he used to illustrate his *History of French Architecture* (4 vols., 1911-21).

Blomfield's substantial history of French classical architecture from 1491 to 1774, though it has of course been superseded from the point of view of scholarly detail, still remains the most lively and sympathetic account of the whole period in English. He draws on a wide range of printed sources and documents and illustrates the buildings clearly and attractively with contemporary engravings, sketches of his own and modern photographs. He rather lamented the tendency, recently imported to France from Germany, but never popular in England, of publishing large portfolios of architectural plates with no plans and little text. He felt that these represented an easy way out and might prevent the student from studying the buildings themselves. He himself had spent a part of every autumn from 1897 in France with his wife and daughter — the same daughter, incidentally, who shattered the dignified carapace of establishment respectability which Blomfield had been at such pains to construct around himself, by shouting a slogan in favour of votes for women at King George V and Queen Mary on the occasion of her presentation at Court in June 1914.[1]

Blomfield seemed to find the same unruffled gentlemanly quality in French post-mediaeval architecture that he had found in English. Anything 'extreme' is somehow unsporting and therefore not architecture: 'The mere caprices of the Court of François I were no more architecture than the discordant efforts of Borromini a hundred years later'.[2] French architecture ended at the same time as in England, shortly after the middle of the eighteenth century, when 'men such as Chalgrin, Brong-

[1] J. Pope-Hennessy, *Queen Mary*, 1959, p.468.
[2] *French Architecture 1661-1774*, I, p.19.

niart, Antoine and Gondouin set about the revival of the antique in its most literal and pedantic form'.[1] He was so obsessed by this idea that he had evidently never looked at their buildings at all. He repeated it again in his contribution to Livingstone's *The Legacy of Greece* (Oxford 1921): 'The national traditions, both of France and England, were lost, Greek architecture became the fashion and the misguided enthusiasms of pedants and amateurs insisted on literal reproductions which completed the extinction of architecture as a vernacular art... Conscious and deliberate tinkering with the art of architecture ended by destroying it'.[2]

Though Blomfield condemned Ruskin on more than one occasion and also severed himself from the Arts and Crafts Movement, it is fascinating to discover that he could nonetheless interpret French classicism as a kind of unselfconscious anonymous craft. This interpretation also lies at the heart of the writings of T.G. Jackson (1835-1924), whose buildings we have already noted as influencing the revival of interest in Elizabethan and Jacobean architecture. Jackson was a pupil of Sir Gilbert Scott but quickly reacted against the doctrinaire approach to style of the Gothic Revival, as can be seen in his little book, *Modern Gothic Architecture* (1873). At the end of his long life he published a three-volume history of Renaissance architecture in Italy, France and England under the title, *The Renaissance of Roman Architecture* (Cambridge 1921-3).

Jackson claimed that his 'contribution to the subject is taken from a rather different point of view' from that of historians like Gotch, Blomfield and Belcher, and that his concern was rather 'to explain the movement by the social history of the age, and to show how one reflects the other'.[3] In practice, however, Jackson's approach is no different from Blomfield's who had already written sensitively about architecture in its social context. In his somewhat Blomfieldian conclusion to his great work, published in his eighty-eighth year, Jackson writes of art that 'To live, it must be natural, spontaneous. It must come to our conception as naturally as our language to our lips; it must be the free

[1] p.xv.
[2] R.W. Livingstone, ed., *The Legacy of Greece*, Oxford 1921, pp.421-2.
[3] *Renaissance of Roman Architecture*, II, pp.v-vi.

expression of our ideas, unfettered by formal rules, and un-
checked by premeditation. It must flow from us unconsciously.
To talk about it is fatal... To bring it into the field of conscious
effort is to kill it... For art really to live it must be vernacular as
it was in the Middle Ages'.[1] The determinedly anti-intellectual
refusal of Blomfield and Jackson to consider theory and ideas
makes their definition of architecture resemble the definition of
a gentleman in which the very act of asking how the concept is
defined, and whether one is a gentleman or not oneself, is sufficient to show that one is not.

Exactly parallel to the writings of Blomfield were those of
John Belcher (1841-1913) and Sir Mervyn Macartney (1853-
1932), in particular their *Later Renaissance Architecture in England,
a series of examples of the domestic buildings erected subsequent to the
Elizabethan period* (2 vols., 1898-1901). Though the authors we
have been looking at in this chapter may be criticised for a
technique which relied too much on purely visual history, their
tremendous industry produced accurate plans of post-mediaeval
buildings which have been the essential foundation of later
research. Both Belcher and Macartney were eminently successful architects associated with the turn to classicism around 1900,
and their sumptuously illustrated folio volumes were frankly
presented as pattern books for other architects. They claim
disarmingly of the buildings they choose to describe that 'No
attempt has been made to classify them or to arrange them in
chronological order, or to trace by examples the growth of
development of Renaissance Architecture. The Editors have
rather sought to illustrate its adaptability to every purpose,
large or small, monumental or domestic'.[2] The frankly unsystematic and unintellectual approach is positively Blomfieldian, as
is the special emphasis on the essentially English qualities of
seventeenth and eighteenth-century architecture in England
which is everywhere 'marked by modesty and restraint, purity
and dignity'. Belcher and Macartney believed that 'a grave and
sober demeanour... [is] reflected in English buildings... a
quiet dignified charm... a sturdy masculine feeling'. Later
Renaissance architecture 'appears to adjust itself to the English
character; there is no need of any extravagant display or

[1] *ibid.*, pp.216-17.   [2] I, p.xi.

extreme severity'.[1] This decent Englishness is in marked contrast to foreign classicism: they thus claim that 'In emotional
France the severity of Classic form was never altogether congenial'; while 'In Germany the new departure was marked by a
ruggedness and stolidity essentially Teutonic'.[2]

Another popular argument in these years is that real English
architecture was killed in the later eighteenth century by
revivalism. Belcher and Macartney, like Blomfield, attack the
Adam brothers for possessing 'too much delicacy of detail', and
claim that 'The demand which then arose for (so-called) "pure
Classic", like the more recent demand for "pure Gothic", was
bound to result in "dead works"'.[3]

In fact, it is scarcely surprising to find similarity of outlook
among these authors. They had been involved in 1896 in
founding the stylish and influential journal, *The Architectural
Review*, which concentrated on the artistic rather than the
technical aspects of architecture. It was run initially by a large
editorial panel including Blomfield, Macartney and Ernest
Newton, but from 1905-20 the editorship was in the sole hands
of Macartney who was responsible for giving it a generally
classical bias. Books on related themes included *London Churches
of the 17th and 18th centuries* (1896) by George Birch, Curator of
Sir John Soane's Museum from 1894-1904, W.J. Loftie's *Inigo
Jones and Wren, the Rise and Decline of Modern Architecture in
England* (1893), and *The Domestic Architecture of England During the
Tudor Period* (2 vols., 1910) by Thomas Garner and Arthur
Stratton. Garner, a partner of the architect Bodley, died in 1906
so that Stratton, who was closely associated with *The Architectural Review*, was chiefly responsible for the book. Anxious to
promote the sympathetic restoration of Tudor country houses as
well as to encourage the Tudor domestic revival in contemporary architecture, he claimed that 'Love of home is a strong
characteristic of the English race, yet as a nation England has
done little to preserve what has been bequeathed from the
past'.[4]

It is no coincidence that most of the books we shall see in this
chapter by authors like Gotch, Blomfield, Macartney, Garner,
Stratton, Birch, Bond and Vallance, were published by Messrs

[1] pp.4-5.   [2] p.xv.   [3] p.4.   [4] 2nd ed., 1929, p.vi.

Batsford. This remarkable firm of architectural publishers and booksellers had been established in 1843 by Bradley Thomas Batsford (1821-1904) who ran it with his two sons, Bradley (1846-1906) and Herbert (1861-1917). His grandson Harry entered the business in 1897 and maintained his uncles's ideals until after the Second World War. He explained in 1943 that 'My Uncle Herbert aimed at appealing to the general public with a series of well-illustrated popular text books on the English House, Cathedral, Parish Church, Village and Manor House. I think he was right. Beauty was no longer merely the privilege of the few, and the average Englishman was beginning to care for the story of his island and the buildings of it'.[1] Herbert Batsford's close friend, the architect Professor Albert Richardson, wrote an obituary of him in 1917[2] which emphasised the importance of Batsfords' revival of the eighteenth-century tradition of the combined bookseller, publisher, editor and patron.

A remarkably close parallel to the work of the Batsford family is afforded by Edward Hudson at *Country Life*, a journal which, as we noted at the beginning of this chapter, played an increasingly important role in making architectural history, or at least that of the country house, look respectable. It was founded and edited by Edward Hudson (1854-1936) who also ran Hudson and Kearns, the family printing business he had inherited from his father. He was passionately dedicated to the traditional patterns of English culture, architecture, craftsmanship and gardening, and though not articulate in print himself conveyed his huge enthusiasm to the country at large through the medium of the articles and illustrations produced by his friends and colleagues for *Country Life*. So successful was his endeavour that Walter (later Lord) Runciman, President of the Board of Trade, declared as early as 1911 that *Country Life* had become 'the keeper of the architectural conscience of the nation'.[3] It was not merely the weekly articles on the English architectural heritage in town and country that helped *Country Life* sustain this august role but also the seemingly endless series of beautifully produced

---

[1] H. Bolitho, ed., *A Batsford Century*, 1943, p.44.
[2] *RIBA Jnl.*, XXIV, 1917, pp.97-8.
[3] C. Hussey, 'The Making of Country Life', *Country Life*, CXVI, 1967, p.55.

books on architecture and related topics which appeared under its imprint for sixty years. A key and characteristic figure in this process was Harry Avray Tipping (1856-1933), gardener and antiquarian, rich bachelor and younger son of Sir William Tipping, MP, of Brasted Place, Kent. For half a century from the 1880s he laid out gardens, mostly at a succession of houses owned by himself, in a stylistic compromise between the informality associated with Gertrude Jekyll, and the formality admired by Reginald Blomfield. His interest in historical research had led him to join the team of authors working on the *Dictionary of National Biography* under Sir Sidney Lee, and in 1907 he contributed the first of his many articles on country houses to *Country Life* where his historical knowledge and insistence on accuracy effected an architectural revolution. The year 1914 saw the publication of his important folio, *Grinling Gibbons and the Woodwork of his Age* and also the launching of his magnum opus, the nine-volumed series of *English Homes*, though publication of this was delayed until after the war.

It should not be thought that the study of mediaeval architecture was neglected in these years, for Lethaby was joined by scholars like Prior and Bond. In 1892 Blomfield had been approached by the publishers George Bell & Sons to write a history of English architecture. Blomfield was prepared to undertake only the period from 1500-1800 and his book on that subject appeared, as we have seen, in two volumes in 1897. He suggested to Messrs Bell that his old friend, E.S. Prior (1852-1932), be invited to write on the mediaeval period. This admirable proposal resulted in the publication of Prior's superlatively good *A History of Gothic Art in England* (1900),[1] uniform in size with Blomfield's two volumes.

Prior was a central figure in the group of Shaw's pupils associated with the rise of the Arts and Crafts Movement in the 1880s. Educated at Harrow and at Gonville and Caius College, Cambridge, he was a founder of the Art Workers' Guild and became its Master in 1906, Secretary of the Arts and Crafts Exhibition Society from 1902-17, and was the architect of a number of more or less eccentric Arts and Crafts buildings in heavily vernacular styles and materials. His interpretation of

[1] Reprinted 1974, The Scolar Press, Ilkley, Yorkshire.

Gothic is close to Lethaby's but he appears in a chapter on the history of 'the English tradition', rather than in the last chapter, because he lacks Lethaby's impressive world view of culture. Indeed, Prior begins his book with a chapter on 'Gothic Art in England and France' which is dominated by his anxiety to correct the impression given by Lethaby — though he does not mention him by name — and also by the American C.H. Moore (1840-1930) and others, that English mediaeval architecture was, to use a phrase of Lethaby's, *'continuously* influenced from France'.[1] Prior claims that his opinions 'are at variance with the assertion of the great French architecture being the mother of all the Gothics, sending her children into all the countries of north-west Europe'. The following paragraph is a beautiful example of the illuminating contrasts Prior can draw between French and English Gothic:

To outside view the French cathedral has the air of a revolution — the erupted mass of a gigantic effort: but the English takes the look more of a constitutional development, a chain of precedent — not a volcano, but a water-worn down shaped through long years by air and water. So great is the French mass of buttressed and contoured outline, that its western towers scarcely break its profiles; but in the English church the suggestion is that of a long ship, so sheer and clear above the hull stand the mast-like steeples.[2]

Elsewhere Prior used the word 'picturesque' to define one of the characteristics of English Gothic in a way which unexpectedly anticipates the later insights of Pevsner. Prior describes 'the more complex developments of the English type, that gave at Salisbury, and afterwards at Wells and Exeter, a peculiar picturesqueness both inside and out'. Unlike Pevsner, he is also particularly responsive to colour in architecture, as is well exemplified in his contrast between Lincoln and Salisbury;[3] on the other hand, he has not grasped the concept of architecture as space which his German contemporaries were developing. What he is ultimately most anxious to prove, both in this book and in his slightly later *The Cathedral Builders in England* (1905), is firstly the Englishness of English Gothic, and secondly that the quality of Gothic is the result of its being a collective endeavour not dependent on the 'taste' of individuals. The preoccupation

[1] p.269. [2] p.82. [3] pp.210-11.

with Englishry is, as we have seen, especially characteristic of
the years round 1900; and the belief in artistic teamwork is the
legacy of the Arts and Crafts Movement. For Prior, Gothic is a
'homely' art: 'Homely, perhaps, but the pleasure of this home-
sense is the true note of the English character'.[1] He finds a
'constant English tradition... since the Conquest, of a native
craftsmanship, free alike from continental importation and
Masonic dictation',[2] and sees 'reflected... [in Gothic] the qualities of the English landscape'.[3] Prior's interpretation of Gothic
in terms of Englishry is far more subtle and under-stated than
Blomfield's cruder interpretation of English Renaissance architecture in similar terms. His belief in the collective nature of
Gothic design, an echo of the romantic socialism of Ruskin and
Morris, is, however, emphatically stated: 'The first symptom of
the decline is the birth of artistic individuality; the segregation
of the artist from the community at large; the making of art a
personal rather than a collective ambition... intellectual formalism may invade the spontaneity of art, and so-called "culture" may insist on what it calls "correctness" or "erudition" or
"naturalism". So came the decline in Greek and Renaissance
art'.[4] He insists that 'in the history of mediaeval art personality
vanishes entirely',[5] and that mediaeval 'art is not the fancy of a
wayward will, but a revelation of human quality in the aggregate'.[6] Having seen in the concentration camps of Soviet Russia
and Nazi Germany exactly what human quality can be like in
the aggregate, our sadder if not yet wiser age can no longer quite
share Prior's faith in collectivism. Nonetheless, Prior shared
Lethaby's conviction that architectural history *mattered* because
it was an aspect of cultural history, and he was consequently
prepared to ask some important fundamental questions. Devoted though he was to the forms of Gothic architecture, Prior
could yet question whether it was the forms themselves that had
the power to move him, or whether it was not rather some inner
truth which lay beyond them: 'it is hard to justify any special
admiration for Gothic architecture, if its forms be separated

---

[1] p.447.   [2] p.v.
[3] *The Cathedral Builders in England*, 1905, p.25.
[4] *A History of Gothic Art in England*, 1900, p.8.
[5] *The Cathedral Builders*, p.21.   [6] *ibid.*, p.22.

from the great truth of Gothic life . . . We conclude that the art of the mediaeval ages was *not* this architectural dress, but something underneath it'.[1] For Pugin, of course, this underlying truth was the Catholic faith. That argument is not one that appealed to Prior, and his explanation of the 'reality' at the heart of Gothic is couched in vaguer Ruskinian terms of 'growth' and 'power'. Prior's role as a practising architect also made him keen to interpret the 'essence' of Gothic in a way that would be applicable to the problems of contemporary architecture. He thus wrote of the 'inner truths' of Gothic architecture that 'These things were not of design, but of growth — such as would appear immediately in our own building, if its learning could be forgotten and we had architecture only for our material needs. It would then depend on the strength and character of those needs whether our building developed the genius of mediaeval building, but at any rate the power of growth would show architecture alive'.[2]

T. Francis Bumpus (1861-1916), Anglo-Catholic ecclesiologist, produced a long flow of popular histories of English and continental cathedrals. His work need only be noted here as another instance of the explanation of style through national character. Condemning French mouldings, in his *A Guide to Gothic Architecture* (1915), as expressive of French character, he is pleased to note that 'English mouldings are just as eloquent of national character . . . English love of detail, and English love of harmony, and English sobriety come out clearly in our mouldings. We see that the soul of the workman is in his sectional lines, which are trenchant, sprightly, or grave, according to the character of the man'. The ideals of the English gentleman, modest and understated, are permanently reflected throughout the whole range of our architectural history: 'all our buildings — whether cathedrals, or parish churches, or houses — are of homely compass, and their effects calm, and in no wise strained'.[3]

Another prolific mediaevalist was Francis Bond (1852-1918). He was a more serious scholar than Bumpus, but his work lacked the charm of Prior's and has a tone which is somehow in keeping with his role as Headmaster of the Hull and East Riding College. He was educated at King Edward's Grammar School,

[1] *ibid.*, p.16.   [2] *ibid.*, p.18.   [3] pp.20-1.

Louth, and Lincoln College, Oxford, and from 1893-1914 was a lecturer, mainly on Gothic architecture, at the Oxford University Extension Delegacy. His principal book was his monumental *Gothic Architecture in England, an Analysis of the Origins and Development of English Church Architecture from the Norman Conquest to the Dissolution of the Monasteries* (1905). Bond was distressed at the lack of interest in architecture which he felt characterised Edwardian England: 'Painting, music, novels, play-acting, count their votaries by thousands. The new symphony by Pole or Russian or Bohemian obtains respectful audience and admiration... Not so with architecture. There was never a time of such blackness of indifference as to the master-art of architecture'. He argues that it was totally different 'In the old England... [where] every village mason could build a church'.[1] Bond's approach is thus tinged by the Englishry we have observed in the course of this chapter, but he was fundamentally concerned by the fact that since the pioneering days of Britton, Pugin, Petit and Willis, the study of mediaeval architecture had atrophied. He also complained that it had especially suffered from the continuing application of Rickman's, to him, false system of classification. His ambition was to make treatment of the subject more systematic and scientific in the sense of Viollet-le-Duc, and more evolutionary in the sense of Darwin. This was important because it meant overthrowing the interpretation of architecture through the concept of style which had been accepted in England since Rickman. Bond complained that 'We have been told for nearly a century that there are four periods of English mediaeval architecture: Norman, Early English, Decorated, and Perpendicular. But there is no such thing'. He also rejected the claim that 'there is in each of the four periods some inward and spiritual significance, which, could it be discerned, would give us the keynote or character of the whole architecture of the time'.[2] For Bond there were no periods but a single organic development which should be studied as Darwin had studied the origin of species. Bond did not want stylistic analysis of successive periods but a comprehensive investigation of the whole of mediaeval architecture under the principal headings of (1) planning; (2) the vault and its abutments;

[1] p.xvii.   [2] p.xx.

(3) drainage; and (4) lighting. This, to do him credit, is what he achieved in his *Gothic Architecture in England*, and it makes a very serious, if scarcely very readable, work of reference.

Bond's immense industry and matter-of-fact approach produced a continuous flow of books on English mediaeval art of which the principal were *Cathedrals of England and Wales* (1899), *Screens and Galleries in English Churches* (Oxford 1908), *Fonts and Font Covers* (Oxford 1908), *Wood Carvings in English Churches* (2 vols., Oxford 1910), *An Introduction to English Church Architecture* (2 vols., Oxford 1913), and *The Chancel of English Churches* (Oxford 1916). Bond was followed by scholars like A. H. Thomson, F. H. Crossley, J. C. Cox, and Aymer Vallance, whose books, often published by Batsfords, appealed to a popular audience as well as to scholars. The Rev. William Howard Aymer Vallance (1862-1943), educated at Harrow and Oriel College, Oxford, and greatly contrasting in character with Francis Bond, was a curious and romantic disciple of William Morris, in all except Morris's socialism. He published two books on Morris in 1897 and could also claim to have 'discovered' Aubrey Beardsley whom he introduced to John Lane, publisher of *The Yellow Book*. He bought Stoneacre at Otham in Kent, a half-timbered yeoman's house with a great hall which, before presenting to the National Trust, he elaborately restored and enlarged in 1920. He published a handsome folio on *The Old Colleges of Oxford* (1912), *Old Crosses and Lychgates* (1920 and 1933), and *English Church Screens* (1936). The last of these, the standard work on the subject, contains an unusual account of the menace posed to the future of screens by women's suffrage, a cause for which Vallance had little sympathy. He describes with doubtless justified asperity how 'Breadsall church, Derbyshire, [was] burnt with its contents including the screenwork, on the night of 4th to 5th June 1914, having been fired by ladies, qualifying for the parliamentary vote'. [1]

Between 1900 and 1924 there appeared the extensive series of Little Guides which covered the English counties in upwards of forty volumes. In their day, they were as familiar and as indispensible to the architectural tourist as Pevsner's *Buildings of England* have since become. The various authors who contribu-

[1] pp.v-vi.

ted to this popular series all shared the Victorian ecclesiological assumption that the most interesting building in any town or village would necessarily be the mediaeval parish church, however completely restored; Georgian architecture is invariably ignored or dismissed as modern and therefore ugly.

This prejudice against the eighteenth century, which seems to reflect a belief that its classicism and its way of life were un-English, is expressed in the establishment in 1908 of the otherwise admirable Historical Monuments Commission. Its aims were 'to make an inventory of the Ancient and Historical Monuments and Constructions connected with or illustrative of the contemporary culture, civilizations and conditions of life of the people of England, excluding Monmouthshire, from the earliest times to the year 1700, and to specify those which seem most worthy of preservation'. The volumes issued by the Commission from 1910 onwards are the handsome outcome of a painstaking and loving dedication to the task of recording the English achievement. Moreover, the gradual abolition of a date limit mirrors perfectly the growth of interest in the history of eighteenth, nineteenth and twentieth-century architecture. Thus in 1921 the absurdly early date limit of 1700 was extended cautiously to 1714; 1946 saw the introduction of a discretionary extension to 1850; and in 1963 all date limits to the Commissioners' discretionary powers were removed.

The Commission had in fact been preceded by two similar bodies: the Victoria History of the Counties of England, and the London County Council Survey of London. Like the Historical Monuments Commission volumes, these made little use of documentary sources, save in the case of major mediaeval buildings, so that most buildings were dated on purely stylistic grounds. The scope of the monumental series of volumes published from 1904 by the Victoria County History is wider than that of the Royal Commission in that it includes topics like geology and natural history and, from the start, had no date limit for buildings. These dignified volumes celebrate a rural England based on the parish system which was already beginning to be a pleasing anachronism before the First World War. The inception of the Survey of London was similarly caused by a reaction against the pressures of modern life which were causing the demolition of countless historic buildings in London. The key figure in the founding of the London Survey Committee was the dedicated Arts and Crafts idealist, Charles Robert Ashbee (1863-1942). A pupil of Bodley, he had come under the influence of Ruskin and Morris and had founded the Guild of Handicraft in 1888 in the East End of London at Essex House, Mile End. Ashbee's Guild, which was accompanied by a School of Handicraft until 1895, specialised in metalwork, silverware and furniture, all designed in a rarified Art Nouveau taste. It was remarkable as a social experiment operating in the East End of London, and was moved bodily to the Cotswolds in 1902 where it had a short life at Chipping Campden before being wound up five years later. It was during the Guild's London period that Ashbee founded in 1894 the Committee for the Survey of the Memorials of Greater London. The object of this Committee, of which Ashbee was chairman, was 'to watch and register what still remains of beautiful or historic work in Greater London, and to bring such influence to bear from time to time as shall save it from destruction or lead to its utilization for public purposes'. The grandiose aim was to compile a register of all interesting buildings and to publish monographs on the most important of them. The first of these monographs, written by Ashbee and published by the Guild and School of Handicraft in 1896, was entitled *The Trinity Hospital in Mile End, an Object Lesson in National History*. The proposed demolition by the Corporation of Trinity House of these charming alms-houses, then believed to have been designed by Sir Christopher Wren, caused a national outcry of a type with which we have become familiar in the 1960s and 70s from the Euston Arch to Mentmore. It is fascinating to find Ashbee defending the building not primarily as a distinguished work of art, but as something deeply embedded in the English way of life, and therefore reflecting 'a certain cultured amateurishness':[1] Trinity Hospital which, like 'Most great architecture bears upon it the mark of what is best in the national character', was also important for Ashbee as rooted in 'the Guild tradition of the middle ages, which brought with it the element of charity and fellowship'.[2] The monograph is accordingly illustrated not only with measured drawings of the buildings but with attractive sketches of

[1] p.24.   [2] p.7.

the interior by Max Balfour with such captions as 'Two Old Captains playing Drafts'. Ashbee thus presses into the service of preserving a classical building of the 1690s a range of sentiment and language which draws on Pugin, Ruskin, Morris, romantic socialism and the Arts and Crafts Movement, as well as on what we have called the religion of 'Englishry'. It is important to remember that the Survey of London's great series of scholarly records of London buildings which is still in progress, with 39 volumes to date, began life as a preservationist movement, exactly like the the National Trust, the Georgian Group and the Victorian Society.

Although the Trinity House pamphlet is described on its title page as 'the first monograph of the Committee for the Survey of the Memorials of Greater London', that honour is generally accorded to the volume on the *Parish of Bromley-by-Bow* which appeared in 1900, edited by Ashbee from material collected by members of the Survey Committee and printed under the auspices of the London County Council. In 1898 the London County Council had acquired from Parliament statutory power to purchase historic buildings or to provide funds for their restoration and maintenance, and it was thus appropriate that it should undertake the responsibility for publishing the Survey. The aim of the work, as stated in Ashbee's Introduction, was 'to stimulate the historic and social conscience of London', and its urgency was well conveyed in his statement that 'A glance through the present volume shows that of the sixteen objects or groups of objects deemed by us to be of sufficient importance to be recorded, six have been destroyed during the compilation of this work, and at least two others threatened with destruction.'[1]

The sale and threatened destruction of Clifford's Inn in 1903[2] was another of the many disasters which drew attention at this time to the total absence of any machinery in England to prevent the destruction of historic buildings. The sad tale of Clifford's Inn was given much prominence in the first two numbers of the *Burlington Magazine*, which had been founded in 1903. A powerful editorial pointed out how 'Great Britain shares with Russia and Turkey the odious peculiarity of being without legislation of any kind for the protection of ancient

---

[1] p.xvi.   [2] Not in fact demolished until 1935.

buildings... such as is possessed to some degree by every other country in Europe, and by almost every State of the American Union'.[1] The Editor drew attention to a useful parliamentary paper presented to the House of Commons in July 1897 which outlined the statutory provision for the preservation of historic buildings which existed in Austria, Bavaria, Denmark, France, Belgium, Italy and Greece.

An unexpectedly important role in the field of preservation was played by the great Marquess Curzon of Kedleston (1859-1925), Viceroy of India from 1898-1905 and Foreign Secretary from 1919-24. His life was dedicated to the pursuit of magnificence but also to the restoration of palatial buildings, so that his Ancient Monuments Preservation Act was the legislation which gave him most satisfaction during his period as Viceroy. He was made an Honorary Fellow of the RIBA in 1904 and subsequently bought two of the finest mediaeval castles in England, Bodiam in Sussex and Tattershall in Lincolnshire, which he bequeathed to the nation after paying for their extensive restoration. He also acquired Montacute and Hackwood on lease, and employed A. S. G. Butler to carry out elaborate modernisations at Kedleston, his family seat in Derbyshire. He was a serious student of architectural history, insisting on the proper consultation of documents, and intended to publish six volumes on major English houses. He produced a full architectural study of Bodiam Castle and, appearing posthumously, of Walmer and Tattershall Castles. His *British Government in India* (2 vols., 1925), contains important accounts of British architecture in India, especially at Calcutta, the former capital.

Lord Curzon combined his intense love of English architecture with an almost mystical faith in England's imperial destiny. The Walpole Society, founded in April 1911, represents a closer parallel to the kind of historical and architectural interests reflected in the Victoria County Histories, the Inventories of the Royal Commission on Historical Monuments and the Survey of London. The Walpole Society had as one of its immediate objectives the publication of George Vertue's notes on the lives of English artists which Walpole had put to such brilliant use in his *Anecdotes of Painting in England*. But the Society

---

[1] *Burl. Mag.*, II, 1903, p.3.

was also founded 'with the object of promoting the study of British Art' in the belief that 'Few realise how intimately our Art is bound up with our past history and with our national life and character'.[1] Here, then, is yet another instance of this national self-consciousness in which we can again discern the impact of the Arts and Crafts Movement, for Lethaby and Prior were both members of the original committee. Indeed, the first annual volume published by the Society in 1912 contained an article by Prior on English mediaeval figure sculpture, and one by Lethaby on London and Westminster painters in the middle ages.

What we have observed in this chapter is that architectural history has been promoted by those who have, in many varied ways, a powerful notion of what architecture ought to look like in the present day: either positive, in the case of the practising architects, or negative, in the case of preservationists. Important new elements were now added to these traditions which we shall investigate in the second section of this chapter.

2 Classicism and the Country House

By the eve of the First World War reaction had already set in against the type and scope of the kind of architectural history we have been describing so far in this chapter. The change is heralded in two distinguished and influential books of 1914: Geoffrey Scott's *The Architecture of Humanism*, and Albert Richardson's *Monumental Classic Architecture in Great Britain and Ireland during the 18th and 19th centuries*. This new approach to architectural interpretation is anti-vernacular, anti-sentimental, anti-associational: it is not concerned to show the reflection in buildings of qualities of Englishness such as decency, fairplay and amateurishness, or indeed any moral or social values at all; nor does it believe that the essence of this Englishness was smothered by the arrival of connoisseurship in the eighteenth century. By contrast, it is concerned to reinstate architecture as a Fine Art with independent laws of its own, and to emphasise classicism as a permanent language which transcends national boundaries.

In his brilliant book, Geoffrey Scott (1883-1929) ruthlessly

---

[1] *Walpole Soc. Annual*, I, Oxford 1912, p.v.

demolished one by one the fallacies which he believed sustained the nineteeth-century English and French approach to architectural theory and, by implication, to architectural history: they were the Romantic, Mechanical, Ethical, and Biological Fallacies, which had been used to justify notions that architecture ought to be expressive of its purpose, structure, materials, or of the national way of life or of the craftsman's temperament, and so on. One of the concepts which Scott introduced in place of the discarded fallacies was architecture as an art concerned primarily with the shaping of space. Clough Williams-Ellis wrote of him: 'Geoffrey had a great feeling for *space* and I recall him often gesturing and posturing to express this feeling when within buildings — especially churches'.[1] This spatial emphasis, it will be remembered, was a cornerstone of the architectural history pioneered in Germany around 1900 by Schmarsow, Riegl, Brinckmann and, later, Frankl, though the German books to which Scott specifically refers in his Preface are Burckhardt's *Civilization of the Renaissance in Italy* and Wölfflin's *Renaissance und Barock*. From Wölfflin and Lipps he derived the theory of empathy to explain the overriding merit of classical architecture: 'The centre of that architecture', Scott claimed, 'was the human body; its method, to transcribe in stone the body's favourable states; and the moods of the spirit took visible shape along its borders, power and laughter, strength and terror and calm';[2] similarly, Wölfflin had argued that 'We always project a corporeal state conforming to our own; we interpret the whole outside world according to the expressive system with which we have become familiar from our own bodies. That which we have experienced in ourselves as the expression of severe strictness, taut self-discipline or uncontrolled heavy relaxation, we transfer to all other bodies... Moreover, it is clear that architecture, an art of corporeal masses, can only relate to man as a corporeal being'.[3]

In 1908 Scott had won the Chancellor's English Essay Prize at Oxford with a paper on *The National Character of English Archi-*

[1] Quoted from A.C. Foster, *The Architectural Aesthetic of Geoffrey Scott*, Cambridge B.A. thesis, 1974.
[2] 2nd ed. 1924, p.239.
[3] *Renaissance and Baroque*, Fontana Library ed. 1964, pp.77-8.

tecture, published that year as a forty-six-page pamphlet. At this date his outlook was still very largely the product of influence from William Morris and Reginald Blomfield. He quoted Morris' celebrated description of England which begins with the words, 'The land is a little land...'; and it is clear that he believes, with Blomfield, in an 'essence' of Englishness expressing itself in 'permanent forces' which *ought* to be reflected in English architecture, but are all too frequently absent from it: the offending periods include Perpendicular, the work of Vanbrugh and of Adam, Strawberry Hill Gothick and Victorian architecture. Of Perpendicular he writes: 'The delight in stained glass led to another defect which was less characteristic. The monumental nature of architecture which, usually, we so jealously safeguarded, was sacrificed; the walls became transparent, and the church a lantern';[1] and of Vanbrugh: 'Scrupulousness in the treatment of material had led us to the faults of the Perpendicular style; here it was the excess of another national quality which spoilt Blenheim. Vanbrugh aimed at emphasising the solid'.[2] He dismisses Adam because he 'had no more touch with permanent forces than the grotesque Gothic of Strawberry Hill'.[3]

The striking change in approach between Scott's Chancellor's Essay, published when he was twenty-six, and his *Architecture of Humanism* of six years later, is due to his contact with the great Bernard Berenson (1865-1959), whose secretary and librarian at I Tatti he now became. Though Berenson is not normally thought of as an architectural historian, the formalist approach of his essay, 'A Word for Renaissance Churches',[4] undoubtedly influenced Scott. Berenson had complained in this paper that few authors writing in English had treated architecture 'from the point of view of the aesthetic spectator',[5] but that they did so rather from that of the builder or from the religious standpoint. Scott was to find himself in complete sympathy with this approach, and with Berenson's isolation of the domed and centrally planned, or Greek-cross, church as the most characteristic expression of the Renaissance aesthetic. Writing of the exquisite church at Todi, Berenson claimed that it was difficult

[1] p.28   [2] pp.40-1.   [3] pp.43-4.
[4] *The Study and Criticism of Italian Art*, 1902, pp.62-76.   [5] p.v.

to believe when visiting it that 'the purpose of the building was other than the realization of a beautiful dream of space. It suggests no ulterior motive . . . Such a building sings indeed not the glory of God, but the Godhead of man'.[1] This resolutely aesthetic interpretation of the centrally planned pilgrimage church, ignoring all functional or symbolical explanations, was not seriously challenged until Wittkower's *Architectural Principles in the Age of Humanism* (1949). Scott repeated this view in two articles[2] on St Peter's in *Country Life* in 1926-7 in which he described the pilgrimage churches of Todi and Montepulciano as 'exercises in the poetry of architecture', though he also emphasised the role of St Peter's as a symbol of the papacy.

As Scott himself complained, his book was often taken to be purely a defence of the then unpopular Baroque architecture. He attempted to argue in the second edition of 1924 that it was simply chance that Baroque, as an architecture of space with a 'purely psychological approach to the problem of design' and with 'a freedom from mechanical and academic "taboos"',[3] happened to be an obvious illustration for his thesis. It is interesting, however, that in Germany the appreciation of space also went hand in hand with an appreciation of Baroque in a way which makes it difficult to be clear which came first. Scott's book was certainly widely used between the wars by architects and historians as a way of making Baroque respectable. Thus Scott himself wrote in 1924: 'I noticed in the literature that appeared on the occasion of the recent Wren Bicentenary, that a number of writers were at pains to present Wren in the character of a great baroque architect. This is, I think the "new angle": it implies a better understanding both of the nature of baroque, and of the true inspiration of Wren'.[4] In the same year, 1924, a no less personal but equally influential interpretation of Baroque appeared in the brilliantly impressionistic *Southern Baroque Art, a Study of Painting, Architecture and Music in Italy and Spain of the 17th and 18th Centuries* by the twenty-six-year-old Sacheverell Sitwell. Sir Osbert Sitwell later wrote that it 'set a

---

[1] p.70.
[2] 'The Vatican Basilica of St Peter's', *Country Life*, LX, 1926, pp.1000-6, and LXI, 1927, pp.16-23.
[3] p.262.   [4] pp.262-3.

whole generation chattering of the Baroque and the Rococo'.[1]

Scott led a colourful life which ought to be explored more fully. He lived luxuriously in Florence and in 1917 became engaged to Lady Sybil Cutting (1879-1943). A daughter of the 5th Earl of Desart and the widow of William Bayard Cutting of Long Island, formerly Secretary to the American Embassy in London, she had acquired in 1911 the historic Villa Medici at Fiesole. In 1923-24 Scott contrived to have an affair with the Hon. Mrs Harold Nicolson (Vita Sackville-West) and within two years he and Lady Sybil were divorced. She married the critic and essayist Percy Lubbock (1879-1965), while Scott went to America to edit Boswell's papers of which he published six volumes before dying from pneumonia in New York on 14 August 1929 aged forty-six. He also published two small volumes of poems and a very carefully-wrought biography of Madame de Charrière, *The Portrait of Zélide* (1925).

In some sense analagous to Scott was the art critic Adrian Stokes (1902-72), for whom the psychoanalytical theories of Melanie Klein played the same role that Lippsian *Einfühlung* had for Scott. After an education at Rugby and Magdalen College, Oxford, Stokes settled in Italy in 1926 where, much influenced by Ezra Pound, he produced his beautiful studies of the early Italian Renaissance, *The Quattro Cento* (1932) and *Stones of Rimini* (1934). His Kleinian approach with its emphasis on the therapeutic role of architecture in a psychological struggle against fantasy, has had little general influence on the development of architectural history though there are many for whom his writings still have a suggestive charm.

Although Scott was undoubtedly a pioneer in the appreciation of Baroque architecture he was not in fact the first Englishman to attempt a serious assessment of the subject. In 1910 the architect and prolific architectural writer, Martin Shaw Briggs (1882-1977), published a remarkable study of the Baroque town of Lecce under the title *In the Heel of Italy: a Study of an Unknown City*, which was later translated into Italian. He subsequently wrote *Baroque Architecture* (1913), which was published in a German translation in the following year. It was important for containing in a single volume in the English language the kind

[1] *Laughter in the Next Room*, 1949, p.61.

of information which had been scattered through Gurlitt's volumes of the 1880s. Writing in 1913, Briggs was still unable to accept the art of Borromini, though he did appreciate the essentially Baroque character of the west towers of St Paul's Cathedral, which are in fact inspired by Borromini.

With Scott's *The Architecture of Humansim*, the other key work of 1914 which turned upside-down all recent notions of architectural history and development was Richardson's *Monumental Classic Architecture in Great Britain and Ireland during the 18th and 19th Centuries*. The whole picture of English architecture so carefully built up by Blomfield and his contemporaries was now reversed as in a mirror-image, so that the period they had most despised, the later eighteenth and early nineteenth centuries, was seen as the triumphant climax of the movement begun by Inigo Jones. According to this new assessment, the grand tradition of buildings represented by the work of Cockerell, Elmes, Pennethorne and Thomson had been wantonly destroyed by the nationalism of the Gothic Revival and of the Arts and Crafts Movement, so that it was left to Richardson and his generation to pick up the pieces and build a new and glorious classical future. Where his immediate predecessors and, indeed, many of his contemporaries, had been nationalist, Richardson was cosmopolitan so that he was able to refer with knowledgeable enthusiasm to the torch of classicism as kept alight by Duc, Hittorff and Labrouste in France, by Schinkel in Germany, and, in his own day, by McKim, Mead and White in North America. The tender vernacularism and sweet Englishry so beloved of authors like Macartney, Prior, and Lena Milman who saw in Wren 'the English clinging to comfort and homeliness... [and] the same tale of tenderness',[1] was ruthlessly scrapped in favour of admiration of what Richardson called the 'indescribable austerity and remoteness' of 'monumental architecture'.[2] Thus Richardson's stately folio, magnificently produced by Batsford, with its fine photographs and plans and its ravishing sepia plates, all devoted to the 'unfashionable' period from 1730-1880, can only be described as epoch-making. It would have been even more so, but for the impact of the First World War.

---

[1] *Sir Christopher Wren*, 1908, p.174.   [2] p.2.

Like Belcher and Blomfield, Richardson was primarily a practising architect, not an architectural historian, so that his books were similarly conceived as propaganda for a particular type of architecture. He was anxious to promote the kind of large-scale urban classicism that was reflected in his Regent Street Polytechnic, designed in 1907 with F.T. Verity in a Parisian style derived from Nénot, and in his neo-Cockerellian New Theatre at Manchester of 1910-12. It was clear to Richardson that the kind of scholarly expertise required to design classical buildings of this kind could not be obtained through the traditional English custom of pupilage in architects' offices which had been current throughout the Gothic Revival: what was needed was a full-blown system of architectural education based on schools of architecture, ideally attached to universities, and modelled on the fountain-head of academic classicism, the Ecole des Beaux-Arts in Paris. Thus it is no accident that a new generation of influential architects were all professors: Adshead and Reilly at Liverpool, Richardson and Simpson in London. Thanks largely to the efforts of these men, it really seemed by about 1912 that England was to be in the main stream of French and American classicism. From 1909 Stanley Adshead (1868-1946) was lecturer in civic design at Liverpool University and Professor in the same subject from 1912-14, thus holding the first university chair of town planning in England. The post had been created as a result of the initiative of Charles Reilly (1874-1948), who was professor of architecture from 1904-34 at Liverpool University in what was the first school of architecture in England. He was a great admirer of English, French and American classicism, and so put to good use the fact that the centre of Liverpool was dominated by Elmes and Cockerell's monumental classical masterpiece of the 1840s and 50s, St George's Hall. Indeed, he later wrote: 'I really think the measured drawings we published of St George's Hall were the beginning of the disproportionate influence of the little Liverpool School [of architecture]'.[1] In 1924 he published a monograph on *McKim, Mead and White*, the first book by an Englishman on American architecture. Of the great upholders of the Beaux-Arts tradition in America he wrote, 'the work of McKim,

---

[1] *Scaffolding in the Sky, a Semi-Architectural Autobiography*, 1938, p.119.

Mead and White will be found, I think, to be one of the great determining forces in the history of the architecture of our own time . . . and in England to-day and for the last ten years or more most of us have been consciously or unconsciously influenced by their work and outlook'. Reilly echoes that cosmopolitan note which we have already observed in Richardson when he claims that 'These noble, reticent buildings of McKim, Mead and White's express a universal spirit such as our present-day civilisation should do, even if it does not. They would be equally at home in London as in New York'.[1] Reilly's *Representative British Architects of the Present Day* (1931) was an idiosyncratic attempt to argue that England was in the forefront of the classical tradition though, rather curiously, it omitted Burnet and Holden.

In the meantime, Adshead had moved to London in 1915 to occupy the newly founded chair of town planning at the University College School of Architecture (the Bartlett), since 1903. Simpson prepared a huge scheme in 1914 for enlarging and completing Wilkins's buildings of the 1820s for University College in Gower Street. Of this he built only the School of Architecture and the Chemistry Building which cleverly blended Wilkins's Greek Revival style with simplified Beaux-Arts details. He was succeeded as Professor in 1919 by Richardson himself who remained there as a resolute defender of classicism until 1946.

The Architectural Review was an important vehicle for propagating a classical view of architecture in these years, and Richardson published in its pages a number of significant historical articles in the years immediately prior to 1914: for example, on Thomas Hope, on the Empire Style in England, on the Neo-Grec, on Krafft, on Hittorff, and on Duc's Palais de Justice in Paris.

In the chastened mood after the First World War the kind of optimism shown by Reilly and Richardson no longer seemed appropriate. Ironically, their ambitions for replanning England's towns and civic centres in a large austere style that would have been as at home in France or America was transferred to the proponents of the Modern Movement in Architecture. The schools of architecture, which men like Reilly had

[1] pp.7-8.

been so anxious to establish, were to play an important part in this process, because architectural education in a school, unlike that received in an office, tends to encourage a kind of doctrinaire paper architecture.

What seemed of immediate importance after 1918 was once more the recording and preserving of the English heritage of building in the face of new economic and social pressures. In 1919 the Church of England dropped a bombshell on the architectural world in the form of a Report of a Commission appointed by the Bishop of London, Dr Winnington Ingram, which proposed the demolition of nineteen city churches, including thirteen by Wren and others by architects such as Hawksmoor and both the Dances. The proposal to redevelop the valuable sites of these historic churches on the grounds that they were not pulling their weight was one of the most barbarous ever made by the Anglican church. Despite this, it took seven years of hard fighting before the measure was dropped. Individuals like Sir Reginald Blomfield, with help from *The Times* newspaper, and institutions like the National Trust, the London Survey Committee and the Society for the Protection of Ancient Buildings, kept the matter firmly before the public eye. Despite the public outcry the measure was carried by 71 votes to 54 in the House of Lords in July 1926, perhaps partly due to the influence of the Archbishop of Canterbury, Dr Randall Davidson, but was finally defeated in the following November in the House of Commons by 124 votes to 27. In the meantime, T.S. Eliot had immortalised the proposals in one of the memorable footnotes to *The Waste Land* of 1922. In otiose comment on his beautiful phrase, 'where the walls / of Magnus Martyr hold / Inexplicable splendour of Ionian white and gold', he wrote ironically, 'The interior of St. Magnus Martyr is to my mind one of the finest among Wren's interiors. (See *The Proposed Demolition of Nineteen City Churches*: P.S. King & Son, Ltd.)'.[1]

In the very year that the Wren churches were saved, the London County Council proposed the demolition of John Rennie's superb Waterloo Bridge of 1811-17. This Greek Doric masterpiece had featured prominently in Richardson's *Monumental Classic Architecture* just twelve years before and there is

[1] *Collected Poems, 1909-35*, 1936, p.81.

little doubt that this book had helped create a climate of opinion favourable to the preservation of a building in the neo-classical style. The demolition of Newgate Gaol in 1902 had similarly drawn attention to the merits of its then little-appreciated architect, the younger Dance; Blomfield published a valuable essay on Dance in *The Architectural Review* in 1904 which he reprinted the following year in his book, *Studies in Architecture*. Blomfield was again prominent in the campaign for preserving Waterloo Bridge, and thought he had achieved victory in June 1932 when the House of Commons refused to vote money for its demolition. However, the Labour majority on the London County Council, led by Herbert Morrison, were determined to flout the Conservative majority in the House of Commons, so that in the end the destroyers won. Work on building a new bridge from designs by Giles Gilbert Scott began in October 1937.

The rehabilitation of Neo-Classicism which had been set under way by Richardson was continued in the 1920s by a greater scholar than he, the architect Arthur Bolton (1865-1945), who was Curator of Sir John Soane's Museum from 1917 until his death. Bolton's researches, like those of Gotch, Blomfield and Richardson, went hand in hand with his architectural practice which was remarkably varied stylistically, ranging from Hurtwood of 1910, an extraordinary Tuscan villa in Surrey, via his Adam Room at the British Empire Exhibition at Wembley in 1924, to the neo-Empire facade he built in Duchess Street, off Portland Place. During Bolton's period of teaching at the Architectural Association School of Architecture, a student called John Swarbrick produced in 1902-3, perhaps at Bolton's suggestion, a Prize Essay on the work of the Adam brothers.[1] Batsford invited Swarbrick to write a book on this subject which appeared at an unpropitious time in 1915 under the title, *Robert Adam and his Brothers: their Lives, Work and Influence on English Architecture*. It is a dull and heavy-handed work which is nonetheless historically important as the first attempt at a documented monograph on this subject. The honour of having produced the first monograph goes to the popular and prolific

[1] *The Life, Work and Influence of Robert Adam and his Brothers. Reprinted from 'Architectural Association Notes',* 1903.

belletrist, Percy Fitzgerald, who produced the facile and chatty *Robert Adam, Artist and Architect: his Works and his System. The Substance of Lectures Delivered at the Society of Arts* ... (1904).[1] Adam particularly needed rescuing from Victorian censure because his ornamental approach to architectural design had deeply offended those two great pundits, Joseph Gwilt and James Fergusson. The generally uncensorious tone of the *History of Architecture* with which Gwilt prefaced his great *Encyclopaedia of Architecture* (1842, 6th ed. 1889) is unexpectedly interrupted by a vitriolic attack on the 'vicious taste of Robert Adam, a fashionable architect, whose eye had been ruined by the corruptions of the worst period of Roman art ... Yet such is the fact, the depraved compositions of Adam were not only tolerated but had their admirers'. His gateway at Syon is dismissed by Gwilt as 'disgraceful'.[2] Fergusson's *History of the Modern Styles of Architecture* (1862, 3rd ed. 1891), took its tone from Gwilt by claiming that the Adam brothers 'stamped their works with a certain amount of originality, which had it been of a better quality, might have done something to emancipate Art from its trammels. The principal characteristic of their style was the introduction of very large windows, generally without dressings ... They also designed Portland Place and Finsbury Square, in the latter of which their peculiar mode of fenestrations is painfully apparent'.[3]

The reassessment of Adam's genius begun by Fitzgerald and Swarbrick was magnificently continued by Arthur Bolton. Installed in the Soane Museum, he had easy access to the collection of nearly 9000 Adam drawings which Soane had acquired in 1833. Bolton put them to admirable use in his fully documented and lavishly illustrated book, *The Architecture of Robert and James Adam* (2 vols., 1922). Here indeed was handsome treatment for architects whose work Blomfield had described in 1897 as 'essentially a morbid development, evidence of the slow decay that was surely overtaking the once magnificent school of English architecture'. Bolton compared the denigration of the Adam style with the parallel denigration in the nineteenth

[1] See also his 'The Life and Work of Robert Adam', *Arch. Rev.*, VII, 1900, pp.147-56, 273-83, and VIII, 1900, 120-8.
[2] New ed., 1891, p.226.   [3] p.65.

century of the Perpendicular style, but he was able to claim that today 'we are beginning to realise that the last half of the eighteenth century, whatever may have been the case in Italy and France, was a great period in England'.[1] Drawing attention to the inaccessibility of much of Adam's domestic work he pointed out, interestingly, that 'Comparatively few people have ever seen a really first class Adam building inside and out'.[2]

Bolton had by now turned his attention to a far more unfashionable designer, John Soane, on whom he published a full and sensitive monograph in 1924, *The Works of Sir John Soane, R.A.* Again, Richardson had led the way when he described Soane ten years before as 'the most original architect of the eighteenth century'[3] in his *Monumental Classic Architecture.* In 1927 Bolton produced a fascinating anthology under the title, *The Portrait of Sir John Soane, R.A. (1753-1837) Set forth in Letters from his Friends (1775-1837)*, and in 1929 came his even more valuable edition of Soane's *Lectures on Architecture*, delivered at the Royal Academy from 1809-36. The *Lectures* was the last in the series of fourteen 'Publications of Sir John Soane's Museum' which were produced as a result of the tireless energy of Bolton in promoting knowledge of Soane.

From the early 1920s Bolton threw himself into the arduous task of editing, with H.D. Hendry, the *Transactions of the Wren Society* in twenty volumes (1923-45). This was a thorough and on the whole scholarly publication of original drawings and documents relating to Wren and his contemporaries. It must be regarded as one of the single most impressive contributions to English architectural history made in the twentieth century.

During the very period that Bolton was busy popularising Soane at the museum which bears his name, the Directors of the Bank of England were equally busy destroying his principal masterpiece. As Pevsner has rightly said, 'The virtual rebuilding of the Bank of England in 1921-37 is — in spite of the Second World War — the worst individual loss suffered by London architecture in the first half of the C20 ... It was the only work on the largest scale by the greatest English architect of about 1800 and one of the greatest in Europe'.[4] It seems that the

[1] I, p.vii.   [2] p.viii.   [3] p.41.
[4] *The Buildings of England, London*, I, 1973, p.182.

original intention of the Directors had been to retain Soane's top-lit Banking Halls in a new building, but that Baker persuaded them to adopt his own more grandiose scheme for their total replacement in a style derived from Soane.[1] As so often, the destruction of a major building served to draw the attention of the public to its merits. Thus in 1930 two architects, H. Rooksby Steele and F.R. Yerbury, published *The Old Bank of England, London*, an admirable and beautifully illustrated survey which reached a wider audience than Bolton's monograph on Soane of 1924.

One popular author who ought not to be entirely ignored is Edwin Beresford Chancellor (1868-1937) who was educated in Paris and at Christ Church, Oxford, and published over forty books, mostly on the topography of London, which helped create a climate sympathetic to eighteenth and early nineteenth-century architecture. One of the most attractive of them is *The Private Palaces of London, Past and Present* (1908), but he also published *The Lives of the British Architects from William of Wykeham to Sir William Chambers* (1909).

In 1924-6 Stanley Ramsey, who was in architectural partnership with Professor Stanley Adshead from 1912, edited nine volumes comprising a series called 'Masters of Architecture'. The subjects chosen for these slender monographs: Inigo Jones, Vanbrugh, Hawksmoor, Chambers, Soane, Bentley, Fischer von Erlach, Gabriel, and McKim, Mead and White, tend to reflect very clearly the new interest in a hard classical tradition which had been especially promoted by Richardson. The books vary in quality and their authors were mostly architects who looked to the classical past for practical guidance in the far from classical 1920s. We have already referred to Reilly's enthusiastic account of the lessons to be learned from McKim, Mead and White. H.V. Lanchester (1863-1953), of the partnership, Lanchester, Stewart and Rickards, wrote on the Austrian Baroque architect, Fischer von Erlach, whose work had inspired their magnificent municipal buildings at Cardiff and Deptford. The weakest in the series is that by Ramsey himself, on Inigo Jones, which simply reflects the cosy Englishry of the years round 1900. Ramsey can state, for example, that 'Of the two men, Palladio

[1] H. Baker, *Architecture and Personalities*, 1924, p.122.

and Inigo Jones, the latter was incomparably the greater architect',[1] and that in Wren's 'most ambitious projects, we find the
domestic or rural touch... Even St Paul's, in spite of its
grandeur, has an intimate and homely air'.[2] The best volume is
Goodhart-Rendel's pioneering monograph on Hawksmoor.
Here we find one of the most remarkable reversals of taste, for,
in Fergusson's *History of the Modern Styles of Architecture*, written in
1862 and republished as recently as 1891, the account of
Hawksmoor's St George-in-the-East, Stepney (1714-29), builds
up to the following climax: 'the term vulgar expresses more
correctly the effect produced than perhaps any other epithet
that could be applied to it';[3] and in Aymer Vallance's *The Old
Colleges of Oxford* (1912), Hawksmoor's work at All Souls is
similarly dismissed as 'a puerile caricature of the kind that only
brings the noble name of Gothic into contempt', and which 'it
would be uncharitable to judge too seriously as architecture'.[4]
Just twelve years later Goodhart-Rendel, in his first book, could
write: 'Hawksmoor's great superiority over his contemporaries,
then, lies in his greater consciousness than theirs of the emotional values of architectural forms'.[5] Goodhart-Rendel's sympathy for a Baroque architect, as well as the language in which
he conveys his admiration, doubtless owe something to Geoffrey
Scott. Goodhart-Rendel's exceptionally sensitive eye helped
him to become one of the most original writers about architecture in twentieth-century England, so that we shall need to
refer to him again.

Further support for this new interpretation of eighteenth-
century architecture now came from a young scholar, Geoffrey
Webb, who produced an important edition of Vanbrugh's
letters in 1928.[6] He ridiculed the Blomfieldian interpretation of
Wren in terms of a 'traditional', 'English', 'vernacular' style,
and instead, perhaps influenced by Richardson's book, emphasised that the importance of Wren lay in establishing a monumental classic architecture. Webb also looked to Geoffrey Scott
for support in defining the Baroque elements in Vanbrugh's
style, quoting from the perceptive description of Michelangelo

---

[1] p.10.   [2] p.19.   [3] II, p.54.   [4] p.48.   [5] p.17.
[6] This appeared as vol. IV of *The Complete Works of Sir John Vanbrugh*, ed. B.
Dobrée and G. Webb, 4 vols., 1926-8.

as a 'proto-Baroque' architect in Scott's articles on St Peter's in *Country Life* in 1926-7.

1928 also saw the publication of the first important monograph on Vanbrugh by H. Avray Tipping and the young Christopher Hussey (born 1899), *The Work of Sir John Vanbrugh and his School, 1699-1736*, which appeared as one of the volumes in the *Country Life* series of English Homes. The preface acknowledges a debt to Webb's edition of Vanbrugh's letters and also emphasises Vanbrugh's role as an originator of the Picturesque Movement in a way that makes it clear that Hussey, who had published his brilliant book on *The Picturesque* in 1927, had an important hand in writing it. The curious argument is also put forward in the preface that 'The Louis XIV, Napoleonic and the Great Wars seem to have led men to require a similar drama and turbulence in architecture and, accordingly, to a sympathy for the designs of this extraordinary genius [Vanbrugh]'. The direct influence of Geoffrey Scott can clearly be seen in the magnificent claim for Vanbrugh that 'Among the architects of humanism who have exalted the emotions and forms of life by their metamorphosis into forms of art he must be set on a level with Michelangelo and Bernini'.[1]

Another great admirer of Scott was Arthur Trystan Edwards (1884-1973), the author of *Sir William Chambers* (1924) which is the only remaining volume in Ramsey's Masters of Architecture series worthy of notice here. Edwards was a pupil of Reginald Blomfield and of Stanley Adshead at the Department of Civic Design at Liverpool, and it is interesting to note that his whole approach in this sensitive monograph — which quite sensibly concentrates almost exclusively on Somerset House — is conditioned by the destruction of Georgian London and its replacement by strident or pompous new commercial buildings, which was so appalling a feature of the 1920s. Thus Chambers is praised at Somerset House for 'making his building so extraordinarily suitable not only to its social purposes but to its natural environment': it 'is the typical river front building which has the humility and the degree of social spirit to line up to the river and to partake of the character of a simple wall emphasising the position of the bank... Chambers saw at a

[1] p.lxii.

glance that this was an occasion for restraint'.[1] What Edwards does not seem prepared to consider is that Chambers unlike, say, Gandon, may simply not have been up to the task of monumental composition on this scale.

It does not come as a surprise to learn that in the same year, 1924, Edwards published *Good and Bad Manners in Architecture, an Essay on Social Aspects of Civic Design.* The key chapter of the four contained in this popular little book was that devoted to the shameful demolition of Nash's Regent Street, which he described quite simply as 'the most beautiful street in the world'. Here, again, was a reversal of opinion, for, since Nash's death in 1835, he had been condemned for his 'sham' stucco by generations of architects who had been taught to believe in 'truth to materials'. Edwards must thus have especially enjoyed claiming that 'This question of stucco is a crucial one', and that 'Painted stucco is an ideal material for street architecture'.[2] The Regent Street saga is yet another example of the way in which the destruction, whether threatened or executed, of a building directs to it the sympathetic eye of both the architectural historian and the general public. Edwards subsequently claimed with some justice that 'This second chapter had a certain influence in creating what was known, for a number of years, as "the Regency cult". In my critical appreciation of the work of John Nash, I was perhaps the first to acclaim him as an architectural genius of the highest order'.[3]

In 1931 *Country Life* published an impressive volume on *Buckingham Palace, its Furniture, Decoration and History.* The bulk of the text was by H. Clifford Smith, but Christopher Hussey contributed the first two chapters which, despite the book's somewhat restrictive title, contained an admirable and fully documented account of the architectural history of the palace, the first scholarly description of a building by Nash.

In 1935 came the first monograph devoted to John Nash. It was by the thirty-one-year-old John Summerson, who was to become the leading architectural historian in England during the next forty years. Like all his work, the book is fully documented and beautifully written. To the disappointment of some of his admirers, Summerson has always been anxious to avoid being labelled as a preservationist. Also, though trained as an

---

[1] pp.9-11.　　[2] 1944 ed., pp.64-5.　　[3] ibid., p.vi.

architect under Richardson at Univeristy College London, he came to believe in the virtues of the Modern Movement in architecture and was one of the first modern architectural historians whose study of past architectural styles was not conditioned by a wish to see them emulated in present-day architecture. He has thus been at pains to dissociate the origin of his interest in Nash from Trystan Edwards's nostalgia for the old Regent Street. His book on Nash, he affirms, was due both to his chance discovery on the Isle of Wight in 1932 of a portfolio of designs by Nash and the Reptons, and also to his being unemployed at the time. So far is he anxious to remove himself from any suspicions of real sympathy for Nash that he describes on the last page of his book how, recently, 'a noble ghost, a fiction of elegance, dignity, and urbanity, rose from the ruins of Regent Street, and to-day the name of Nash is accorded more honour than his contemporaries would have believed possible'.[1] The disappointment caused by Summerson's detached tone was expressed by the reviewer of the book in *The Architectural Review* for May 1935, who complained that with his 'deliberate understatements... Mr. Summerson has stressed nothing'. The reviewer's concern to give practical application to architectural history was emphasised in his concluding sentence where, deploring 'the chaos of modern Regent Street', he claimed that 'If today there were an architect living of anything like Nash's calibre, the great problem of the epoch, the housing problem, would be as good as solved'.[2]

In the year of Trystan Edwards's *Good and Bad Manners*, 1924, a very similar book called *The Pleasures of Architecture* was published by the extrovert architect, Clough Williams-Ellis (1883-1978) and his wife, Amabel. This was intelligent and attractive propaganda for a modern *Beggar's Opera* type of classicism, civilised and gentle. It was also extremely popular. Clough Williams-Ellis became increasingly alarmed at the degradation of the English scene by ribbon-development, bungalows, petrol-stations, badly-designed signs and advertising. The result was a polemical little book, *England and the Octopus* (1928), which alerted many to a problem to which no satisfactory solution has yet been found.

Polemics were the order of the day, and the 1930s, though

[1] p.276.   [2] LXXVII, 1935, p.222.

rich in architectural journalism, were a lean time for architectural history. *The Architectural Review*, elegant, stylish, amusing and influential, played an important part in the 1930s both
in popularising the Modern Movement and in creating opposition to the demolition of Georgian buildings. In 1934-5 Osbert
Lancaster published an entertaining series of articles on the
architectural decline of an imaginary seaside resort, in which he
developed the theme of *England and the Octopus*. These formed
the basis of his book, *Progress at Pelvis Bay* of 1936. In the
following year Robert Byron (1905-41) published an equally
devastating article in *The Architectural Review* under the title
'How We Celebrate the Coronation'. This surveyed the range of
superb classical buildings in London which had recently been
demolished or were under threat of demolition: Carlton House
Terrace; Pembroke House, Whitehall Gardens; houses in
Abingdon Street; All Hallows, Lombard Street; Waterloo
Bridge; the Adelphi; Sir Joseph Banks's house in Soho Square;
Sir Joshua Reynolds's house in Leicester Square; Kingston
House, Kensington Gore; Chesterfield, Devonshire, and Dor-
chester Houses; one side of Bedford Square; and Munster
Square. Byron was not afraid to point the finger of accusation at
the guilty parties: 'The Church; the Civil Service; the Judicial
Committee of the Privy Council; the hereditary landlords; the
political parties; the London County Council; the local coun-
cils; the great business firms; the motorists; the heads of the
national Museum — all are indicted'.[1]

How We Celebrate the Coronation was also published as a
pamphlet in 1937 by the Architectural Press, publishers of *The
Architectural Review*. Earlier that year Robert Byron and Lord
Rosse had founded the Georgian Group in the hope of calling a
halt to further widespread destruction. Educated at Eton and
Oxford, Byron was a dynamic and bizarre figure in the fashionable intellectual world which had originally been associated
with the name of Harold Acton at Oxford in the 20s. He became
a passionate enthusiast for Byzantine civilization, publishing on
that subject *The Station, Athos: Treasures and Men* (1928) and *The
Byzantine Achievement* (1929). Later his interests extended further
east, and his last book, *The Road to Oxiana* (1937), recorded his

[1] LXXXI, 1937, p.223.

travels in Perisa and Afghanistan in search of the origins of Islamic art. In the meantime he had published a short book of aesthetics, *The Appreciation of Architecture* (1932) and a superb account of Lutyens's buildings at New Delhi in *The Architectural Review*.[1] From 1932, in which year the Commissioners for Crown Lands announced their intention of demolishing Carlton House Terrace, he played a prominent role in the campaign to preserve what was Nash's principal surviving contribution to the urban scene in London. It was from the circle of those fighting for the preservation of Carlton House Terrace that the first members of the Georgian Group were drawn. Most unfortunately for Sir Reginald Blomfield's reputation as the grand old man of English classicism, it was, ironically, his schemes for replacing Nash's stucco terraces with a monumental pile of Portland stone, that Byron and his friends were attacking. One portion of his vast plan, no. 4, Carlton Gardens, was in fact constructed from 1934 in which year he published *Modernismus*, a withering attack on modern architecture. Unfortunately, Blomfield's arguments were not especially clever or coherent and the book has never been well regarded. It was perhaps unwise of him to attack two such very different and esteemed books as Geoffrey Scott's *The Architecture of Humanism* and Manning Robertson's *Laymen and the New Architecture* (1925). However, he made some good points: for example, his criticism that concrete, 'unlike brick and stone, becomes more ugly every year of its life. In cities its surface soon becomes intolerable. If it is smooth, the effect is greasy, and if rough, indescribably squalid';[2] he also sensibly condemns a certain modern view of architecture which postulates 'a new world in which collectivism is to take the place of individualism, and architecture will grow of itself, because form will no longer be a matter of considered design so much as a spontaneous development from what is supposed to be the purpose of the building and the nature of the materials employed'.[3]

By a curious irony, Blomfield's best-known design is that for the electricity grid pylon. However, *Modernismus* failed because it was written by the wrong man at the wrong moment. Those with influence in the architectural world were now interested

[1] LXIX, 1931, pp.1-30.   [2] p.77.   [3] pp.69-70.

both in the history and the preservation of Georgian architecture, and were often also admirers of the Modern Movement like P. Morton Shand who was an influential contributor to *The Architectural Review* at this time. Typical was John Betjeman (born 1906), best-known of the group of architectural journalists and polemicists of the 1930s. In 1933 he founded a series of illustrated county histories called the Shell Guides. These were expressly intended to counteract the antiquarian and mediaeval stance of the Little Guides by drawing attention to the merits of Georgian and early Victorian architecture, and to the evils of over-restoration. In the same year, aged twenty-six, he published *Ghastly Good Taste, or a Depressing Story of the Rise and Fall of English Architecture*, an entertaining if puzzling book. It is marked by a dichotomy between the 'Englishry', in precisely the Blomfieldian sense, with which much of it is informed, and the praise of the latest Bauhaus modernism, which is the climax of the book. He can thus write: 'Do not despise the English Sunday. When it is gone, like the elegant terrace or the simple brick house in the High Street, it will be missed. Sunday is sacred to Protestantism, and Protestantism purified our architecture';[1] he can claim, like T.G. Jackson, that architecture must be unselfconscious, but can also state that James Gibbs, who placed the classical Radcliffe Camera in the heart of a Gothic setting, 'would also have had the courage to build today as sincere an essay in modern materials in its place'.[2] The same combination of preservationism and modernity is expressed even more forcefully in his pamphlet of 1939 on *Antiquarian Prejudice*. Attacking the buildings of his day for exemplifying 'the timidity miscalled "tradition" but really antiquarianism, which enslaves be-knighted architects', he urged architects to imitate the example of Soviet Russia in producing 'an honest, plain structure of steel, glass and/or reinforced concrete'.[3]

This is clearly not the voice of the Betjeman who has found so central a place in the warm heart of the British public in the 1960s and 70s. Something happened in the Second World War to change his outlook.

[1] p.63   [2] p.58.   [3] pp.16-17.

3 The Second World War

The fashionable enthusiasm for Soviet Russia of progressive intellectuals in the 1930s became enforced as the national orthodoxy following this country's alliance with Stalin in 1941. For five years the country was flooded with pro-Soviet propaganda in which, stimulated by the language of 'total reconstruction', *The Architectural Review* was associated with a general campaign in which the need to rebuild bomb-damaged buildings was somehow confused with a desire to build a new collectivist society and to replace all nineteenth-century urban housing with blocks of flats. In January 1943 Finsbury Borough Council, who had commissioned the celebrated Health Centre from Lubetkin in 1937, could erect a monument to Lenin in Holford Square from designs by the same architect.[1] In 1941 John Summerson, generally so careful to avoid committing himself to anything, published an essay called 'The new Ground-work of Architecture', which was twice reprinted during the course of the war. It was written in the belief that 'the change in the world-outlook for architecture is so deep, so fundamental', that all traditions have to be abandoned: 'This loose bondage to the past is usually called "tradition". It is architectural Toryism. It is the Royal Academy point of view. It is the line of least resistance, defended, like other Tory lines, by platitudes, catch-phrases, and every form of easy lip-service — everything but clear thought'.[2] He writes that 'Today we are, I hope, not interested in accumulating vast family fortunes and cresting them with expensive frills. Certainly we do not want to be artificial... The architecture of today must be the architecture not of a class but of the community itself. The need for parade vanishes. We are rediscovering architectural beauties deeper and subtler than any which the fourteenth or eighteenth centuries knew, but of which the Greeks had, perhaps, more than a glimpse'.[3]

As well as creating a climate of opinion which helped ensure the return of a Labour government in 1945 and the accompany-

---

[1] See *The Architects' Journal*, 21 January, 1943, p.48.
[2] A.F. Scott, ed., *Modern Essays, 1939-41*, 1942, pp.22-3.
[3] pp.26-7.

ing period of 'post-war reconstruction', the war was also bound
to create a counter-reaction in favour of the preservation of all
those deeply English and traditional things which it was supposed that a German victory, unlike a Soviet alliance, would
necessarily destroy. Thus, in terms of architectural history a
new lease of life was given to the veneration of 'the English
tradition' which we investigated at the start of this chapter.
Harry Batsford and his nephew, Brian Cook, had already
launched their 'The British Heritage Series' and 'The Face of
Britain Series' before the war. Messrs Collins now produced
their 'Britain in Pictures' series, which eventually contained
over 100 titles, published during and shortly after the war. It
included John Betjeman's *English Cities and Small Towns*, Edmund Blunden's *English Villages*, Vita Sackville-West's *English
Country Houses*, and John Piper's *British Romantic Artists*. Here
was a celebration of the English achievement, of the national
heritage and way of life, which was implicitly bound up with the
war effort. An architectural parallel at government level was
the establishment in February 1941 in the face of extensive
bomb damage of the National Buildings Record with the aim of
providing a complete photographic survey of historic buildings.
It operated during the war from All Souls College, Oxford,
under the direction of Walter Godfrey and John Summerson.
What began as a war-time exercise soon became an essential
tool for architectural historians, and today, renamed the
National Monuments Record, it comprises over a million
photographs. In 1942 Summerson published in collaboration
with J.M. Richards *The Bombed Buildings of Britain*. Richards
(born 1907), who had been a member of the staff of *The
Architectural Review* from 1935 and was an admirer of the social
reconstruction carried out in Soviet Russia, published in 1940
An Introduction to Modern Architecture, a slim Penguin volume
which was soon to be found in the pockets of all those anxious to
Build a Better Britain. But Richards's wartime absence from
England made him nostalgic for the old country so that,
forgetting the charms of all those health centres and penguin
pools that had appealed to the young in heart, he published in
1946 *The Castles on the Ground*. This brilliant and beautiful
account of the cosy delights of English suburbia represented a

turning-point equivalent to the one which is evident in the career of John Betjeman.

Sensitively illustrated by John Piper, *The Castles on the Ground* was an exercise in nostalgia which sought to recreate a golden period identified with the English middle class. Its publication had been preceded by a few months by a very different book which identified a similarly golden world with the upper class: Evelyn Waugh's *Brideshead Revisited* (December 1944). As Waugh explained in 1959 in the preface of the revised edition, it was originally written in 'a bleak period of present privation and threatening disaster — the period of Soya beans and Basic English', and at a time when 'It was impossible to foresee . . . the present cult of the English country house. It seemed then that the ancestral seats which were our chief national artistic achievement were doomed to decay and spoliation like the monasteries in the sixteenth century. So I piled it on rather'.[1] Brideshead Castle is indeed the country house to end all country houses, a rich and impossible amalgam dominated by a dome by Inigo Jones and containing a Baroque tapestry-hung hall, a Chinese drawing room, a Pompeiian parlour, a Soanesque library and an art nouveau chapel. *Brideshead Revisited* was nonetheless a powerfully influential and popular novel which helped create an atmosphere that was receptive to the kind of popular architectural history of which much was published by Batsford and is especially associated with the names of Sacheverell Sitwell and James Lees-Milne. Prevented from indulging in his usual travels, Sitwell (born 1897), spent the war at Weston Hall, Northamptonshire, where he devoted the time not spent in the service of the Home Guard to writing *British Architects and Craftsmen*. Finished in 1943 though not published until spring 1945, this popular book had been through four editions by 1948. Sitwell later confirmed[2] that it had been written with a view to preventing further needless destruction of historic buildings. It can be seen as an architectural parallel to *Brideshead Revisited* with its heady nostalgic introduction which is similarly a reaction against the realities and the propaganda of the war:

[1] 1960 ed., pp.9-10.   [2] In the preface to the rev. ed. of 1960.

It is of no use now, when we have come so far, to argue that the past was contemptible for its illiteracy, or for its legal use of torture. For there are the prisons and the concentration camp, and we know how minds can be perverted by mass-education. We know, too, that standards of life were improving before the war, but have we not lost in other ways as much as we have gained? Can we get it back again? Is not the life of the individual in our large towns, near the cinema and the fried-fish shop, with the air-raid shelter opposite, hideous and shameful compared with that of any savage? Is our's to be a world only of dog-races and the cup-final? When we consider the spiritual values in our council houses, should we not envy the Papuan and the black fellow of the Torres Straits? The golden age is dying even now, before our eyes, among the Stone Men of Malekula and the dancers of Orokolo. In New Guinea our steel birds drop their bombs among the birds of paradise, and the blessings of civilization have been brought to the built-up terraces of the living Stone Age. Let us consider, rather, our own glorious past and draw profit from it for the future.[1]

Sitwell's search for the essence of Englishry was identical with that of the Edwardians we saw at the beginning of this chapter. To him all the riches of English architecture 'have to the full, our national habit of reticence or self-effacement', and he claimed that 'We are looking in these pages for the link joining Hampton Court Palace of red brick and Portland stone, with the humble mariners' almshouses or hospital at Old Yarmouth, with its flag pole in front of it; for the connection between St Paul's Cathedral and any Methodist chapel or Quaker meeting house; for the secret shared, in common, by the Painted Hall at Greenwich Hospital, and the print of a bluejacket, "penny plain and twopence coloured", in the window of the toy shop at Hoxton. We are searching for the national genius, expressed in architecture and its lesser arts'.[2]

The career of James Lees-Milne (born 1908) expresses very effectively the creative preoccupation with the fate of the country-house which has dominated and formed a whole branch of architectural history from the war onwards. Educated at Eton and Magdalen College, Oxford, Lees-Milne joined the staff of the National Trust in 1936; in 1941, having been discharged from the army for health reasons, he became

[1] p.1.   [2] p.10.

responsible for dealing with the many owners of historic houses who, rightly or wrongly, were coming increasingly to feel that the only way of preserving them would be to hand them over to the National Trust. His two volumes of diaries covering the years 1942-5, published as *Ancestral Voices* (1975) and *Prophesying Peace* (1977), constitute one of the most entertaining of all by-paths in recent architectural history. They reveal the author's profound detachment from Churchill's war aims which, if publicly expressed at the time, might almost have landed him in internment. Lees-Milne was one of those who saw that the only ultimate victors in the war would be the Communists and socialists. As a Catholic of pacifist outlook who was shocked by our policy of unconditional surrender, he did not feel especially committed to the preservation of the English political establish-ment, and in 1944 he recorded with interest the anti-Catholic sentiments of the then Duke of Devonshire who complained that 'Papists owe a divided allegiance. They put God before their country'.[1] In the age of egalitarianism that was being ushered in by wartime propaganda, Lees-Milne's devotion to the country house was bound to have political overtones; and since the war it has indeed been difficult for the architectural historian who is concerned with, and may be primarily inspired by, preserva-tion, to keep politics out of architecture. We can see the implica-tions of this in some of Lees-Milne's own post-war books: *The Age of Adam* (1947), *Tudor Renaissance* (1951) and *The Age of Inigo Jones* (1953), all published by Batsford. The prefaces to the first two of these have an apocalyptic war-time tone: in *The Age of Adam* we are reminded of the wholesale destruction of our historic buildings by 'bishops, aldermen and captains of com-merce' before the war and by Hitler during it: thus today, 'while we are still allowed by those little subfusc men at West-minster to retain a semblance of our native sanity, we may yet soothe our minds — starved like our bellies — in nostalgic reflections upon that earlier, less progressive age, when politics was a game, society an art and art a religion. And so our last solace is to let our minds drift, as often as they may, upon delicious tides of retrogression, away from the present quagmire of existence, towards the quickened elegance of eighteenth-

[1] *Prophesying Peace*, 1977, p.94.

century living'.[1] *Tudor Renaissance*, dedicated to Michael and Anne Rosse — Lord Rosse was a founder of the Georgian Group and its chairman from 1946-68 — contained in its preface a special emphasis on the ever-increasing threat to the survival of the country house:

Of the three hundred or so greatest English country houses still in private occupation in 1939, I calculate that today less than a third, perhaps just a quarter, are inhabited by the families of their former possessors. Their fate, and indeed that of the remainder (now mostly depleted of their furniture and works of art), can easily be foreseen, unless drastic measures are immediately taken to stave it off — by the Government. Thus we are faced with the absurd paradox that only the instrument of these monuments' destruction can now be turned to their salvation.[2]

It should not be thought that the interest in architectural history stimulated by the war was expressed only in terms of the country house. For example, the following books were all published during or immediately after the war in the period 1944-8: A.H. Gardner, *Outline of English Architecture*, T.D. Atkinson, *Local Style in English Architecture*, F.H. Crossley, *English Church Design, 1040-1540 A.D.*, A. Needham, *How to Study an Old Church*, John Harvey, *Henry Yevele 1320-1400, the Life of an English Architect* and *Gothic England, a Survey of National Culture 1300-1550*, Katharine Esdaile, *English Church Monuments, 1510-1840*, Marcus Whiffen, *Stuart and Georgian Churches outside London, 1603-1837*, John Summerson, *Georgian London*, Donald Pilcher, *The Regency Style*, Antony Dale, *Fashionable Brighton, 1820-1860*, Ralph Dutton, *The English Interior, 1500-1900*, and Martin Briggs, *Men of Taste, from Pharaoh to Ruskin*. Messrs Batsford, who, in gravely inconvenient circumstances, published all but two of the books in this list have thereby put the country greatly in their debt. However, an interesting sidelight on the history of taste is revealed by the fact that in 1947 the firm refused to publish the final chapter of Martin Briggs's book which consisted of an account of Hitler and Mussolini as patrons of art and architecture. Though Briggs claimed that his study was 'perfectly cool and impartial', Batsford argued that its publication would be 'injudicious in the climate of opinion then prevail-

[1] p.v.   [2] p.v.

ing'.[1] This climate of opinion did not, incidentally, prevent *The Architectural Review* from publishing in the same year an interesting article contributed by three leading architects from Soviet Russia under the title, 'Reconstruction in the U.S.S.R.'[2]

Apart from Summerson, the most distinguished of this group of authors who were publishing books in the years 1944-8 is John Harvey (born 1911). He writes as an architect, trained by his father and by Sir Herbert Baker, and in his first book, *Henry Yevele* (1944), which must be the first full-length biography of an English mediaeval architect, explains that he is 'advocating the study of the fourteenth century as a means of solving the problems of the twentieth, and especially the architectural problems'. He believes that Gothic, as the true national style, ought to be revived, but not in the spirit of the Victorian Gothic Revival because 'The nineteenth century was less fitted to understand Gothic life than any period for some fifteen hundred years'.[3] He thus disapproves not only of the Gothic Revival but of the entire classical tradition in English architecture, describing in truly Puginian language how from the sixteenth century

The disruptive results of artistic dictation by the dead hand of classic Rome soon became apparent, and architectural invention tended to disappear, giving place to the monotonous game of piecing together bits of the classic orders in new ways, an occupation worthy of some mechanical contrivance designed in the Academy of Lagado, rather than of the human brain. The Roman Renaissance imposed a terrible handicap on architectural genius, hardly to be surmounted by a Wren, but regret for past mistakes is useless; only the production of a genuine national architecture could be accepted as a proof of 'true repentance', and for such a proof it is never too late.[4]

In 1950 Harvey produced the first general survey in English of Gothic architecture throughout Europe, *The Gothic World 1100-1600, a Survey of Architecture and Art*. It is a fascinating study with an interpretation distinctly reminiscent of Worringer's in which vast antitheses are drawn between Mediterranean man

---

[1] *Men of Taste*, 1947, pp.vi-vii. Extracts from the offending chapter were published in *The Builder*, CLXIV, 1943, pp.86-7, and CLXVIII, 1945, pp.350-1, where they were advertised as forming part of the forthcoming *Men of Taste*.

[2] CI, 1947, pp.177-84.   [3] p.vi.   [4] p.76.

and 'the northern soul'.[1] Harvey's *Gothic England, a Survey of National Culture 1300-1550* (1947) is an exercise in cultural history which draws on all the resources of rhetoric and scholarship to present a persuasive and heady account of mediaeval architecture, sculpture, painting, music, poetry, cookery and social life. He does not hesitate to present the whole development in culturally holistic terms in which every phenomenon is seen as an inevitable reflection of something else: 'The same feeling pervades the whole of the social life of the age: at a time when a salad had fourteen ingredients apart from its dressing, how many forms of decoration might be found in a chapel?'[2] Religion, curiously, tends to be omitted from this great cultural package, and remains a subject about which Harvey is somewhat cool: 'The Church was heavily handicapped by being irrevocably committed in theory to the whole Bible; in the days of its greatest power it could have made its position practically impregnable had it been able without loss of face to jettison the Old Testament'.[3] An analogy with Worringer, which we have noted above, is again suggested by Harvey's underplaying of religion. For Worringer, 'the Christian system always remained merely a substitute for the form which Northern man could not previously create by his own energy. There could therefore be no question of an absolutely complete absorption into Christianity'.[4] Whereas Pugin, whose approach Harvey's at many points resembles, interpreted the forms of Gothic as an expression of the truths of Christianity, Harvey sees them as Blomfield might have done, as dependent on deep and permanent traits in the English character: 'Much that is fundamental in English character and temperament was then essentially what it is now',[5] and 'This extraordinary national spirit is not confined to the Gothic age, it is found before and since'.[6]

These early books of Harvey's were written against the background of the war with its barbarisms, privations and emphasis on national endeavour. His approach is thus coloured by an understandable reaction against the realities of life in the mid-1940s in favour of an escape to a sun-lit Gothic past, and by

---

[1] p.130.   [2] p.154.   [3] p.12.
[4] *Form in Gothic*, 1927 ed., pp.86-7.
[5] p.vii.   [6] p.8.

an equally understandable reaction against the bleakness of modern architecture which he singles out for special attack in *Henry Yevele*. We have noted similar kinds of reactions in the work of those who, unlike Harvey, were not primarily scholars: Sacheverell Sitwell, James Lees-Milne and Evelyn Waugh. However, Harvey's architectural interpretation on the basis of 'Englishry' sets him apart from authors like Waugh and Lees-Milne who, as Catholics, were less likely to be attracted by the worship which we have described as 'the religion of England'. It would indeed be culturally difficult for Catholics to accept belief in the presence of permanent traits in the English character because that would seem to imply acceptance of the most characteristic expression of that belief, the national Protestant church established in the sixteenth century as an attempt, necessarily temporal, to create a church coterminous with the nation.

The nationalist interpretation still finds a place in Harvey's recent study, *The Perpendicular Style 1330-1485* (1978). One of the reasons for his especial praise of this style is that he sees it as the expression of a political and social system which he admires, and which lasted 'until the tragic end of the Plantagenet dynasty in 1485'. He argues that 'The success or failure of individual sovereigns, politically speaking, was reflected in the vicissitudes of the style. Perpendicular was an art expressing to the full the national form taken by the aspirations of the ruling dynasty'. It was also a direct consequence of the national character: 'Its shapes were mostly straightforward and could be made to appeal to the commonsense strain in the English character. It might have been in response to this practical attitude that in the period of the style the typical steeple lost its pointed spire and became a square tower, bluntly shaking an English fist into the sky'.[1] He also explains that 'The reaction away from Curvilinear and the artistic licence which was its logical outcome lay in fundamental traits of the English character, full of practical common-sense'.[2]

It is thus possible to see Harvey's approach as involving the invocation of a kind of Churchillian Protestantism as a permanent feature of the English character, and reading it back

[1] pp.18-19.   [2] p.159.

into the Catholic Middle Ages as an explanation of Perpendicular. But whether this account of his approach be just or no, it is not the essence of his truly remarkable achievement as an architectural historian. This rests rather with his *English Mediaeval Architects, a Biographical Dictionary down to 1550* (1954) which we shall consider in the next chapter.

A welcome feature of the late 1940s and early 1950s was the series of 'Architectural Biographies' and 'Introductions to Architecture', the latter edited by Hugh Casson, which were published by Art & Technics Ltd. The Biographies were especially successful, including excellent studies of Soane by John Summerson, Holland by Dorothy Stroud, and Archer by Marcus Whiffen. The idea of publishing these miniature monographs with barely fifty pages of text each was an admirable one which ought to be revived. The sister series of 'Introductions' was less successful though it contained attractive volumes on *Tudor* by John Harvey, *Georgian* by Albert Richardson, and *Regency* by Paul Reilly.

In the next chapter we must leave this comfortable English world and return to the 1930s to investigate the consequences of the arrival in this country of exiled art historians following the rise to power of Hitler.

V
The Establishment of Art History

1 The Impact of Germany

Most of the architectural history which has concerned us in the previous chapter was written by English gentlemen, many of whom were also architects and who generally came from privileged backgrounds. Since historical and architectural scholarship was rarely the central activity of their careers, their writings were prompted by a desire to serve a variety of ends: notably the enrichment of their own architectural practice, or the cause of preservation. It is with no wish to denigrate the very real merits and charms of this tradition to say that by continental, especially German, standards it looked extremely amateurish. Though they had generally been expensively educated at public schools and at the colleges of Oxford and Cambridge, these authors had not acquired any formal training in their subject for the simple reason that it was not taught in any schools or universities. However, the concept of 'art history', as used in the title of this chapter, would imply to a German a professional scholar who had been taught art history as an intellectual discipline in a university, and who had led a life dedicated to this subject and to no other. The first steps to establishing this pattern in England were the founding of the Courtauld Institute of Art in 1932, and the arrival of the Warburg Library in the following year. These two institutions had very different origins and characters and it was simply an historical accident, the rise to power of Hitler, that brought them together in a cross-fertilisation of the greatest consequence for the development of architectural history in this country.

The Courtauld Institute was founded as a result of the endeavours of Viscount Lee of Fareham (1868-1947) and his friend Sir Samuel Courtauld (1876-1947), the industrialist and

collector who for twenty-five years was the Chairman of
Courtaulds Ltd. Courtauld had formed a magnificent collection of French Impressionist paintings which he hung in his
superb house, no. 20, Portman Square, a beautifully restored
Adam mansion. This became 'a great London centre for the arts
of painting and music'[1] and, after his wife's death in December
1931, he gave it to London University to be a school of
appreciation and understanding of the arts in which teachers
would be trained and a wider audience stimulated by public
lectures. His proposals were united with the scheme for endow-
ing a Chair in the History of Art at London University which
had been initiated in 1928 by Lord Lee in conjunction with Sir
Joseph (later Lord) Duveen and Sir Martin Conway. Lee, who
had been Minister of Agriculture and First Lord of the Admiral-
ty, had already given Chequers Court, with its collections, to
the nation as a home for the Prime Minister. He was now bent
on giving his extremely catholic collection of pictures to London
University where it could play a teaching role analogous to that
of the Fogg Collection at Harvard.

A committee was set up including Sir Martin Conway and Sir
Robert Witt, who both owned superb collections of photo-
graphs which they intended giving to any future Department of
History of Art, Lord Lee, Professor Albert Richardson, Profes-
sor Ernest Gardner and Henry Tonks. The munificence of
Samuel Courtauld soon made their proposals a reality: W. G.
Constable, who specialised in the history of Italian and English
eighteenth-century art, was the first Director of the Courtauld
Institute, a post which carried with it a Chair of History of Art in
London University; and James Mann (1897-1963), whose special subject was the history of armour, was Deputy Director and
Reader in History of Art. But there the difficulties began. The
absence of any kind of accepted English tradition into which
such an Institute could fit necessarily caused frictions. Courtauld, as a rich collector who wanted the general public to share
his enthusiasms, tended to be impatient of the characteristic
caution and reserve of the academic approach; in some traditional academic quarters art history was not thought sufficiently
serious as a scholarly discipline; others, notably John Betjeman,

---

[1] Obituary of Courtauld by T.S.R. Boase in *Burl. Mag., XC, 1948, p.29.*

thought it too serious by half; there was also a world of art connoisseurship, associated with the *Burlington Magazine*, which tended to regard with mild suspicion this new intrusion into their territory of an historical and academic approach. The character of the *Burlington Magazine*, however, was complex and it should by no means be regarded as wholly hostile to the Courtauld Institute. Described by Summerson as 'one of the milestones on the road from Connoisseurship to Art History',[1] the magazine had been founded in 1903 partly as a result of the efforts of Roger Fry (1866-1934), England's first professional art historian in a German or Berensonian sense. It was intended as a counterpart to the *Gazette des Beaux-Arts* or the *Repertorium für Kunstwissenschaft*, but immediately encountered grave financial difficulties and was only saved by Fry's tour of America from November 1904 when he persuaded prominent collectors, such as Pierpont Morgan, to provide generous endowment. Fry was co-editor with Sir Lionel Cust from 1909-19. A somewhat ambiguous welcome was given to the Courtauld Institute in an editorial of December 1930, and the same issue carried a warmer welcome in the form of a letter from Roger Fry. In an editorial of September 1937 Herbert Read published anonymously what Lord Lee described as 'a mean and sneering attack on the Courtauld Institute in general, and its new Director, Tom Boase . . . in particular'.[2] Disappointed at not getting the Directorship himself, Read took advantage of the occasion to expose to public gaze the academic and personal difficulties the Institute was encountering in its early years. W.G. Constable, who was described by Lord Lee as 'consumed with personal ambition [which] swelled and festered into an almost insane jealousy of anyone who held any other comparable post',[3] was succeeded as Director in 1937 by T.S.R. Boase whose qualifications were not immediately apparent. Herbert Read had witheringly written of Boase that 'His name is unknown to the world of art studies, but his researches into the history of the mediaeval Papacy have no doubt given him a methodical and scholarly

---

[1] *What is a Professor of Fine Art?*, University of Hull, 1961, p.11.
[2] A. Clark, ed., *'A Good Innings', the Private Papers of Viscount Lee of Fareham*, 1974, p.340. (First published 1939 in a privately printed edition of 10 copies.)
[3] *ibid.*, p.321.

mind which should be of great value in the administration of an institution which must in future pretend to learning or lose all public respect. The appointment will surprise our foreign colleagues, who are not familiar with our English eccentricity in such matters'.[1]

The attack naturally drew forth a response from Lord Lee who defended both Boase and the Institute in the October issue of the *Burlington Magazine*, although the December issue contained letters supporting Herbert Read's views from Ellis Waterhouse and David Talbot Rice. We have spent a little time with the early years of the Courtauld Institute because its teething troubles show very clearly how alien a subject art history was at that time in this country. In the meantime its importance had been eclipsed by that of the Warburg Institute. The tradition of Anglo-American connoisseurship which was variously reflected in the founding of both the *Burlington Magazine* and the Courtauld Institute was revitalised by the dramatic arrival in 1933 of Fritz Saxl with the entire Warburg Library, of Rudolf Wittkower, of Nikolaus Pevsner and, three years later, of Ernst Gombrich. Saxl (1890-1948), who was already in close contact with Aby Warburg by 1910, studied under Dvořák in Vienna and Wölfflin in Berlin. Like Erwin Panofsky, he followed a line from Hegel and Riegl, rather than from Wölfflin, which encouraged him to study the transformations of classical themes as expressive of different philosophies. One of the fundamental questions which Warburg had taught him to ask was how men in the Renaissance interpreted the Gods which they depicted in their art, and how their interpretations differed from those of antique artists and also those of artists in the post-Winckelmann era. Saxl became Warburg's assistant in Hamburg in 1913 and played a large part in turning Warburg's immense and ever expanding private library into a scholarly institute. Warburg had begun building up a library in 1886 of books relating, however remotely, to the survival of the classical tradition. During Warburg's illness in 1920-24, Saxl had been in charge of both the Library and the Institute, and following Warburg's death in 1929 became first Director of the Warburg Institute. In 1933, in the face of discrimination against Jews, Edgar Wind

---

[1] *Burl. Mag.*, LXXI, 1937, p.108.

(1900-71), a member of the staff of the Institute since 1928, came to England to negotiate with London University on the Institute's behalf; in the same year, with the financial and moral assistance of Lord Lee, Samuel Courtauld and the Warburg family in America, the Warburg Institute arrived by ship in London from Hamburg. The extraordinary cargo consisted of six scholars, 60,000 books in six hundred boxes, a quantity of iron shelving as well as reading desks, book-binding and photographic apparatus. These scholars were, of course, acutely conscious that their ways of thought were as foreign to the English as the languages — mainly German and Italian — in which the books in their library were written. Nonetheless, the experiment worked: in Saxl's words, 'The arrival of the Institute coincided with the rising interest in British education in the study of the visual documents of the past. The Warburg Institute was carried by this wave, and its methods of studying the works of art as an expression of an age appealed to some younger scholars. A number of German refugees who had not belonged to its staff became its collaborators and enlarged the contact with English scholars'.[1] In 1936 the University of London agreed to house the Institute, but in 1941 the library had to be evacuated to Denham; in 1944 the Institute was officially incorporated into the University and its members were given regular positions: Wittkower now became a Reader and Gombrich a Senior Research Fellow and, eventually, Director from 1959-76. It was housed first of all in the Imperial Institute in South Kensington and, from 1958, in less attractive but purpose-built premises in Woburn Square, Bloomsbury, where it was joined by the magnificent collections of Courtauld, Lee of Fareham, Witt, and Roger Fry.

Like Warburg himself, Saxl and Gombrich were not architectural historians. Rudolf Wittkower (1901-71), however, interested himself in architectural history from an early age, and his impact on its study in this country has been profound. His outlook tended to be less Warburgian than that of Saxl or Gombrich, and he could claim British citizenship because, though he was born in Berlin, his father had been born in

[1] E.H. Gombrich, *Aby Warburg, an Intellectual Biography, with a Memoir on the History of the Library by F. Saxl*, 1970, p.337.

England. He studied at Munich University and gained his
Ph.D. at Berlin University for a thesis written under Adolf
Goldschmidt on the minor quattrocento painter, Domenico
Morone. A more vital influence on the direction of his scholarship was the ten years he spent in Rome from 1922 where he was
an assistant, and later Research Fellow, at the Bibliotheca
Hertziana, the German art-historical research institute, from
1922. The escape from Berlin to the south seems to have helped
open his eyes to Baroque architecture in the same way that Italy
had awaked Winckelmann and Pater, for example, to new
cultural apprehensions. Put less dramatically, Wittkower
brought to the first-hand study of Roman buildings and archives
the insights of Gurlitt, Schmarsow, Brinckmann and Frankl. At
this time the current edition of Baedeker still spoke of 'the
degenerate Renaissance known as Baroque', and warned travellers 'to . . . beware of being led captive by art essentially flimsy
and meretricious'. No one has been more influential in overthrowing that view than Wittkower. And it was in the pages of
Baedeker that he first did so, for he was invited to revise the
account of the arts in Rome for a new edition of Baedeker in
1927. His first major article, on Michelangelo's dome of St
Peter's, appeared in 1933,[1] and was followed in 1934 by his
study of Michelangelo's Laurentian Library in Florence,[2] a
brilliant definition of the distinction between Mannerism and
Baroque which is one of the key contributions to architectural
history in the first half of the twentieth century.

During the 1930s Wittkower fundamentally altered our understanding of the development of Italian architecture from
1500-1700. If the revision he undertook of Baedeker helped make
Baroque architecture acceptable to a generation of tourists in
Rome, then for a more scholarly audience he established a
definition of Baroque which went far beyond the pioneering
work of his ultimate master, Heinrich Wölfflin. For Wölfflin
Rome had always been the natural centre and norm, but
Wittkower altered this balance by emphasising for the first
time the vital role of the North Italian tradition in the creation

[1] 'Zur Peterskuppel Michelangelos', *Zeitschrift für Kunstgeschichte*, 2, pp.348-
70.
[2] 'Michelangelo's Bibliotheca Laurenziana', *Art Bulletin*, XVI, pp.123-218.

of Baroque architecture — though even he did not extend his interests to the neglected subjects of Spain, Flanders and Holland in the seventeenth century. With his Hegelian or, at any rate, Wölfflinian turn of mind, Wittkower tended to interpret the two currents in Italian architecture as a Roman thesis and a North Italian antithesis, and therefore attempted to argue for a necessary synthesis (or symbiosis as he calls it in his post-Darwinian way) in the form of the architecture of Carlo Rainaldi (1611-91), which thus assumes a prominence in his account of Italian Baroque scarcely sustained by Rainaldi's actual talent. He published a pioneering article in 1937[1] on Rainaldi and Italian Baroque architecture, and after the war his interests flowered in important articles on Juvarra, Vittone and Guarini and, of course, in his monumental study of *Art and Architecture in Italy 1600-1750* (Harmondsworth 1958).

On his return from Italy Wittkower accepted a temporary lectureship at Cologne in 1932, but in the following year he settled in England where Saxl soon gave him an unpaid post in the Warburg Institute. In 1937 the *Journal of the Warburg Institute* was launched, the first academic periodical in the history of art ever published in this country. Wittkower was co-editor from 1937 to 55, first with Edgar Wind, then with Anthony Blunt, T.S.R. Boase, Frances Yates and E.H. Gombrich. The Second World War affected Wittkower and the Warburg Institute with a new appreciation of 'the English tradition', just as it had the English authors discussed in the last chapter. Thus, as Sacheverell Sitwell's incarceration in Northamptonshire helped produce his *British Architects and Craftsmen*, so the evacuation of the Warburg Library to Denham encouraged Wittkower's interest in English art which resulted in his important paper of 1943, 'Pseudo-Palladian Elements in English Neo-Classicism',[2] and also the superb book he produced in collaboration with Fritz Saxl, *British Art and the Mediterranean* (Oxford 1948). The book preceded the article chronologically for it was the record of a travelling exhibition of photographs arranged by Saxl and Wittkower for the Warburg Institute in 1941. Their inspiring and beautifully produced book is one of the most outstanding

[1]   *Art Bulletin*, XIX, pp.242-313.
[2]   *JWCI*, VI, 1943, pp.154-64.

achievements of twentieth-century art history in this country:
certainly there could be no more triumphant justification of the
characteristic method of the Warburg Institute in its cultural
and iconographical study of the migration of classical symbols.
After the emphatically insular history, generally unintellectual
in approach, which we investigated in the last chapter, *British Art
and the Mediterranean* — written by two immensely distinguished
German scholars at a time when Britain was at war with
Germany — came as a revelation. Here was an essentially
European outlook which also treated art history as intellectual
history. The preface recalls the origins of the book in the
photographic exhibition of 1941: 'At a period when inter-
European relations were disrupted by the war, it was stimulating to observe in the arts of this country the age-long impact of
the Mediterranean tradition on the British mind', a sentence in
which the key word, perhaps, is 'mind'. By contrast, it was as
recently as 1934 that Blomfield had written: 'For myself I am
prejudiced enough to detest and despise cosmopolitanism... I
am for the hill on which I was born; France for the French,
Germany for the German, England for the Englishman',[1] and
had also earlier expressed dislike of architectural photography.

The book celebrated in photographs with full explanatory
captions the impact of Greece and Italy on British art from
prehistoric times to the present day. This vast scope was made
possible not only by the learning of Saxl and Wittkower, but by
their ability to draw together assistance from a brilliant circle of
friends and colleagues: they acknowledge the help of nearly
forty scholars in the preface, amongst which figure prominently
the names of those associated with the Warburg and Courtauld
Institutes like Blunt, Mann, Webb, Whinney, Wind and Yates.
The first part of the book, up to 1500, was written by Saxl and
the second half by Wittkower. Saxl's lifelong interest in the
meaning of the imagery in mediaeval astrology and mythology
brought an unfamiliar emphasis to the presentation of English
mediaeval art. From the point of view of the development of
architectural history, Wittkower's account of the eighteenth
century was of seminal importance. The preface had already

[1] *Modernismus*, p.82.

whetted the reader's appetite: 'Special stress has been laid on the eighteenth century. Contact with the South was then particularly close, and generated ideas which colour many of our thoughts today'. The illuminating emphasis on topics like Lord Burlington, the Greek Revival and the Picturesque — which were virtually ignored by Sitwell in *British Architects and Craftsmen* — helped determine the course of much writing on architectural history after the war.

Wittkower himself published a number of extremely important papers on Palladio and English Palladianism, beginning with 'Pseudo-Palladian Elements in English Neo-Classicism' which might be regarded as the first scholarly paper of its kind in an English journal. Not only had the subject of Palladianism been curiously ignored, but Wittkower's typological approach, in which he confined himself to analysis of the Palladian window motif and rusticated surrounds to windows and doors, was also extremely novel.

Novelty was again the keynote of what is arguably his most important contribution to architectural history, *Architectural Principles in the Age of Humanism*, which first appeared in 1949 as volume 19 in the *Studies of the Warburg Institute*. Here was another vindication of the value of the Warburgian tradition of analysing in a literary or intellectual fashion the meaning of symbols. This had been given important expression by Richard Krautheimer, the distinguished German émigré in America, who published a suggestive article in the *Warburg Journal* in 1942, entitled 'Introduction to an "iconography of Mediaeval Architecture"'.[1] By studying contemporary texts as well as the buildings, Wittkower was able to overthrow the accepted interpretation of Renaissance architecture in terms of purely hedonist and aesthetic theory, and to show that Renaissance churches, especially centrally-planned ones, reflected a complex religious symbolism. The extremely favourable reception of a book so academic in presentation seems to have taken Wittkower by surprise. A second edition appeared in 1952 and a revised edition ten years later which was itself reprinted in 1967. Reyner Banham had already tried to explain its popularity,

[1] V, 1942, pp.1-33.

especially with architects, as early as 1955 in his celebrated article, 'The New Brutalism':[1]

> The general impact of Professor Wittkower's book on a whole generation of post-war architectural students is one of the phenomena of our time. Its exposition of a body of architectural theory in which function and form were significantly linked by the objective laws governing the Cosmos (as Alberti and Palladio understood them) suddenly offered a way out of the doldrum of routine functionalist abdication, and neo-Palladianism became the order of the day. The effect of *Architectural Principles* has made it by far the most important contribution — for evil as well as good — by an historian to English Architecture since *Pioneers of the Modern Movement*.

However, while it may have become fashionable for smart architects to be seen with copies of Wittkower's abstruse study, it seems doubtful whether it can actually have influenced the forms of modern architecture to any significant degree.

Before leaving the impact of the continental scholars who arrived in London in the 1930s we should glance at three who, for different reasons, stayed here very briefly. The most distinguished of these was Werner Weisbach (1873-1953), who had published pioneering studies of Baroque and Mannerist art from 1919 onwards. In 1939 he delivered three lectures at London University which were published in book form two years later as *Spanish Baroque Art* (Cambridge 1941). Weisbach explained for the benefit of his English audience the distinction between Renaissance as *'ein Stil des Seins'* (a style of 'being') and Baroque as *'ein Stil des Werdens'* (a style of 'becoming'), borrowing this terminology from Paul Frankl's *Das System der Kunstwissenschaft* (Brno 1938). Weisbach also disposed of the popular notion that the Jesuits were responsible for the Baroque style of church architecture.[2] His aim was to show how Baroque architecture, sculpture and painting in Spain were an expression of

---

[1] *Arch. Rev.*, CXVIII, 1955, pp.355-61. See also C. Rowe, 'The Mathematics of the Ideal Villa, Palladio and Le Corbusier compared', *Arch. Rev.*, CI, 1947, pp.101-4, and 'Mannerism in Modern Architecture', *Arch Rev.*, CVII, 1950, pp.289-99.

[2] See also R. Wittkower and I. Jaffé, ed., *Baroque Art, the Jesuit Contribution*, New York 1972.

Spanish character and history, and faced with the extraordinary individuality of Spanish art it would be difficult for even the most Wölfflinian critic to escape invoking some such interpretation.

Our knowledge of seventeenth-century classical architecture in England was extended by two foreign scholars who had been directly influenced by the Warburg Institute in London. Eduard Sekler's *Wren and his Place in European Architecture* (1956) was conceived in 1948 when the author was returning to his native Vienna after spending two years in England. Struck by the contrast between English and continental Baroque, he clearly set out in his book the eclectic range of European sources on which Wren drew. Even more striking was Per Palme's *Triumph of Peace, a Study of the Whitehall Banqueting House* (1957), written in London with the help of Gombrich, Wittkower, Summerson and Pevsner, as a thesis for a degree at Uppsala University. In this ambitious but somewhat prolix work, Palme achieved his declared aim of setting a building in its historical and social as well as its aesthetic context. In true Warburgian fashion, he analysed the complex symbolism of the building and its decoration, explaining its role in the elaborate diplomatic and royal ceremonial of the day.

One outstandingly good book which ought to be mentioned here is *The Architectural Setting of Anglican Worship* (1948), by G.W.O. Addleshaw, a Canon Residentiary of York, and Frederick Etchells, the architect who translated Corbusier's *Vers une architecture* in 1927. Though produced outside any tradition of German-inspired art-historical scholarship, this profound study of the meaning of the forms and arrangements of Anglican churches, showing how they are related to changing liturgical conceptions, has a lasting place in the literature of architectural iconography.

1949, the year which saw the publication of Wittkower's *Architectural Principles in the Age of Humanism*, can also be seen as a lesser milestone in modern art history as marking the start of the Oxford History of English Art. This ambitious enterprise, the first of its kind, was intended to cover the entire artistic history of England in eleven volumes by different scholars from the Celto-Saxon period to the present day. It was edited by T.S.R. Boase (1898-1974), the Oxford don and mediaeval historian who,

amidst some controversy, had become the second Director of
the Courtauld Institute in 1937, a post he held for ten years
before returning to Oxford. The Oxford History was a deliberately self-conscious product of the combination of German
professional art-historical ideals, and the English tradition of
inspired amateurism. It was thus given the purposefully
nationalist scope of English rather than British art, and foreign
contributors were carefully excluded. Amongst the contributors
were David Talbot Rice (1903-72), educated at Eton and Christ
Church, close friend of Robert Byron with whom he visited
Mount Athos in 1926, Gloucestershire squire and Professor of
Fine Art at Edinburgh University from 1934 until his death;
Oliver Millar (born 1923), a student at the Courtauld Institute
and Assistant Surveyor of the King's Pictures from 1947; Joan
Evans (1893-1977), a scholar of unusually wide scope and
markedly independent approach, who had acted as External
Examiner in History of Art at London University from 1938-46;
and Margaret Whinney (1897-1975), who became a Reader in
the History of Art at the Courtauld Institute in 1950.

The first volume to be published, Joan Evans's *English Art
1307-1461* (Oxford 1949), carried a lengthy and tendentious
editor's preface, not repeated in subsequent volumes, in which
Boase drew attention to the absence in this country of academic
acceptance of *Kunstgeschichte* and to the English distrust of
Stilkritik. Acknowledging the value of the English tradition of
connoisseurship with its emphasis on deciding the date and
provenance of individual artistic objects, he implied not that
stylistic criticism was over but that it had hardly begun.[1] One
ambition he was anxious to achieve was to establish the history
of art and architecture 'as part of the general history of England'.[2] What this meant in practice was that stylistic description
was excluded from the titles of the volumes, and that the starting
and closing-points of the first eight volumes, i.e. up to 1714,
were determined by the reigns of English monarchs: this did not
turn out to be a specially helpful arrangement.

In the meantime, the significance of the Oxford History had

---

[1] A point made in a slightly patronising editorial welcoming the series in the
Burl. Mag., XCII, 1950, p.63.
[2] p.v.

been exceeded by that of the Pelican History of Art, edited by
Nikolaus Pevsner. This was a world history of art in forty-eight
volumes with an appropriately international range of contributors. Whence arose this monumental scheme, so totally unlike
anything we have already seen in the English art-historical
scene? The answer lies to a great extent in the vision and energy
of its editor, Nikolaus Pevsner (born 1902), whose contribution
to the establishment of art history we have delayed discussing
till now because it was rather different in kind from that of Saxl,
Wittkower and Gombrich. Though he had published books on
Baroque painting and architecture while still in Germany, he
gravitated on his arrival in England not towards the world of
Saxl and the Warburg Institute, but to that characterised by the
refugee architect Gropius and the promotion through journalism
of Modern Movement architecture and design. The immediate
fruits of this were two pieces of propaganda, *Pioneers of the
Modern Movement from William Morris to Walter Gropius* (1936)
and *An Enquiry into Industrial Art in England* (Cambridge 1937), in
which 'modern', i.e. Bauhaus-inspired, design and socialism
were projected as part of a single package: thus, 'unless a further
levelling of social differences takes place in this country, no
steady development towards the aims of the Modern Movement
is possible'.[1] Reyner Banham claimed that *Pioneers of the Modern
Movement* was 'the precise bridge between the New Architecture
and the New Art-criticism', in that it was perhaps the first
English art-historical book which treated 'an historical period
as a whole'[2] by offering an interpretation based on the *Zeitgeist*.
It could, however, be argued that these books of Pevsner's are
not a reflection of the best qualities of the German art-historical
tradition but, on the contrary, demonstrate some of the pitfalls
into which the art-historian can be led by an unthinking
acceptance of the notion of the *Zeitgeist*.

A happier product of the influence of German art-historical
technique was Pevsner's *An Outline of European Architecture* (1943),
a lively little Penguin book characterised by the interpretation of
architecture as space which had already had a long history in
Germany. Its importance for our purpose at the moment lay in its

[1] *An Enquiry*, p.202.
[2] 'Pelican World History of Art', *Arch. Rev.*, CXIV, 1953, p.286.

popularity: it had already been through four editions by 1953 and had evidently replaced Banister Fletcher in most schools of architecture as the most widely-read popular history of architecture. It had thus helped to create the kind of audience which made it possible for its author, as well as its publisher, Sir Allen Lane, to envisage a History of World Art on the scale of the Pelican series launched in 1953. A year or so earlier, Pevsner had persuaded Lane to publish his epoch-making *Buildings of England* series, which appeared in forty-six volumes between 1951 and 74. These wonderfully helpful books have opened up a world of delight to countless thousands, and it is now impossible for anyone at all seriously interested in architecture to travel in any English county without the relevant 'Pevsner'.

Leaving aside for the moment the English archaeologists, A.W. Lawrence and J. Ward-Perkins, and also John White, who wrote the Pelican History of Art volume on *Art and Architecture in Italy 1250-1400* (1966), only three English architectural historians have contributed volumes to Pevsner's Pelican History of Art series: Geoffrey Webb, Anthony Blunt and John Summerson. As an undergraduate at Magdalene College, Cambridge, Geoffrey Webb (1898-1970) had been influenced by E.S. Prior's lectures as Slade Professor and by his *A History of Gothic Art in England* (1900). He later became a friend of Roger Fry, of Saxl and of Wittkower, and was one of the earliest lecturers at the Courtauld Institute from 1934-37, as well as being on the staff of the Cambridge School of Architecture from 1928-39 and 1946-48. Like some of the contributors to the Oxford History of English Art, he thus represents the impact of *Kunstgeschichte* on the English tradition, but he did not achieve the same success as some of his colleagues. Though he was appointed Slade Professor of Fine Art at Cambridge in 1938-9 and 1946-8, it became clear that there was no permanent job for him in the University, nor a Fellowship at his college, and he became Secretary to the Royal Commission on Historical Monuments (England) in 1948. The almost impossibly wide scope of his otherwise attractive contribution to the Pelican History of Art, *Architecture in Britain: the Middle Ages* (1956), unfortunately served to diminish its usefulness.

Anthony Blunt (born 1907), who contributed *Art and Architecture in France 1500-1700* to the Pelican series in 1953, was

appointed Director of the Courtauld Institute in 1947 in succession to Boase, and is one of the few recent English art-historians
who has concerned himself with the study of continental rather
than English architecture. After his early adoption of · com-
munism, his distinguished career has been especially associated
with the study of Poussin, but one of his earliest books was the
first monograph in any language on the greatest of French
classical architects, François Mansart (1598-1666). Consisting
of a series of lectures delivered at the Warburg Institute in 1940,
this was published in the following year as volume 14 in the
Studies of the Warburg Institute. In 1958 he published a monograph on Philibert de l'Orme as the first volume in a series
entitled *Studies in Architecture*, which he and Rudolf Wittkower
edited for the publisher, Desmond Zwemmer. By 1979 eighteen
volumes had appeared, the majority on post-mediaeval architecture in Italy and France, the work of English, American, and
one German, scholars. The publication on this impressive scale
of the fruits of advanced architectural scholarship is due to the
vision of Desmond Zwemmer, who is primarily a bookseller not
a publisher. But for the accident of his generosity and devotion,
the dissemination of architectural knowledge since the late
1950s would have been very considerably less.

The third of the three English scholars who have written on
architecture in the Pelican History of Art is Sir John Summerson
(born 1904). His masterly *Georgian London* (1945), which
arose out of a course of lectures prepared for the Courtauld
Institute in 1939, was a turning point in the use of documentary
sources in eighteenth-century architectural history. He followed it with the no less brilliant Pelican history of *Architecture in
Britain 1530-1830* (1953). With the possible exception of Jackson's writings, this was the first general survey of English post-
mediaeval architecture since Blomfield's two-volumed history
of 1897. It benefited greatly from the new understanding of
continental architecture, especially Mannerism and Baroque,
which had been achieved largely thanks to foreign scholars in
the half century since Blomfield. Not until that understanding
had been established was it possible to move away from the
tradition which went back at least to Blomfield of describing
English architecture from Jones to Soane as 'Renaissance'.
Geoffrey Webb played an important role in popularising the

notion of English Baroque with his edition of Vanbrugh's letters in 1928, which we have already noted, and, twenty years later, with his *Baroque Art* (British Academy Lecture, 1947). The skilful way Summerson plays the game of source-hunting reflects an art-historical technique which stemmed from the Warburg and Courtauld Institutes. In Summerson's case it served the additional role of showing how much English seventeenth and eighteenth-century architects had relied on a variety of pattern books. This was in contrast to the older approach, associated with Blomfield and Jackson, of interpreting architectural style as a spontaneous, unselfconscious vernacular.

2 The Impact of Colvin

The third component which it is possible to discern in Summerson's approach is related to the impact of the great lexicographer of British architects, Howard Colvin (born 1919). The contribution made by Colvin in his great *Biographical Dictionary of English Architects, 1660-1840* (1954) needs to be discussed in a different section of the present book from that which had as its central theme the impact of the Warburg and Courtauld Institutes. Colvin approaches architectural history not as a study with speculative implications rooted in *Kulturgeschichte*, but as an arena for the establishment of documented facts, an approach which was still in the early 1950s more characteristic of the study of mediaeval history than of architecture. The contrast could not be more clearly conveyed than by the two nearly contemporary prefaces by Boase, in the first volume of the Oxford History of English Art in 1949, and by Colvin five years later in his *Dictionary*. Whereas Boase implied that English art historians ought to learn the technique 'by which analysis of styles provides not only a precise instrument of attribution but also an indication of phases of emotional temperament',[1] Colvin expressly dissociated himself from stylistic attribution, and explained that 'Many attributions based on mere speculation I have felt at liberty to ignore, however wide their currency, and however distinguished their sponsors'.[2] In the place of speculation he constructed a corpus of knowledge about English archi-

---

[1] p.v.   [2] p.xii.

tecture based on such extensive research in archives of all kinds and in all places that it seems scarcely possible for one man to have carried it out single-handed, especially by the age of thirty-five.

It is hardly an exaggeration to say that Colvin's *Dictionary* changed the face of English architectural history. A professional academic and a mediaeval historian by training — his first book was a study of *The White Canons in England* (Oxford 1951) — he applied the techniques familiar in the study of mediaeval history to the study of post-mediaeval architecture, and thereby rendered architectural history academically respectable. That is the essence of Colvin's revolution. It was also a curiously conservative kind of revolution for it represented in some sense a return to the origins of English art history in the notes on architects and artists assembled by George Vertue (1684-1756) which, as we have seen, were elaborated by Horace Walpole in his *Anecdotes of Painting in England*.

In 1955 Colvin published an article in the journal of the British Records Association which surveyed the slow growth of the use of documents by architectural historians, and set out very clearly for the benefit of future research workers the location and the character of the various types of archives which are likely to contain information about architects and their work. He complained at the same time that architectural history was academically 'a marginal subject . . . pursued by a few enthusiasts with scarcely any of the facilities for instruction and publication which are enjoyed as a matter of course by other historical and archaeological disciplines'. He noted that one advantage of the present situation was that 'the total number of serious architectural historians in this country today is so small that they nearly all know one another personally, and when, in default of a professional journal of architectural history, they publish an article in *Country Life* or the *Architectural Review*, they are actually paid for what they write'.[1]

Steps were soon taken to give architectural history a professional status by the foundation in 1956 of the Society of Architectural Historians of Great Britain, in which an annual journal, *Architectural History*, was to play an important part. The

[1] 'Architectural History and its Records', *Archives*, II, no. 14, 1955, p. 300.

Society, which was affiliated to the American Society of Architectural Historians, founded in 1940, was addressed at its inaugural meeting in June 1957 by Howard Colvin on the subject of 'The Study of Architectural History in England'. A fine series of scholarly and fully documented books on English post-mediaeval architecture, which shows no sign of abating, now began to flow from authors like Dorothy Stroud, John Fleming, John Harris, J. Mordaunt Crook, Mark Girouard, Kerry Downes, M.H. Port, and several others.

Two other important dictionaries of English artists also appeared in the early 1950s. The first was the *Dictionary of British Sculptors 1660-1851* (1951, rev. ed. 1961) by Rupert Gunnis (1899-1965), the result of fourteen years of archival research in which he was helped and, on occasion, accompanied by Howard Colvin. In 1954 John Harvey published his memorable *English Mediaeval Architects, a Biographical Dictionary down to 1550*, which was a parallel to Colvin's research into post-mediaeval architecture. Just as Colvin's *Dictionary* had been rooted in a tradition which began with Vertue and Walpole and was continued in the nineteenth century by Wyatt Papworth's *Dictionary of Architecture* and the contributions to the *Dictionary of National Biography*, so Harvey was indebted to the pioneering work of Dallaway, Britton, Wyatt Papworth and Lethaby in establishing the names of most of the great mediaeval masters of architecture. Both Colvin and Harvey were able to draw on the extensive documentary research carried out between the two world wars by Professor Douglas Knoop and G.P. Jones into the history of the building trades in England up to the end of the seventeenth century. Harvey also benefited from an impressive work by L.F. Salzman, *Building in England down to 1540, a Documentary History* (Oxford 1952), which continued the tradition of Knoop and Jones. It sheds an interesting light on the history of English taste that the writing of this book was completed as early as 1934, at which time no publisher could be found to take it. Salzman made clear his resolute aim not to be 'concerned with artistic deductions from existing buildings but with contemporary documentary evidence on the actual processes of buildings'.[1] This limited ambition did not satisfy Harvey who wanted to

[1] p.v.

raise on the basis of documentary fact a body of stylistic criticism and attribution. His valiant and delightful attempts to achieve this end have been dogged by the problems of inadequate documentary information and by doubts as to whether individual artistic personality was a sufficiently recognised concept in the Middle Ages to justify present-day attempts at stylistic attribution. His work has thus been coolly received by Pevsner,[1] but the questions he raises are central ones, and it is a pity that there has been so little attempt to answer them. There has been no flowering of mediaeval architectural scholarship following his *Dictionary* as there has been of post-mediaeval studies following Colvin's *Dictionary*. Indeed, the years between Geoffrey Webb's *Architecture in Britain: the Middle Ages* of 1956 and Harvey's own *1he Perpendicular Style* of 1978 saw the publication of no major book by an English scholar on a period of post-Conquest mediaeval architecture. The greatest contribution in this field has in fact been due to Colvin who has edited from 1963 the *History of the King's Works* (six volumes to date) which provide an all too rapid précis of the story of public building in England from the Middle Ages to the mid-nineteenth century.

It may be appropriate to mention here the patient enquiry into the history of vernacular and ordinary domestic architecture, as well as of building materials, which is well demonstrated in W.J. Arkell's *Oxford Stone* (1947), *Studies in Building History, Essays in Recognition of the Work of B.H.St.J. O'Neil*, E.M. Jope, ed.(1961), Alec Clifton-Taylor's *The Pattern of English Building* (1972), Eric Mercer's *English Vernacular Houses* (1975) and D. Cruickshank and P. Wyld's *London: the Art of Georgian Building* (1975).

While the impact of Colvin's emphasis on documentary and archival research was shaping a new generation of architectural historians, John Harris (born 1931) was developing a parallel expertise based on the discovery and identification of architectural drawings. The victory of the Modern Movement in the 1940s meant that English architects now deliberately rejected all tradition, so that the historic collection of drawings assembled by the Royal Institute of British Architects came to be seen rather as an archive for architectural historians than a

[1] *Arch. Rev.*, CXVIII, 1955, pp.259-60.

source of inspiration for architects. Sharing freely his endless architectural discoveries with his colleagues, John Harris put to brilliant advantage his position at the RIBA Drawings Collection, from 1956 onwards and as adviser to the American collector of British art, Paul Mellon, from 1965-78. The Drawings Collection now became the true centre of research into English post-mediaeval architecture, especially after its rehousing in 1971 in an elegant Georgian mansion next door to the Courtauld Institute of Art in Portman Square, a move which further emphasised the gap between historical knowledge of architecture and its present-day practice. John Harris's *Sir William Chambers* (1970) was perhaps the first architectural monograph to contain a fully documented catalogue raisonné of the kind long familiar in monographs on painters, but probably his greatest achievement so far is the RIBA Drawings Catalogue of which the first volume was published in 1969. Sixteen volumes have been contributed to date by a variety of scholars. Harris was also closely involved in the founding of the Furniture History Society in 1964 with its important journal *Furniture History*. The systematic use of archives in establishing information about furniture designers is another reflection of the Colvinian approach which has borne immense fruit in the last fifteen years.

VI
Victorian and
Neo-Classical Studies

The gradual rise of a sympathetic reassessment of Victorian architecture seems to need a new chapter because it occurred in circles which were generally only marginally connected to the art-historical world which we have investigated in the last chapter. In the 1920s it began to be fashionable for Oxford undergraduates to look at the hitherto despised Victorian architecture with amused affection. The mood of this world, which included men like Evelyn Waugh, Robert Byron, Harold Acton and Brian Howard, is well conveyed in Christopher Hollis's recollection that 'Harold Acton also collaborated in those days with Robert Byron in organising a display of early Victorian domestic ornaments but for some unexplained reason it met with the disapproval of the authorities and was banned by the Proctors'.[1] Towards the end of the decade appeared the brilliant study by the twenty-five-year-old Kenneth Clark, *The Gothic Revival, an Essay in the History of Taste* (1929), which, he claimed, was indebted to Geoffrey Scott and Goodhart-Rendel. His approach was characterised more by amusement than affection, and he was criticised by Goodhart-Rendel for his claim that 'The Gothic Revival is one of the very few styles which we cannot swallow; and if we believe in objective values at all, we are justified in thinking that these styles are devoid of merit'.[2] Goodhart-Rendel was also inclined to disbelieve in the antithesis which Clark claimed existed between the theories of Pugin and of Geoffrey Scott: might it not be the case, Goodhart-Rendel argued, that 'all the pleasure-giving qualities of form and pattern are due to unconscious ethical associations'?[3]

---

[1] C. Hollis, *Oxford in the Twenties, Recollections of Five Friends*, 1976, p.102.
[2] *The Gothic Revival*, 1950 ed., p.100.
[3] In his review of the book in *Arch. Rev.*, LXV, 1929, p.303.

Clark's tone was echoed in Dudley Harbron's oddly named *Amphion, or the Nineteenth Century* (1930), which deserves at least a mention as the first, though admittedly not very helpful, history of Victorian architecture. The author, an architect from Hull, illustrated the text with a series of inept drawings by himself.

The essay by Goodhart-Rendel which Clark acknowledged in *The Gothic Revival* was his 'English Gothic Architecture of the Nineteenth Century', published in 1924 in the RIBA *Journal*.[1] He might also have added another pioneering article by the same author on 'The Churches of Brighton and Hove', which had appeared in *The Architectural Review* in 1918.[2] Harry Stuart Goodhart-Rendel (1887-1959) was an extremely complex figure whom we have already come across as the author of a brief but influential monograph on Hawksmoor in 1924. He was the only child of Harry Chester Goodhart (1858-95), a man of unusual gifts who was a Fellow in Classics at Trinity College, Cambridge, from 1881-91 and subsequently Professor of Humanity at Edinburgh University until his tragically early death from pneumonia. He was a man of tremendous strength of character, though intensely reserved in manner, of whom an obituarist wrote in 1891 how, in his rooms, 'even the chair covers were designed and worked by himself; he made his own fishing-rods, and at least one suit of clothes... He combined the artist's brain with the skill and strength of an artisan'.[3] He was a tutor of the ill-fated Prince Albert Victor, the Duke of Clarence, who, somewhat surprisingly, acted as his best man on his marriage in 1886 to the eldest daughter of the first and last Lord Rendel (1834-1913). An immensely wealthy member of Lord Armstrong's engineering and armaments firm, Lord Rendel acquired Hatchlands, Surrey, in 1889, an early Adam house, and also a villa at Cannes. He left a life interest in all this property, as well as in the bulk of his fortune, to his grandson, Harry Stuart Goodhart, who assumed the additional surname and arms of Rendel on his mother's second marriage, to his tutor, in 1902. His father's premature death acted as a constant warning to the young Harry Goodhart-Rendel who, with the active assistance of his mother, took elaborate precautions to

[1] XXI, 1924, pp.321-39. [2] XLIV, 1918, pp.23-9 and 59-63.
[3] Obituary in the *Cambridge Review*, XVI, 1895, p.294.

avoid suffering a similar fate. Spending less than a year at Eton, on grounds of health, he eventually went up to Trinity, Cambridge, to read music, which was then the guiding passion in his life. His modern tastes clashed with those of his master, Sir Donald Tovey, and, possibly influenced by his cousin by marriage, Halsey Ricardo, a talented Jewish architect, he turned to architecture. He received a little training in 1909 from Sir Charles Nicholson, Bart., the church architect, and from that year until his death half a century later practised as an architect in London and at St Raphael in the South of France, adopting a variety of styles, including the 'Modern' style. During the two world wars he served as an officer in the Grenadier Guards. Life in the Brigade suited him perfectly and he was justly proud of the Squad Drill Primer, which he published in 1918. He was received into the Roman Catholic Church in 1924 and subsequently designed several Catholic churches.

Country squire and professional architect, dedicated Guards officer and pioneer architectural historian, Catholic convert as much at home in France as in England, travelling about in a chauffeur-driven Rolls Royce, sporting an astrakhan coat and an eye-glass, Governor of Sadlers Wells, Vice-President of the Royal Academy of Music and President of the RIBA, Goodhart-Rendel fits into no conceivable pattern but seems invented to serve as a warning to historians dedicated to the concept of the *Zeitgeist*. It is to help explain his unique position that we have enlarged on his no less unique background, his odd but talented father and his somewhat bizarre upbringing. His own personality will also guide us through the maze of apparent contradictions to an understanding of the nature of his contribution to architectural history: his rigorous intellect on the one hand appreciated order and precision, which helps explain his devotion to the Brigade of Guards and to the Catholic Church as well as to the buildings of, for example, Cockerell, Duc and Bentley; and, on the other hand, abhorred sloppiness and cant, which is why he did not admire the essentially Picturesque character of much English architecture in the later nineteenth century, or the false moralising of the Modern Movement.

Though he regarded himself primarily as an architect, Goodhart-Rendel's influence has been almost entirely as an historian. What that influence rests on, apart from the slender but suggestive study of Hawksmoor, is a handful of major articles on Victorian and Edwardian architects, a remarkably complete annotated card-index of nineteenth century British churches, which can now be consulted at the National Monuments Record and the RIBA Library, and a book of lectures written in 1934 but not published till towards the end of his life, *English Architecture since the Regency, an Interpretation* (1953). It may sound a slender enough basis for his considerable reputation but there can be no doubt that Kenneth Clark was not only expressing the feelings of his own generation when he described Goodhart-Rendel in 1950 as 'the father of us all'.[1]

In his first published articles on 'The Churches of Brighton and Hove' (1918), Goodhart-Rendel already spoke like a prophet to 'a generation not yet awakened to what was great in the "Gothic Revival"'.[2] He would have been influenced by two important articles on William Butterfield which had already been published in the same journal in 1900[3] by his cousin, Halsey Ricardo, following Butterfield's death in that year. Butterfield's most significant buildings had been produced from the 1840s to 60s, and Ricardo's bold attempt to revive interest in his architecture as an example primarily of masterful conviction and only secondarily of the Gothic Revival, is of exceptional interest for its date. Goodhart-Rendel will also have known T. Francis Bumpus's 'A Modern View of London Church Architecture' which appeared serially in the *British Architect*, vols. 54-6, 1900-1.[4] Bumpus used some of this material in his two-volumed *London Churches, Ancient and Modern*, of which the second volume, published in 1908, remained almost the only account in English of the Victorian Gothic churches of London until the publication in 1938 of the Rev. Basil Clarke's *Church Builders of the Nineteenth Century, a Study of the Gothic Revival in England*, with a preface by Goodhart-Rendel's master, Sir

[1] *The Gothic Revival*, 1950 ed., p.6.

[2] XLIV, 1918, p.23.

[3] VII, 1900, pp.259-63, and VIII, 1900, pp.15-23.

[4] See also Bumpus's 45 articles in *The Architect*, September 1899-December 1901, vols. LXII-LXVI, on 'Stained Glass in England since [i.e. during] the Gothic Revival, with some account of the churches referred to'.

Charles Nicholson. In his book, which is a forceful Anglo-Catholic tract, Bumpus enthused over the churches of Butterfield, Street, Brooks and Pearson but reserved his highest admiration for the more recent work of Bodley, G.G. Scott, junior, and Sedding. A similar emphasis, though without the Anglo-Catholicism, marks Hermann Muthesius's remarkable but still comparatively little-known book, *Die neuere kirchliche Baukunst in England* (Berlin 1901). In his *A Guide to Gothic Architecture* (1915), which was ostensibly a study of mediaeval architecture up to the end of the Decorated style, Bumpus actually illustrated his points by frequent references to Victorian churches in both text and plates. As an immensely prolific and popular author, Bumpus relied to some extent on plagiarism and his works contain unacknowledged quotation from Eastlake and Sedding.

Goodhart-Rendel described architecture with the eye of a practising architect and liked writing about the way a building worked. What he admired was, first, rationalism, which is not the same as functionalism, and, secondly, toughness when combined with a certain poetry. This made him especially receptive to certain currents in Edwardian architecture, and he published important papers on the work of Temple Moore (1926),[1] Beresford Pite and Halsey Ricardo (1935-6),[2] as well as an equally pioneering and more influential study of 'Rogue Architects of the Victorian Era' (1949),[3] which included the eccentric experimentalists like E.B. Lamb, John Shaw, James Wild, Bassett Keeling, Greek Thomson, E.S. Prior and James Maclaren, who have since come into favour.

The 1930s saw the rise of the extraordinarily influential and mysterious John Betjeman (born 1906). Mysterious because, in Summerson's words, he 'has not written even one book about Victorian architecture nor ever to my knowledge promoted any serious general claims for its qualities. Yet his name has become an illuminant and sanction; through him, kindliness toward Victorian architecture is permitted to thousands whose habits of mind would drive them in a quite other direction'.[4] With

[1] *Arch. Rev.*, LIX, 1926, pp.12-17 and 59-63.
[2] *RIBA Jnl.*, XLIII, 1935-6, pp.117-28.   [3] *RIBA Jnl.*, LVI, 1949, pp.251-8.
[4] J. Summerson, *Victorian Architecture, Four Studies in Evaluation*, New York 1970, p.16.

Betjeman what had been a private joke at Oxford in the 20s became a slightly more public joke in the world of architectural journalism in London dominated by *The Architectural Review.* The atmosphere is beautifully encapsulated in Evelyn Waugh's novel, *A Handful of Dust (1934),* with its clever frontispiece of the resolutely Gothic Hetton Abbey and its recurring chapters called 'English Gothic'. Anthony Last, the squire of Hetton, was convinced that 'the time would come . . . when opinion would reinstate Hetton in its proper place. Already it was referred to as "amusing", and a very civil young man had asked permission to photograph it for an architectural review'.[1] The civil young man might well have been John Betjeman who was on the staff of *The Architectural Review* in the early 1930s. Osbert Lancaster (born 1908), who was also on the staff of the same journal, soon produced his *Pillar to Post* (1938) and *Homes Sweet Homes* (1939), which described Victorian architecture, among many other things, with devastating but somehow sympathetic irony.

In the meantime, however, the influence of Nikolaus Pevsner was beginning to be felt at *The Architectural Review.* In 1936, the year which saw the appearance of the first of his many articles for the *Review*, he published his *Pioneers of the Modern Movement from William Morris to Walter Gropius*, a widely influential book at which we have already glanced in a different context. Here was architectural history with a mission on a scale that had scarcely been seen since the days of Pugin. It was an attempt to persuade the English to accept the Modern Movement as the only style in which a modern man ought to express himself. In order to establish the historical authenticity of the new Movement, a surprising pedigree was contrived for it in the work of men like Morris, Shaw and Voysey. This led to an historical approach which granted recognition only to buildings or objects which were regarded as in the Line of Progress to the Authentic Modern Movement. Pevsner's claim that there was a necessary connection between acceptance of the International Modern Style and sympathy with the Gothic Revival was emphatically proclaimed in December 1945 in a special issue of *The Architectural Review* devoted to the Gothic Revival. The editorial introduction described the contents as 'an interim

[1] p.29.

statement on the new aesthetic and historical approach to Gothicism, an approach made possible only by the now unchallenged establishment of the modern movement as the style of our century'.[1] Reyner Banham was still making the same point in the same journal eight years later.[2] Despite these claims, the two men who, apart from Pevsner himself, were most responsible for arousing interest in the Gothic Revival — John Betjeman and Goodhart-Rendel — were expressly associated with opposition to modern architecture. This point was underlined by the publication in 1953 of Goodhart-Rendel's *English Architecture since the Regency*, with its marked hostility to the ideals of the Modern Movement. Not surprisingly, it was vigorously attacked in a leading article in *The Architectural Review* by Pevsner himself. The language in which Pevsner condemns Goodhart-Rendel's lack of enthusiasm for the Modern Movement is fired with a missionary zeal: 'Mr. Goodhart-Rendel blasphemes this mystery, because he lived through it and could not recognise it', and the subjects of the book are referred to slightingly as 'Mr. Goodhart-Rendel's friends, the Victorians'.[3]

In the later 1950s and 60s the mood changed and greater harmony prevailed. The principal reason for this new sense of solidarity was the suddenly increased threat to Victorian buildings posed by the intensive urban redevelopment which accompanied post-war prosperity and the property boom. The Victorian Society, founded in 1958, channelled together for the first time the interests that were variously represented in enthusiasm for the nineteenth century: romantic nostalgia, active preservation, and academic research. The Society began at a meeting on 5 November 1957 called by the Countess of Rosse, with the active support of John Betjeman and Christopher Hussey, at 18, Stafford Terrace, Kensington, which was, and is, one of the most remarkable Victorian interiors in London, having remained virtually untouched since its elaborate decoration in the fashionable taste of the 1870s for Lady Rosse's grandfather, the artist Edward Linley Sambourne. It was Lady Rosse's husband, the 6th Earl of Rosse (born 1908), who, with Robert Byron, had founded the Georgian Group in 1937, following the threat to

[1] XCVIII, 1945, p.149.   [2] CXIV, 1953, pp.285-8.
[3] 'Originality', *Arch. Rev.*, CXV, 1954, pp.367-9.

Nash's Carlton House Terrace. The prominent role played by members of the same family somehow serves to emphasise the rapid revolutions in taste, characteristic of the twentieth century, by which previously unfashionable periods swing back into favour. As recently as 1945, F.H. Crossley, in his *English Church Design, 1040-1540 A.D., an Introduction to the Study of Mediaeval Building*, had been able, when describing specific architects such as Sir Gilbert Scott, G.E. Street and Temple Moore, to dismiss them confidently with the words, 'These styles were sufficiently trite when applied to the erection of churches, but became absurd when applied to secular buildings such as the Law Courts'.[1] Even Reginald Turnor in his *Nineteenth Century Architecture in Britain* (1950), evidently regarded the whole story as the unfolding of a tragedy.

It may be appropriate at this point to put special emphasis on the major role played by Christopher Hussey (1899-1970) in bringing his knowledge and enthusiasm to the cause of preservation of English architecture, including Victorian buildings, and the degree of respectability his presence thereby gave the movement. Like Goodhart-Rendel, he was an hereditary landowner and not an art-historian in the modern sense, but the weekly articles which he contributed to *Country Life* for exactly fifty years on all aspects of English architecture, towns and villages, landscapes and gardens, sustained the role of the journal as 'the keeper of the architectural conscience of the nation'. As a young man he had rediscovered the process whereby his grandfather had created both the house and the romantic landscaped garden at Scotney Castle, Kent, in the 1830s as an expression of the theories of the English Picturesque Movement. His appreciation of the link between the view from the window in the library at Scotney and the books on its shelves, formed in John Cornforth's words, 'the basis of his aesthetic experience',[2] and found perfect expression in his books on *The Picturesque* (1927) and *English Country Houses, Late Georgian, 1800-1840* (1958). Working under Edward Hudson, the owner and editor of *Country Life* until his death in 1936, Hussey came to share his intense enthusiasm for the work of Sir Edwin

[1] p.1.
[2] Obituary of Hussey, *Country Life*, CXLVII, 1970, p.767.

Lutyens (1869-1944). This flowered in *The Life of Sir Edwin Lutyens* (1950), the finest architectural biography in the English language. Together with his sensitive monograph of 1931 on the architecture of Lutyens's Scottish parallel, Sir Robert Lorimer (1864-1929), it established Hussey as an expert on Edwardian and early twentieth-century architecture as well as on Georgian and Early Victorian.

With the Victorian Society in the 1950s and 60s, as with the Georgian Group in the 1930s, the mounting destruction of familiar buildings served to attract the sympathetic attention to them of both the general public and of professional scholars. Though it was founded just too late to help preserve Collcutt's Imperial Institute from demolition by London University from 1957 onwards, the Victorian Society was surrounded in its earliest years by a blaze of publicity while it fought prolonged but unsuccessful battles for the preservation of the Euston Arch and the Coal Exchange, which were both finally demolished in 1961-2. The rapid growth in numbers of the Society was more spectacular than that of the Georgian Group and somewhat resembled the success of the Cambridge Camden Society in the 1840s: from under 600 in 1961 it had risen to 1700 by 1968 and to nearly 3000 ten years later. During the 1950s members benefited from the admirably thorough inventories compiled by the American Professor Henry-Russell Hitchcock (born 1903), *Early Victorian Architecture in Britain* (2 vols., New Haven, Conn. and London, 1954), and *Architecture: 19th and 20th centuries* (Harmondsworth 1958). Peter Ferriday, who had published an admirable monograph on *Lord Grimthorpe 1816-1905* (1957), rebuilder of St Albans Cathedral, edited in 1963 a varied collection of essays under the title *Victorian Architecture*, with an introduction by John Betjeman. The odd state of Victorian studies at this time is reflected in the unusual combination of contributions which included one that seems to have been an elaborate fake and others from authors either dead or non-existent.

As early as 1952 an important exhibition of *Victorian and Edwardian Decorative Arts* had been organised at the Victoria and Albert Museum by Peter Floud (d.1960), the Keeper of the Circulation Department. As Floud's introduction to the cata-logue made clear, the exhibits were selected in accordance with

Pevsnerian orthodoxy in which special emphasis was placed on what was regarded as sincerity and originality. Floud further explained that 'we have deliberately eliminated what was merely freakish or grotesque. At the same time we have purposely left out a whole host of Victorian designers whose work was unashamedly based on the copying of earlier styles'.[1] Amongst those on whom this exhibition made a lasting impact was Charles Handley-Read (1916-71). With his wife Lavinia (d.1971), he now set about forming an astonishingly rich collection along similar lines, though prompted by an understanding of the important role played in Victorian furniture design by architects, amongst whom Burges featured with arresting prominence. Their collection was commemorated in an exhibition, accompanied by a substantial catalogue, which was held at the Royal Academy of Arts in 1972 under the title *Victorian and Edwardian Decorative Art*.

Three further exhibitions on a major scale with equally impressive catalogues were organised by the Victoria and Albert Museum: *Victorian Church Art* (1971-2), *'Marble Halls', Drawings and Models for Victorian Secular Buildings* (1973), and *High Victorian Design* (1974-5). Though the last of these travelled between five museums in Canada, the authorities of the Victoria and Albert Museum unfortunately prevented its display in its home of origin. Part of the importance of these exhibitions consisted in their emancipation from the ambition of excluding from our understanding of Victorian design anything that in 1952 had been considered insincere, grotesque or imitative.

The great variety of serious studies of Victorian architecture published during the 1960s and 70s by authors such as Girouard, Summerson, Crook, Saint, Muthesius, Pevsner, Stanton, Thompson and Macaulay reflects an even more striking change of attitude. Robert Furneaux-Jordan's *Victorian Architecture* (Harmondsworth 1966) could be regarded as a tract for busy students in schools of architecture who wanted to be told how the development of socialism was reflected in Victorian design. It even ended up with photographs of early Modern Movement architecture in Germany as the goal towards which Victorian architecture was moving until its progress was held up by

[1] p.5.

Lutyens. With the publication only twelve years later of an authoritative book with the same title by Roger Dixon (born 1935) and Stefan Muthesius (born 1939), we are in a different world, dominated by explanation and description rather than by social value-judgements. In the meantime, Paul Thompson's *William Butterfield* (1971), by its careful study of patronage, had exposed the inadequacies of the explanation of apparent crudity in some Victorian design as the consequence of crude un-educated patrons. John Summerson, who had published important papers on Butterfield and Pugin in *The Architectural Review* in 1945 and 48, now produced three short books on Victorian architecture. He seems to enjoy having a problem to worry over, and as early as 1937 had produced an article on the special kind of failure which he believed Wren's achievement represented.[1] A similar approach to Sir John Soane characterised his provocative paper of 1951, 'Soane: the Case-History of a Personal Style'.[2] His distinguished mind, ever questing and worrying, now found especially sympathetic those nineteenth-century authors and architects who had expressed doubts about the merit of the architecture of their day. Thus Summerson's *Victorian Architecture, Four Studies in Evaluation* (New York 1970) interprets the subject in terms of failure: 'I believe that any such students, adventuring into Victorian architecture, will have to ponder this problem of failure. There is no avoiding it, and I doubt if there is any point in trying to find a politer name'.[3] His view is not at the moment shared by the younger generation, and in their admirable *Victorian Architecture* (1978) Dixon and Muthesius do not so much as mention the concept of failure.

The long-awaited critical assessment of Edwardian architecture, presaged in Goodhart-Rendel's *English Architecture since the Regency* (1953), has begun to take shape in a variety of ways. An early, admirable but entirely unique expression of this interest was Peter Anson's *Fashions in Church Furnishings, 1840-1940* (1960, rev.ed. 1965), a perceptive study which has wider implications than its title would suggest, since it covers aspects of the history of architecture and of costume. It may be salutary

---

[1] 'The Tyranny of Intellect, a Study of the Mind of Sir Christopher Wren in Relation to the Thought of his Time', *RIBA Jnl.*, XLIV, 1937, pp.373-90.
[2] *RIBA Jnl.*, LVIII, 1951, pp.83-91.   [3] p.17.

to recall that this brilliant, entertaining and reasonably well-documented book, published when its author was in his 70s, should have emerged from a world right outside that of the art-historical scholarship we have been investigating for two chapters. Born in 1889, Anson belonged to the ecclesiological tradition which had produced Bumpus and Clarke and which stretched back to Pugin. He was indeed a Puginian figure: Catholic convert and enthusiastic sailor, first an Anglican then a Catholic monk, maritime artist and author of over thirty books exclusively concerned with religion or the sea, he would have concurred with Pugin's statement: 'There is nothing worth living for but Christian Architecture and a boat'.[1]

The first scholarly monograph on a turn of the century architect was *Charles Rennie Mackintosh and the Modern Movement* (1952, 2nd ed. 1977), by the architect Thomas Howarth, who was then teaching architecture at Manchester University. In 1968 Robert Macleod, also an architect by training, published another monograph on Mackintosh, and three years later a study called *Style and Society, Architectural Ideology in Britain, 1835-1914*, in which he traced the history of, as well as identified himself with, the view that architecture is an anonymous mechanical service which should not be concerned with style.

A variety of presentations of the whole Edwardian period has been attractively presented in the following publications: Alastair Service's *Edwardian Architecture and its Origins* (1975) and *Edwardian Architecture* (1977); Nicholas Cooper's *The Opulent Eye, Late Victorian and Edwardian Taste in Interior Design* (1976); the special double number of *Architectural Design* in 1978, devoted to a record of Gavin Stamp's exhibition, *London 1900*, at the RIBA Drawings Collection; and the Survey of London volumes on *The Grosvenor Estate in Mayfair*, 1978 and 1980.

The traditional art-historical scholarship associated with the kind of books we have referred to so far has been accompanied by a parallel investigation of urban development in the nineteenth century. These studies, which stand on the borderline between architectural history, sociology and the history of various types of technology, are especially associated with Professor H.J. Dyos (1921-78), who succeeded Pevsner as Chair-

---

[1] Quoted from his obituary in *The Builder*, X, 1852, p.605.

man of the Victorian Society in 1976.[1] By contrast, a more visual approach to urban architecture is contained in a fine series of generally well-documented surveys which concentrate on Neo-Classical and Victorian buildings.[2]

It should be emphasised that the great majority of historians mentioned in this chapter have been actively concerned in fighting battles against the destruction of Victorian and Edwardian buildings. Whereas in the nineteenth century new discoveries in architectural history often went hand in hand with new developments in the practice of architecture, in recent years they have gone hand in hand with new developments in preservation.

It may be appropriate to take in with Victorian studies the development of interest in Neo-Classicism, since there is a certain overlapping of subject matter. What do we mean by Neo-Classicism, a word which, incidentally, does not appear in the Concise Oxford Dictionary? The difficulty we have in answering that question explains the challenge presented by the whole subject. Scholars have found it absorbing to study because its subject matter is complex in theme and form, international in scope, includes furniture, interior decoration and garden design, and has an important theoretical basis incorporating rationalism in France, and the Picturesque Movement in England.

We saw in the first chapter how, following logically from the

---

[1] The studies include H.J. Dyos, *Victorian Suburb, a Study of the Growth of Camberwell* (Leicester 1961), A. Briggs, *Victorian Cities* (1963), A. and P. Smithson, *The Euston Arch and the Growth of the London, Midland & Scottish Railway* (1968), J.R. Kellett, *The Impact of Railways on Victorian Cities*, H. Hobhouse, *Thomas Cubitt – Master Builder* (1971), J. Summerson, *The London Building World of the Eighteen-Sixties* (1973), J.N. Tarn, *5% Philanthropy, an Account of Houses in Urban Areas, 1840-1914* (Cambridge 1975), and D.J. Olsen, *The Growth of Victorian London* (1976).

[2] Maurice Craig's *Dublin 1660-1860* (1952), modelled on Summerson's *Georgian London* (1945); Quentin Hughes's *Seaport, Architecture and Townscape of Liverpool* (1964); A.J. Youngson's *The Making of Classical Edinburgh* (Edinburgh 1966); A. Gomme and D. Walker's *Architecture of Glasgow* (1968); A. Gomme, M. Jenner and B. Little's *Bristol, an Architectural History* (1979); and, with a wider scope, D. Linstrum's *West Yorkshire, Architects and Architecture* (1978).

attempts at defining Renaissance and, more particularly, Baroque art, German critics around 1900 turned their attention to post-Baroque art which they called *'Klassizismus'* or Neo-Classicism. Following in the historiographical footsteps of Wölfflin and Riegl, Kaufmann carried out pioneering research into the work of Boullée, Ledoux and Lequeu. In his concern to relate stylistic and social change, Kaufmann was increasingly determined to present their work as prefiguring the twentieth century: for example, in an article of 1936 on 'Claude Nicolas Ledoux: a Pioneer of Modern Architecture in the Eighteenth Century', he wrote of Ledoux that 'The effects which he proposed were almost the same which are being used by the architects of today . . . simplicity, sincerity and dignity'.[1] It was in this guise that the concept of Neo-Classicism was introduced into this country by Nikolaus Pevsner and by Helen Rosenau. From 1941 until shortly after the war, Pevsner contributed a number of articles and reviews to *The Architectural Review* under the pseudonym 'Peter F.R. Donner' (*Donner* being German for 'thunder'), including one in October 1941 in which he drew parallels in text and illustrations between Ledoux and Le Corbusier. This Kaufmannesque approach informed his interpretation of Neo-Classicism two years later in his celebrated *An Outline of European Architecture*, where he described the work of architects like Soane and Gilly, who were inspired by Ledoux, as possessing 'the crispness and precision of the dawning machine age',[2] and 'close to a new style of the new century'. 'Why', Pevsner agonises, 'is it then that a hundred years had to pass before an original "modern" style was really accepted? How can it be that the 19th century forgot about Soane and Gilly and remained smugly satisfied with the imitation of the past?'[3]

In three articles[4] shortly after the war, Helen Rosenau also applied the Kaufmann doctrine to an interpretation of Ledoux, Lequeu and Boullée, and in 1953 published for the first time the text of Boullée's manuscript, *Architecture. Essai sur l'art,* trans-

---

[1] *Parnassus*, VIII, Oct. 1936, p.18.

[2] 1945 ed., p.199.   [3] p.201.

[4] *Burl. Mag.*, LXXXVIII, 1946, pp.163-8; *Arch. Rev.*, CVI, 1949, pp.111-17, and CXI, 1952, pp.396-402.

lated into English under the title *Boullée's Treatise on Architecture*.

The 1950s were also important for the broad but scholarly studies by Hautecoeur, Summerson and Hitchcock which, for the first time, gave a European perspective to the whole development of Neo-Classicism. Hautecoeur's detailed studies of the period from 1750-1815 appeared in 1952-3 as volumes IV and V in his stately if somewhat inventory-like series, *Histoire de l'architecture classique en France*; the fifth and concluding part of Summerson's *Architecture in Britain 1530-1830* (1953) was called 'Neo-Classicism and the Picturesque: 1750-1830'; while H.-R. Hitchcock's *Architecture: 19th and 20th centuries* (1958) adopted the German phrase, 'Romantic Classicism', to describe European Neo-Classicism. Christopher Hussey's two volumes on *English Country Houses, Mid-Georgian, 1760-1800* (1956) and *Late Georgian, 1800-1840* (1958), incorporated many of Summerson's insights into a fruitful discussion of Neo-Classicism and the Picturesque. It should not, however, be forgotten that thirty years before, Hussey had produced *The Picturesque: Studies in a Point of View* (1927), which was one of the key books in the whole twentieth-century reassessment of the eighteenth century. In identifying the Picturesque Movement as the fundamental English contribution to eighteenth-century aesthetics and design, Hussey had isolated an area of research which is still far from fully explored. The present author's *Thomas Hope (1769-1831) and the Neo-Classical Idea* (1968), and J. Mordaunt Crook's *The Greek Revival, Neo-Classical Attitudes in British Architecture 1760-1870* (1972), were attempts at clarifying the curiously interlocking phenomena of the Greek Revival and the Picturesque. Picturesque gardens and their buildings have been the subject of a number of valuable studies, and the whole subject of garden design now has its own scholarly journal, *Garden History* (1972-). H.D. Clark (d.1971), who was landscape consultant for the Festival of Britain in 1951, published a paper on 'Eighteenth-Century Elysiums. The Role of "Association" in the Landscape Movement' (1943),[1] and *The English Landscape Garden* (1948), which were a development from Elizabeth Manwaring's pioneering *Italian Landscapes in Eighteenth Century England* (New York 1925). Clark's work was followed by Dorothy Stroud's monographs on

[1] *JWCI*, VI, 1943, pp.165-89.

Capability Brown (1950, new ed. 1975) and *Humphry Repton* (1962), and by Christopher Hussey's *English Gardens and Landscapes 1700-1750* (1967). The most stimulating study on this subject is Kenneth Woodbridge's *Landscape and Antiquity, Aspects of English Culture at Stourhead, 1718-1838* (Oxford 1970). Some interesting paths are explored in the collection of essays edited by Pevsner as *The Picturesque Garden and its Influence outside the British Isles* (Dumbarton Oaks 1974), and Peter Willis has published an elaborately documented monograph on the garden designs of Bridgeman (1978).

In *The Picturesque* Hussey had also drawn attention, perhaps for the first time in this country, to the buildings and designs of Boullée and Ledoux, locating the origins of their 'Cult of the colossal' in the work of Piranesi. Hussey's attention had been directed to Boullée and Ledoux not by any German account of Neo-Classicism, but by Henry Lemonnier's paper of 1910 on 'La mégalomanie dans l'architecture à la fin du XVIIIe siècle'. [1]

The interpretation of Boullée and Ledoux associated with Kaufmann, Pevsner and Rosenau was undermined in 1960 by Wolfgang Herrmann's revolutionary article [2] proving that in many cases the 'advanced' aspects of Ledoux's designs were only added by him in the course of preparing engravings of them for publication in the 1780s and 90s. This new chronology for Neo-Classicism naturally encouraged investigation for the first time of what Boullée and Ledoux had actually built in the 1760s and 70s, as well as of the crucial theoretical basis which had been established earlier in the century in the writings of Cordemoy and Laugier. This change of emphasis was reflected in the writings of three distinguished architectural historians, Robin Middleton, Wolfgang Herrmann and Pérouse de Montclos. Following his training as an architect in South Africa, Middleton came to England to write a doctoral dissertation under Pevsner on Viollet-le-Duc. So far from discovering that Viollet was primarily a 'pioneer of the Modern Movement', Middleton showed in 1958 [3] how he could only be interpreted

---

[1] Which he cites from H. Lemmonier, *L'art moderne*, Paris 1912.

[2] 'The Problem of Chronology in Ledoux's Engraved Designs', *Art Bulletin*, XLII, 1960, pp.191-210.

[3] *Viollet-le-Duc and the Rational Gothic Tradition*, Cambridge Ph.D. dissertation, 1958.

properly as the heir to a great eighteenth-century tradition of Neo-Classical theory based on idealist analyses of Greek and Gothic practice. Middleton's extensive paper of 1962-3 on 'The Abbé de Cordemoy and the Graeco-Gothic Ideal: a Prelude to Romantic Classicism',[1] has been the basis on which subsequent interpretations of French eighteenth and nineteenth-century architectural theory have been based. Joseph Rykwert's *On Adam's House in Paradise, the Idea of the Primitive Hut in Architectural History* (New York 1972) was an important and unusual study along similar lines, reflecting its author's penchant for the arcane.

This emphasis on the crucial early years of Neo-Classicism, rather than on its late expression in the eccentric abstract projects of Boullée and Ledoux, was similarly expressed in Herrmann's *Laugier and 18th century French Theory* (1962); in Pérouse de Montclos's admirable monograph on Boullée published in 1969;[2] in John Harris's stimulating article of 1967 on 'Le Geay, Piranesi and International Neo-classicism in Rome 1740-1750';[3] and in Svend Eriksen's monumental *Early Neo-Classicism in France, the Creation of the Louis Seize Style* (1974), translated from the Danish by Peter Thornton, Keeper of the Department of Furniture and Woodwork at the Victoria and Albert Museum. In 1978 two English architectural historians made further contributions to our understanding of the earlier years of continental neo-classicism: John Wilton-Ely in *The Mind and Art of Giambattista Piranesi*, and Christopher Tadgell in *Ange-Jacques Gabriel*. By contrast, the present author's *The Life and Work of C.R. Cockerell, R.A.* (1974) was concerned with showing the way in which the eighteenth-century classical tradition was developed into the Victorian era by a great master.

The mammoth exhibition, *The Age of Neo-Classicism*, organised by the Council of Europe in 1972 and ambitiously staged in the Royal Academy, the Victoria and Albert Museum and

[1] *JWCI*, XXV, 1962, pp.278-320, and XXVI, 1963, pp.90-123.

[2] *Etienne-Louis Boullée, 1728-1799, de l'architecture classique à l'architecture révolutionnaire*, Paris 1969. H. Rosenau, in *Boullée and Visionary Architecture*, London and New York 1976, still interprets him in the Kaufmannesque way; for an account of this book, see D.J. Watkin 'Insidious Collectivism', *Apollo*, October 1976, pp.321-3.

[3] *Essays in the History of Architecture Presented to R. Wittkower*, 1967, pp.189-96.

Osterley Park House, drew together in memorable form, and with a memorable catalogue, the various areas of European scholarship in architecture, town-planning and the whole range of decorative and applied arts. Concentrating on broad synthesis rather than minute definition, the exhibition was important for its effortless incorporation of the Empire Style and the nineteenth-century classicism of Schinkel and Klenze, all of which had been excluded by Hugh Honour from his attractive book, *Neo-Classicism* (Harmondsworth 1968). Mario Praz (born 1896), in his delightfully eccentric *Gusto Neoclassico* (Florence 1940), translated as *On Neoclassicism* (1969), had vigorously defended his favourite Empire Style from Italian critics such as Adolfo Venturi. But Honour's opposition to it seems to be a direct echo of that of Giedion and Kaufmann who saw it as a false, unreal and immoral style which blocked the path of progress from Ledoux to Le Corbusier.[1]

A broader approach than Honour's informed the complex study of Neo-Classicism published by Robert Rosenblum as *Transformations in Late Eighteenth Century Art* (Princeton 1967). Another broad survey, glancing at Russia and North America as well as Europe, was published by Robin Middleton and the present author as *Architettura Moderna* (Milan 1977). Despite its title, this deals exclusively with the period 1750-1870. Hoping to avoid over-reliance on the descriptive term 'Neo-Classicism', and emphasising the importance of rationalist theory in France and of the Picturesque Movement in England, the authors try to show what continuity can be said to exist between architectural theory and practice in the eighteenth and nineteenth centuries.

[1] See 'Napoleon and the Devaluation of Symbols' in Giedon's *Mechanization Takes Command;* and Kaufmann's reference to 'the morbid style of the Empire', in 'Three Revolutionary Architects', p.515.

VII
Some Recent Tendencies

One of the more striking characteristics of recent architectural history has been the increasingly determined attempt to relate buildings to the society in which they were produced, and to the way of life for which it is believed that they and their contents were originally intended. This is an especially challenging and stimulating field though it is beset with difficulties, firstly because social and political history is an extremely complex subject in itself which few architectural historians will have time to master in depth or over a wide period; and secondly, and more importantly, because even if the architectural historian is expert in social, political and economic history, it remains far from clear to what extent and in what ways this is reflected in architecture. Sometimes there seems to be a direct connection, at others very little, so that it is difficult to establish any set of laws or even range of predictions. A Baroque style of interior decoration adopted on the continent to glorify absolute monarchy and the Catholic Church could be adopted at Chatsworth in the 1680s by the avowed enemy of those institutions, the archetypal Whig and Protestant 1st Duke of Devonshire; similarly, the Painted Hall at Greenwich looks like an apotheosis of absolute monarchy and the Catholic Church but is, of course, exactly the reverse.

The continued interest in Marxist theories in the 1960s and 70s, which itself would scarcely have been predicted in the 1950s, has undoubtedly helped encourage a belief that there is a direct and obviously predictable relation between social and economic conditions and architectural forms. This approach has been especially associated in art history with the work of Arnold Hauser and of Dvořák's pupil, Frederick Antal. It has been well summarised in a survey of recent art-historical writings by W. Eugene Kleinbauer who writes that

Hegelians and Marxists alike postulate that reality is essentially historical and evolutionary in character, and that the evolutionary process is determined by the Hegelian dialectic of thesis, antithesis, and synthesis. For both, the laws that determine the evolution of cultural institutions, and the natural processes in organic and inorganic nature, are identical ... Since in Marxist Leninism, art 'expresses' or 'reflects' reality, and reality is a revolutionary development, Marxists argue that changes in art are evolutionary and revolutionary.[1]

It ought, however, to be pointed out that there is no reason why an architect, artist or patron should not escape from, rather than 'express', what the ruling orthodoxy of the day regards as 'reality'.

The new emphases in architectural history have been especially associated with renewed interest in the history of the country house. It may be no coincidence that three of the writers who figure prominently in this movement, Mark Girouard (born 1931), John Cornforth (born 1937) and Marcus Binney (born 1944), have all been architectural editors of *Country Life*, where they have had perforce to see architecture as part of a social scene, albeit a rapidly changing one. One book which emphatically demonstrated the merits of an approach to architectural history as social and cultural history was *The Victorian Country House* (Oxford 1971), by Mark Girouard. He followed this triumphantly successful study, which had grown out of his articles on Victorian country houses for *Country Life*, with *Sweetness and Light, the 'Queen Anne' Movement 1860-1900* (Oxford 1977). This book gives rise to a moment's unease in its concern to make the sociological glove fit the architectural hand. The first chapter contains a certain amount of determinist, somewhat tendentious sociological comment arguing for the emergence of a 'progressive' type of person in the 1870s and 80s who rejected the social, political and religious standards of his parents, and who would inevitably favour the fresh, supposedly 'forward-looking' style of Nesfield and Shaw. We are assured, for example, that

The children or grandchildren of the men who had made the money were reacting against the values they had been brought up to accept ... From the

---

[1] *Modern Perspectives in Western Art History*, New York 1971, p.27.

1860s there was a steady lessening of tension. Literally and metaphorically the next generation could afford to relax. Their views grew less dogmatic, their manners smoother, their prose lighter, and their morals easier ... they needed a new life style ... Fathers who had spent their lives reading the Bible and making money with equally dedicated intensity very probably had agnostic children ... Both aesthetes and progressives tended to do without religion ...'.[1]

One of the troubles is that the architects do not really fit into this neat image: Shaw, Nesfield, Bodley and Scott, junior, were all either Conservative or Christian or both.

Girouard's *Life in the English Country House, a Social and Architectural History* (New Haven, Conn. 1978) is a brilliant and stimulating study which, as its author would be the first to admit, marks only the beginning of our understanding of this complex and curiously ignored subject. Naturally, some of his historical and social assumptions have been questioned by social and political historians[2] but this has not involved any serious undermining of his achievement. Another useful study to be mentioned in this context is Malcolm Airs's *The Making of the English Country House: 1500-1640* (1975). With a much wider range is Judith Hook's *The Baroque Age in England* (1976), an absorbing study by an author who has been trained as an historian, not an art historian.

Another aspect of recent architectural history has been a reaction against the preoccupation with isolated 'prestige' buildings in favour of study and understanding of the whole complex anonymous web of the urban environment. Reyner Banham (born 1922), the first Professor of the History of Architecture in this country, has been particularly associated with this movement. His inaugural lecture delivered at University College London, in December 1970 was entitled, 'At Shoo-fly landing: Architecture is that which changes land-use'. A study of the history of the municipal pier at Santa Monica, California, it was influenced by John Maass's attack on recent American architectural history in the American *Journal of the Society of Architectural Historians* (March 1969), which we investigated in chapter II. Banham's subsequent book, *Los Angeles: the Archi-*

[1] pp.3 and 7.
[2] Prof. L. Stone in the *Times Literary Supplement*, 10 November, 1978, p.1298; and D.N. Cannadine in the *Cambridge Review*, C, 9 February 1979, pp.77-8.

tecture of Four Ecologies (1971), which is a eulogy of what he calls 'instant architecture in an instant environment',[1] will undoubtedly represent for some the unacceptable face of the preoccupation of the 1960s with environmental studies. The more than acceptable face is represented by the achievement of H.J. Dyos (1921-78) who published *Victorian Suburb, a Study of the Growth of Camberwell* (Leicester 1961) and established the series of 'Studies in Urban History', which included C.W. Chalklin's *The Provincial Towns of Georgian England, a Study of the Building Process 1740-1820* (1974), A. Sutcliffe's *The Autumn of Central Paris, the Defeat of Town Planning 1850-1970* (1970), and J.H. Baxter's *St Petersburg: Industrialization and Change* (1976). With Michael Wolff, Professor of English and Victorian Studies at the University of Massachusetts, Dyos edited the stimulating and suggestive work, *The Victorian City, Images and Realities* (2 vols., 1973), which contained valuable essays by John Summerson, D.J. Olsen, Nicholas Taylor and others. Olsen subsequently published *The Growth of Victorian London* (1976), which brilliantly explored the collective tissue of a great nineteenth-century city, while Paul Thompson's *The Voice of the Past, Oral History* (Oxford 1978) investigated another new approach to social history.

The interest in the interlocking patterns of environment and social activity which we have noted in this chapter has been reflected in the study of interior design and furnishings, including the use and arrangement of furniture. A good example of this is the fascinating pioneering study by John Fowler (d. 1977) and John Cornforth, *English Decoration in the 18th Century* (1974, rev. ed. 1978). Cornforth subsequently published an instructive and attractive volume of contemporary water-colours and drawings entitled *English Interiors, 1790-1840, the Quest for Comfort* (1978), the conception of which owed much to *An Illustrated History of Interior Decoration* (1964) by Mario Praz. *English Decoration in the 18th Century* is rooted in the first-hand knowledge of country houses acquired by Cornforth on the staff of *Country Life* from 1961, and by Fowler as an interior decorator specialising in historic country houses. 'Both authors', as they state in their preface, 'are concerned about the problems of preservation, restoration and presentation of country houses, and indeed that

[1] p.21.

is why they began to work on the book'.[1] Cornforth had discovered the inadequacy of conventional architectural history for dealing with these and related problems, in connection with the arrangement and decoration of interiors in country houses owned by the National Trust. The Department of Furniture and Woodwork at the Victoria and Albert Museum is becoming increasingly involved with the historical aspects of this problem, and the Department's Keeper, Peter Thornton, has published an impressive study of *Seventeenth-Century Interior Decoration in England, France and Holland* (New Haven, Conn. 1978). The arrangement of the contents and the decoration of historic houses like Clandon and Sudbury, in National Trust owner-ship, and Apsley House, Ham House and Osterley, in the charge of the Victoria and Albert Museum, have been funda-mentally altered as the result of extensive documentary and other research. The result, inevitably controversial, is apt to give the interiors a determinedly instructive air so that they begin to look like learned reconstructions in museums. Though we gain new insights into seventeenth and eighteenth-century social ceremony, we lose the sense of life and warmth, and of continuous use and development through the centuries down to, and including, the present. There, of course, lies the rub. The sense which the modern researcher has of being able to do what he will with the interiors of these old houses has undoubtedly been heightened by the political and economic circumstances which have come close to destroying — as they were intended to — the possibility of anyone ever living in them again in style. From the mid-1960s, the urgency of the threat to the survival of country houses with their contents and their land became increasingly clear. As the uniquely rich product of a society which saw the family as the stimulus to achievement and the channel of its transmission, country houses have been amongst the chief victims of the ultimately Marxist policies of successive Liberal and Labour governments throughout the twentieth century in persistently and deliberately eroding the concept of the family and private property as the basis of society.

Armed with their new knowledge of how country houses have been used in the past, architectural historians have played an important role in the campaign for preserving and finding new

[1] p.7.

uses for country houses. An especially brilliant example of this was the popular exhibition at the Victoria and Albert Museum in 1975, *The Destruction of the Country House*, with the accompanying book of the same title, edited by Roy Strong, Marcus Binney and John Harris. This was not only a popular success with a long-term practical influence on public opinion, but the research which lay behind its lists and photographic records of destroyed country houses, made it a valuable tool for the architectural historian. The great sale at Mentmore in 1977, to which Marcus Binney and others directed the attention of the nation, served to emphasise the lessons of the exhibition of 1975; and in the same year Marcus Binney founded a new preservation society with the title SAVE Britain's Heritage.

Conservation has indeed been the mood of the 1970s, beginning with the admirable *Lost London, a Century of Demolition and Decay* (1971) written by Hermione Hobhouse, who became Secretary of the Victorian Society in 1976. This contains an urgent plea for the future extension of conservation as well as a useful summary of its recent history. Attitudes to conservation can be a fascinating record of changing estimates of the contrasted merits of past and present-day culture. The generally recognised failure of modern architecture, whether public or domestic, to provide a civilised or humane environment has helped create a climate of opinion which assumes that almost any new building will be worse than anything it replaces. Furthermore, social and political changes profoundly altered many of the traditional patterns of life and manners in the 1960s and 70s, so that preservation of the architectural fabric of English life became a sometimes almost unconscious reaction against these changes. Here, it was felt, were at any rate a few landmarks which people of all political parties could agree on preserving from the wreckage of the old world. What even the Victorian Society would not have preserved in 1958 would have been top priority for preservation ten years later. In the course of a lecture on 'Victorian Conservanda' to the London Society and the Victorian Society in 1958, Goodhart-Rendel said, 'I read in *The Times* newspaper some months ago that Mr. John Summerson had said that he would see no harm in the destruction of Lady Burdett-Coutts's Columbia Market, Bethnal

Green; I think in saying so he was quite right... To encumber
perpetually whatever acreage the building covers with a market
that nobody ever wanted to use, and that nobody has ever
wanted to look at except as a curiosity, would be obviously a
misappropriation of space.[1] The subjective nature of such
judgements is suggested by the fact that in the same lecture he
takes as axiomatic the preservation of Tite's Royal Exchange, a
market scarcely less useless and probably less interesting architecturally than Darbishire's Columbia Market. But Goodhart-
Rendel doubtless felt more at home with the Royal Exchange as
the product of a classical tradition to which he belonged himself
and which was rooted in the work of Cockerell. Exactly twenty
years after this lecture, Dixon and Muthesius wrote of the
fancifully Gothic Columbia Market in their *Victorian Architecture*, that 'its destruction in the early 1960s was one of the most
serious losses of Victorian architecture'.[2] In 1979 Marcus Binney at SAVE opened a campaign to prevent the replacement
with a modern commercial block of Lloyd's in Leadenhall
Street, London, a vast classical pile of 1928 by Sir Edwin
Cooper. He thus put himself in advance of some of the pundits of
the architectural world who had previously supported him, so
that his campaign was condemned in *Building Design* and elsewhere. But the development of architectural history is at the
moment marching hand in hand with conservation, and
younger architectural historians, many of them sharing the
general dissatisfaction with modern architecture, are beginning
to look with sympathetic attention at the work of traditionalist
architects between the wars. Here is a new and fruitful area for
research which should offer an interesting contrast to the field of
mediaeval architecture which similarly needs exploring further.
At the time of writing there are no less than eight books on
Sir Edwin Lutyens (1869-1944) scheduled for publication in the
next few years by English and American architectural historians. These authors will be able to take comfort from *The
Aesthetics of Architecture* (1979) by the young English philosopher,
Roger Scruton. This is the most brilliant defence of humanist
aesthetics and, in particular, of classicism, since Geoffrey Scott,

[1] *Victorian Conservanda*, repr. from *Jnl. of the London Soc.*, February 1959, p.3.
[2] p.110.

though Scruton's range is greater and his vision in some ways more profound.

If this is a bad period for practising architects, since they have temporarily suppressed the credibility of their profession by their barbarous Utopian dreams, it is a boom period for the architectural historian who feeds, vulture-like, on the decaying remains of the civilisation which the planners, the politicians and the architects have helped destroy. The intense public interest in the social life and architecture of the English middle and upper classes up to the Second World War, which can be gauged from the success of numerous television serials and even of Girouard's *The English Country House, a Social and Architectural History* (1978), may itself have had some effect in civilising the mood and designs of a number of present-day architects. This interest in history and this dissatisfaction with the tone of modern life and architecture have at last helped bring about a reawakening of interest in professional architectural circles in the visual side of architecture and in the problem of 'style'. In 1970 Summerson could argue that present-day appreciation of Victorian architecture, of 'even the magisterial creations of Cockerell or Butterfield's noblest churches', would always be an exercise beset by intense problems: 'Since an interest in choice of style is to us something totally unreal, an exercise of this kind is very difficult'.[1] Yet only ten years later at the Cambridge School of Architecture, where from the 1960s architecture had been dethroned in favour of 'Land Use and Built Form', second-year undergraduates were set the project of designing a house in three styles: the Arts and Crafts style of Baillie Scott and his contemporaries at the turn of the century, the 'International Style' of the Modern Movement in the 1930s, and the recent American style associated with fashionable architects like Venturi and Rauch.

Behold, I make all things new[2]

---

[1] *Victorian Architecture*, New York 1970, p.6.
[2] *Revel.*, xxi, 5.

Select Bibliography

The place of publication is London unless otherwise stated.

J.S. Ackerman, 'Western Art History', in J.S. Ackerman and Rhys Carpenter, *Art and Archaeology*, New Jersey 1963, pp.123-231

B. Allsopp, *The Study of Architectural History*, 1970

F. Antal, 'Modern Art History', *Burl. Mag.*, XCI, 1949, pp.49-52 and 73-5

G. Baldwin Brown, *The Care of Ancient Monuments*, Cambridge 1905

M.W. Barley, *A Guide to British Topographical Collections*, Council for British Archaeology 1974

E.S.de Beer, 'Gothic: Origin and Diffusion of the Term; the idea of style in Architecture, *JWCI*, XI, 1948, pp.143-62

I. Berlin, *Historical Inevitability*, 1954

F. Bernabei, *Pietro Selvatico, nella critica e nella storia dell arti figurative dell'Ottocento*, Vicenza 1974

A. Blunt, *Some Uses and Misuses of the Terms Baroque and Rococo as Applied to Architecture*, Oxford 1972

M. Borissavliévitch, *Les théories de l'architecture, essai critique sur les principales doctrines relatives à l'esthétique de l'architecture*, Paris 1926

R. Branner, 'Gothic Architecture' (general review of recent books), *JSAH*, XXXII, 1973, pp.326-33.

J. Burckhardt, *Reflections on History*, 1943
—— *Judgements on History and Historians*, 1959 (intro. by H. Trevor-Roper)

Burckhardt and the Renaissance, Kansas 1960 (conference pamphlet)

P. Burke, *The Renaissance Sense of the Past*, 1969

Burlington Magazine, CIII, 1961, pp.163-5, editorial on 'Art History in Modern British Universities'

E.H. Carr, *What is History?*, 1962

W. Cole, *A Journal of my Journey to Paris in the Year 1765*, 1931 (ed. F.G. Stokes)

—— *The Blecheley Diary of the Rev. William Cole, 1765-67*, 1931 (ed. F.G. Stokes)

P. Collins, *Changing Ideals in Modern Architecture, 1750-1950*, 1965

H.M. Colvin, 'Architectural History and its Records', *Archives*, II, no.14, 1955, pp.300-11

K.J. Conant, 'The Care of Historic Monuments in France', *JSAH*, I, 1941, pp.13-14 and 17

Lady Congreve, Obituary of H. Avray Tipping, *Country Life*, LXXIV, 1933, p.566

J.M. Crook, 'Christopher Hussey: a bibliographical tribute', *Arch. Hist.*, 13, 1970, pp.5-29

Dictionary of National Biography, 1885-1971

J. Dobai, *Die Kunstliteratur des Klassizismus und der Romantik in England, 1700-1840*, 3 vols., Bern 1974-7

D.C. Douglas, *English Scholars*, 1939

G. Erouart and G. Teyssot, intro. to E. Kaufmann, *Trois architectes révolutionnaires, Boullée, Ledoux, Lequeu*, transl. by F. Revers, Paris 1978

L.D. Ettingler, *Art History Today*, London 1961

J. Evans, *A History of the Society of Antiquaries*, Oxford 1956

N. Finch, *Style in Art History, an Introduction to Theories of Style and Sequence*, Metuchen, N.J. 1974

D. Fleming and B. Bailyn, ed., *The Intellectual Migration: Europe and America, 1930-1960*, Cambridge, Mass. 1969, especially C. Eisler, '*Kunstgeschichte* American Style: a study in Migration', pp.544-629

P. Frankl, *The Gothic, Literary Sources and Interpretations through Eight Centuries*, Princeton 1960

J. Gantner, ed., *Jakob Burckhardt und Heinrich Wölfflin, Briefwechsel und andere Dokumente ihrer Begegnung 1882-1897*, Basel 1948

G. Germann, *Gothic Revival in Europe and Britain: Sources, Influences and Ideas*, 1972

Geschichte und Theorie der Architektur, vol.13, *Hommage à Giedion, Profile seiner Persönlichkeit*, Basel and Stuttgart 1971

D. Gifford, ed., *The Literature of Architecture: the Evolution of Architectural Theory and Practice in 19th-century America*, New York 1966

E.H. Gombrich, 'Style', *International Encyclopaedia of the Social Sciences*, New York 1968, vol.15, pp.352-61
—— *In Search of Cultural History*, Oxford 1969
—— *Aby Warburg, an Intellectual Biography*, 1970
—— 'The Logic of Vanity Fair, Alternatives to Historicism in the Study of Fashions, Style and Taste', *The Philosophy of Karl Popper*, P.A. Schilpp, ed., 2 vols., Illinois 1974, II, pp.925-57
—— *Art History and the Social Sciences*, Oxford 1975

A. Hauser, *The Philosophy of Art History*, New York 1959

W. Herrmann, *Laugier and 18th-Century French Theory*, 1962

H.-R. Hitchcock, *American Architectural Books...before 1895*, Minneapolis 1946 and 62

A.G. Holt, *A Documentary History of Art*, 2 vols., New York 1957-8

M.C.W. Hunter, 'The Study of Anglo-Saxon Architecture since 1770: an Evaluation', *Proceedings of the Cambridge Antiquarian Society*, LXVI, 1976, pp.129-39

C. Hussey, 'Gardener and Antiquary' (H. Avray Tipping), *Country Life*, LXXIV, 1933, pp.567-8
—— 'Edward Hudson, an Appreciation', *Country Life*, LXXX, 1936, pp.319-20

H. Huth, 'The Evolution of Preservationism in Europe', *JSAH*, I, 1941, pp.5-12

G.G. Iggers, *The German Conception of History: the National Tradition of Historical Thought from Herder to the Present*, Middletown, Conn. 1968

JSAH, vol.2, No.2, 1941, special issue on 'History in Architectural Education'

JSAH, XXVI, 1967, pp.178-99, 'Architectural History and the Student Architect: A Symposium'

E. Kaufmann, 'At an 18th-Century Crossroads: Algarotti vs. Lodoli', *JSAH*, 4, 1944, pp.23-9
—— review of M. Raval and J.C. Moreux, *Ledoux* (Paris 1945), *Art Bulletin*, XXX, 1948, p.288

W.E. Kleinbauer, *Modern Perspectives in Western Art History: an Anthology of 20th-Century Writings on the Visual Arts*, New York 1971

G. Kubler, *The Shape of Time, Remarks on the History of Things*, New Haven, Conn. 1962

O. Kurz, 'Barocco: storia di una parola', *Lettere Italiane*, XII, 1960, pp.414-44

S. Lang, 'Principles of the Gothic Revival in England', *JSAH* 25, 1966, pp.240-67

P. Léon, *La vie des monuments français, destruction, restauration*, Paris 1951

A.G. Lough, *The Influence of John Mason Neale*, London 1962

A.O. Lovejoy, *Essays in the History of Ideas*, Baltimore and London 1948

J. Maass, 'Where Architectural Historians Fear to Tread', *JSAH,* XXVIII, 1969, pp.3-8

H.A. Millon, 'Rudolf Wittkower, *Architectural Principles in the Age of Humanism*: its Influence on the Development and Interpretation of Modern Architecture', *JSAH*, XXXI, 1972, pp.83-91

P. Murray, intro. to H. Wölfflin, *Renaissance and Baroque*, Fontana Library ed. 1964

O. Pächt, 'Alois Riegl', *Burl.Mag.*, CV, 1963, pp.188-93

W.M. Palmer, *William Cole of Milton*, Cambridge 1935

E. Panofsky, 'Three Decades of Art History in the United States', *Meaning in the Visual Arts*, New York 1955

H. Park, *A List of Architectural Books Available in America before the Revolution*, Los Angeles 1973

N. Pevsner, 'An Un-English Activity? Reflections on Not Teaching Art History', *The Listener*, XLVIII, 1952, pp.715-16
—— 'William Whewell and his Architectural Notes on German Churches', *German Life and Letters, a Quarterly Review*, n.s., XXII, 1969, pp.39-48
—— *Ruskin and Viollet-le-Duc, Englishness and Frenchness in the Appreciation of Gothic Architecture*, 1969
—— *Some Architectural Writers of the Nineteenth Century*, Oxford 1972

S. Piggott, *William Stukeley, an Eighteenth-Century Antiquary*, Oxford 1950

I. Prozzillo, *Francisco Milizia, Teorico e Storico dell'Architettura*, Naples 1971

R.B. Pugh, ed., *General Introduction, The Victoria History of the Counties of England,*Oxford 1970

H.H. Reed, *The Golden City*, New York 1960, rev.ed. 1971

W.D. Robson-Scott, *The Literary Background of the Gothic Revival in Germany*, Oxford 1965

The Earl of Ronaldshay, *The Life of Lord Curzon*, 3 vols., 1928

F.J. Roos, *Bibliography of Early American Architecture*, Urbana, Ill. 1943 and 68

G.S. Rousseau, 'Traditional and Heuristic Categories: a Critique of Contemporary Art History', *Studies in Burke and his Time*, XV, no.l, 1973, pp.51-96

J. Rykwert, *On Adam's House in Paradise, the Idea of the Primitive Hut in Architectural History*, New York 1972

L. Salerno, 'Historiography', *Encyclopaedia of World Art*, vol. VII, 1963, pp.507-59

L. Freeman Sandler, ed., *Essays in Memory of Karl Lehmann*, New York 1964

F. Saxl, *A Heritage of Images, a Selection of Lectures*, 1970 (intro. by E.H. Gombrich)
Fritz Saxl A Volume of Memorial Essays, ed. D.J. Gordon, 1957 (intro. by G. Bing)

M. Schapiro, 'New Viennese School', *Art Bulletin*, XVIII, 1936, pp.258-66
—— 'Style', *Anthropology Today*, Chicago 1953 (ed. A.L. Kroeber)

J. von Schlosser, *Die Kunstliteratur*, Vienna 1924

R. Schneider, *Quatremère de Quincy et son intervention dans les arts 1788-1830*, Paris 1910

G. Scott, *The Architecture of Humanism*, 1914 (rev.ed.1924, reprinted 1980 with intro. by D.J. Watkin)

R.V. Scruton, *The Aesthetics of Architecture*, 1979

A.E. Shipley, *'J.' A Memoir of John Willis Clark*, 1913

J. Summerson, *What is a Professor of Fine Art?*, Hull, 1961
—— ed., *Concerning Architecture*, 1968

A. Hamilton Thompson, *A Bibliography of the Published Writings of Sir W. St. John Hope... with a Brief Introductory Memoir*, Leeds 1929

L. Venturi, *History of Art Criticism*, 1936, new ed. New York 1964

S. Waetzoldt, *Bibliographie zur Architektur im 19. Jahrhundert*, 8 vols., Nendeln 1977

W. Waetzoldt, *Deutsche Kunsthistoriker von Sandrart bis Rumohr*, Berlin 1965

E. Waterhouse, 'An Un-English Activity. II. Art as a "Piece of History"', *The Listener*, XLVIII, 1952, pp.761-2

D.J. Watkin, 'Architectural Writing in the 1930s', *Architectural Design*, October 1979
—— *Morality and Architecture*, Oxford 1977

K.J. Weintraub, *Visions of Culture*, Chicago 1966 (Burckhardt, Huizinga, *et al.*)

J.F. White, *The Cambridge Movement*, Cambridge 1962 (reprinted 1979)

E.R. de Zurko, *Origins of Functionalist Theory*, New York 1957

Index

197